Nature Conservation in Europe

Nature Conservation in Europe

POLICY AND PRACTICE

Peter Bromley

E & FN SPON
An Imprint of Chapman & Hall

London · Weinheim · New York · Tokyo · Melbourne · Madras

Published by E & FN Spon, an imprint of
Chapman & Hall, 2–6 Boundary Row, London SE1 8HN, UK

Chapman & Hall, 2–6 Boundary Row, London SE1 8HN, UK

Chapman & Hall GmbH, Pappelallee 3, 69469 Weinheim, Germany

Chapman & Hall USA, 115 Fifth Avenue, New York, NY 10003, USA

Chapman & Hall Japan, ITP-Japan, Kyowa Building, 3F, 2-2-1 Hirakawacho, Chiyoda-ku, Tokyo 102, Japan

Chapman & Hall Australia, 102 Dodds Street, South Melbourne, Victoria 3205, Australia

Chapman & Hall India, R. Seshadri, 32 Second Main Road, CIT East, Madras 600 035, India

First edition 1997

© 1997 Peter Bromley

Typeset in 10/12pt Times by Mews Photosetting, Beckenham, Kent

Printed in Great Britain by Cambridge University Press

ISBN 0 419 21610 3

∞ Printed on acid-free paper, manufactured in accordance with ANSI/NISO Z39.48-1992 (Permanence of Paper).

Contents

Preface   xi

1   Introduction   **1**

Part One   Europe and the World   **5**

2   Europe and the world   **7**
     References   9

3   Europe and the environment   **10**
     Planning in western Europe   12
     The growth of environmentalism   17
     Other issues   22
     Towards an environmental policy   24
     References   26

4   The European Community   **28**
     Origins and foundations   29
     The structure of the Community   36
     Administrative procedures   45
     Summary   50
     References   51

5   European legislation   **52**
     Underlying principles   53
     Environmental Action Programmes   55
     Other principles   59

Environmental legislation   61
Community Agricultural Policy   74
European Environmental Agency   78
A summary of European nature conservation policy   79
References   80

6   **The environment, Europe and the world**   **83**
    Organizations   84
    International conventions   92
    World conservation strategies   102
    Summary   108
    References   109

Part Two The European Member States   **111**

7   **An introduction**   **113**
    Policies into practice   114
    An overview   116
    References   119

8   **Austria**   **120**
    Political structures   120
    Environmental responsibilities   122
    Land designations   124
    Other issues   128
    Summary   129
    References   129

9   **Belgium**   **131**
    Political structure   131
    Environmental responsibilities   135
    Land designations   136
    Other issues   140
    Summary   142
    References   142

10 **Denmark**   **144**
    Political structure   144
    Environmental responsibilities   146
    Land designations   150
    Other issues   152
    Summary   154
    References   154

11   Finland   **156**
      Political structure   156
      Environmental responsibilities   157
      Land designations   159
      Other issues   163
      Summary   164
      References   165

12   France   **166**
      Political structure   166
      Environmental responsibilities   169
      Land designations   174
      Other issues   179
      Summary   182
      References   183

13   Germany   **185**
      Political structure   186
      Environmental responsibilities   188
      Land designations   190
      Other issues   194
      Summary   197
      References   198

14   Greece   **199**
      Political structures   199
      Environmental responsibilities   203
      Land designations   206
      Other issues   209
      Summary   212
      References   213

15   Irish Republic   **215**
      Political structure   215
      Environmental responsibilities   217
      Land designations   220
      Other issues   224
      Summary   226
      References   227

16   Italy   **229**
      Political structures   229
      Environmental responsibilities   232
      Land designations   236

Other issues   240
Summary   243
References   243

17   Luxembourg   **245**
Political structures   245
Environmental responsibilities   247
Land designations   249
Other issues   250
Summary   252
References   253

18   Netherlands   **254**
Political structures   254
Environmental responsibilities   256
Land designations   260
Other issues   262
Summary   265
References   265

19   Portugal   **267**
Political structure   267
Environmental responsibilities   269
Land designations   272
Other issues   276
Summary   280
References   280

20   Spain   **281**
Political structure   282
Environmental responsibilities   285
Land designations   288
Other issues   292
Summary   295
References   296

21   Sweden   **297**
Political structure   297
Environmental responsibilities   298
Land designations   301
Other issues   304
Summary   307
References   307

22   **The United Kingdom**   **309**
      Political structure   309
      Environmental responsibilities   312
      Land designations   315
      Other issues   319
      Summary   321
      References   322

Part Three Conclusions   **323**

23   **Developments**   **325**
      Expansion of the Community   327
      Subsidiarity   327
      Integrated rural development   328
      Regionalization   329
      Fifth Environmental Action Programme   330
      European Environmental Agency   330
      Nature conservation   331
      Sustainability   332
      Agriculture   333
      Taxation and finances   333
      References   334

24   **Some conclusions**   **335**
      References   337

References   **338**

Appendices   **339**

Appendix A Rio Declaration on Environment and Development
      (Agenda 21)   **341**
Appendix B Glossary of abbreviations   **345**

Index   **347**

Preface

This book, like the European Union itself, has been a long time in the gestation and occasionally has been overtaken by events. For example, while the book was being created, the European Community became the European Union and it also expanded from 12 to 15 members. The response to the latter event was to go on a new round of research to find the necessary information to cover the new additions (Austria, Finland and Sweden, but not Norway ... again!) But the response to the former event was to continue to refer to the European states collectively as the European Community. This was for a number of reasons, but most important of which was the fact that by far the majority of references and texts used in the preparation of this book refer to the European Community and not the European Union or the European Economic Community. For the sake of consistency, therefore, the term European Community is used throughout.

While this book reflects a watershed both in Europe and in the nature conservation movement 'post Rio', it is also evident that both issues continue to unfold and develop. The push for European monetary union is still around, as too is the counteracting push in the opposite direction. The demand for ever tighter environmental controls will continue as will the belief that too much or too little is being done to protect our environment in all its forms. None the less, it appears as if there is a new framework for conservation which puts the environment at the heart of any development proposals; this will be the beneficial legacy of the Rio Summit despite some of its other shortcomings. The European Community, too, has begun to interlink conservation with broader economic and 'quality of life' issues. At the level of the individual member states, some of the more forward-looking ones are already doing this.

The book also reflects another watershed in that for a number of years, after the re-unification of Germany and the economic boom of the late 1980s, the trauma of wars in the former Soviet Union and the former

Yugoslavia and the Europe-wide recession have all put pressure on the good intentions of the Member States to act together and to protect the environment. How conservation will fare in this new climate will be of interest.

For these and other reasons, the creation of the book has been a little like running up an escalator that is moving in the opposite direction. The fact that I have been able to move faster than the escalator and actually reach the top is due, in great part, to many people.

I must thank Liz Hyatt for her hard work and dedication against all the odds (and my writing and sometimes ambiguous instructions) in typing the manuscript. I would also like to thank Ian Wall for the illustrations. Further thanks go to David, Gail, Vera, Jim and Nick for the photographs and for their continued support and help in general. I would also like to thank the various people who shone their own inimitable lights into the dark labyrinth that is the European Community, notably they are Deborah Newton-Cook and Jane McDonnagh.

Finally, I would like to thank Gillian, Patrick, Philippa and Ruth for putting up with books, reference material and the stacks and stacks of paper which took over our inadequate study and eventually the dining-room also. It is to them that this book is dedicated, with much affection.

At the time of writing, the second Earth Summit has just commenced in the United States amid widespread acceptance that little progress has been made towards the biodiversity and 'greenhouse' gas targets set in Rio. Calls for renewed efforts have been coupled with accusations of a lack of commitment. Against this background, it is quite clear that the environment is only slowly becoming an integral consideration in economic development and decision making. In these circumstances, the need for specific conservation legislation and protective land designations will remain paramount as is emphasized in this book.

Peter Bromley

No man is an Island, entire of itself; everyman is a piece of the continent, a part of the main; if a clod be washed away by the sea, Europe is the less, as well as if a promontory were, as well as if a manor of thy friends or of thine own were; any man's death diminishes me, because I am involved in mankind; And therefore never send to know for whom the bell tolls; It tolls for thee.

John Donne (1571–1631)
Devotions, Meditation XVII

Everything that live Lives not alone nor for itself.

William Blake (1757–1827)
The Book of Thel, xi, 26

This book is dedicated to
Gillian, Philippa, Ruth and Patrick;
to my Mother and Father
and to the memory of Jennie Potts
who told me to 'go for it'

Introduction

It is said that you have to be mad or brave or both to be a goal keeper in any sport. The same could be said of attempting to write about two subjects as enormous as nature conservation and Europe in the same book. None the less, madness prevails and here is the book. However, it would be unrealistic to entrust myself with such a broad canvas as 'nature conservation in Europe' without defining the parameters within which I have operated and constructed this book.

It is most appropriate to define the two key concepts in the book. First, nature conservation: throughout the text, nature conservation is perceived and dealt with as a land-based or species-based issue. However, given the way that environmental policies have developed in many countries, it is difficult to draw a line between, say, policies for the creation of national parks and policies for pollution control. Particularly at the level of the European Commission, nature conservation is an indistinguishable element of broader environmental policies. If a line is drawn which appears arbitrary, this must be accepted, because a line needs to be drawn somewhere. Wherever possible, though, the criteria used to define what is nature conservation (as opposed to, say, farm or agricultural policies) is taken from relevant organizations, particularly national or European governments. Where the other policy areas have such an overwhelming impact on nature conservation that they cannot be ignored (and again, agricultural policy is a valid example) they are included.

Furthermore, nature conservation in many European countries is virtually inseparable from landscape or amenity conservation. So, where nature conservation is part of a broader land-based policy framework, the latter is described and analysed. Indeed, this is more usually the case, and so 'nature conservation' is used as a 'catch-all' for landscape, nature and cultural conservation of natural and semi-natural areas.

So much for nature conservation, but what about Europe? When the idea for this book began to form in my mind, the boundaries of Europe were already shifting. What was formerly known as Eastern Bloc Europe was beginning to enter pan-European discussion about economics, environmentalism and politics. So what is Europe; where is Europe? Again, pragmatism prevails. This text tries to compare and contrast, so a necessary prerequisite of this is that comparable information is available. For this reason alone, the focus for the book is the European Community. This is for two reasons; first, the European Commission has standard legislation which is enacted across the EC; second, the individual countries that make up the EC have similar methods of recording and providing information on their policies. These two factors mean that comparison is possible – but still not easy!

These two broad definitions cover the bulk of the text. By being selective in the first two parts of the book (although Part Three does expand the definitions and the horizons) it has been possible to avoid too much oversimplification. However, it is inevitable that some simplification does occur. For this I can only offer the excuse that I wanted to write a text that was somewhat shorter than Tolstoy's *War and Peace*, Proust's *A la recherchè de temps perdu* and the *Complete Works of Shakespeare* combined! The references used in the text will offer more detail. This book is concerned with the national and international overview.

Another inevitable characteristic of the book is that it can only be as good as the information that is available; and, as anyone knows, the quality of information varies, particularly across national frontiers. Furthermore, it is also inevitable that information will be more accessible to the author if it is (1) geographically and (2) linguistically close to hand.

Finally, the more common terms, such as growth, development economies and so on, all have a series of interpretations. As an environmentalist, I am not necessarily happy with the conventional definition of growth or development (because, as we shall see later, growth is often matched by a decline in environmental quality, and a loss to the natural environment). However, as the conventional definitions are used throughout the European Community, they are used here.

After that long list of apologies, it is worth restating what the book does achieve, rather than what its shortcomings are.

The text follows the development of the European Community, and the gradual emergence of an environmental policy. Following this, the environmental policy *per se* is discussed against the backdrop of the communities internal legislative and administrative methodology. In this way, the text follows one logical route through what, at times, seems an illogical process of policy development – 'policy by initiative' it has been called.

Rather than break up this process of focusing down on the environmental policies of the European Community, the text then follows this process by focusing on the nature conservation policies of each individual member state. (Defining 'member state' is, in itself, a difficult task in a rapidly changing world!)

In order to widen the debate, the book concludes by broadening the discussion to encompass the changes that are surrounding the European Community and environmental legislation.

Finally, a constraint has been set on the timescale covered by the book. The Treaty of Rome, and the years and events immediately preceding the Treaty in 1955, represent the start point. The end point was more difficult to determine. With the Maastricht Summit in 1991, which was designed to finalize or develop themes of the 1987 Single European Act, a watershed was reached for several reasons. First, Denmark rejected the outcome of the summit in a referendum in that country in 1992. Also, the Soviet States and 'Eastern Europe' began to experience a difficult period following the break up of the Soviet Union and the Communist Bloc, thereby distracting and presenting new, urgent issues for the Member States. Similarly, Yugoslavia experienced horrendous civil war, thereby destroying any immediate notions of expanding member states. Finally, the Rio Summit in 1992 focused world attention on environmental issues, which faced the European Community with several dilemmas – whether to sign en-bloc any subsequent treaties, how to implement policies, and what emphasis to place on the environment against a backdrop of world recession (or indeed economic surplus), European civil and international wars and 'break-away' tendencies in the community. Given all of these various factors, a watershed was reached between 1992 and 1995. It is debatable, therefore, whether the environment will play a leading role in the community in the late 20th and early 21st centuries as the community struggles for its international purpose in other arenas. For this reason, 1995 has been taken as a break-off point. Anything else would enter into the realms of commentary on current situations – a job best left to serious journalists, political commentators and, of course, politicians.

PART ONE

Europe and the World

Europe and the world | 2

The history of the European Community has been one of continual and varied debate about the Member States' relationship with each other, and the collective communities' relationship with the wider world. The wider world has, in itself, been variously seen as: the rest of Europe; the Eastern Bloc; and the whole of the world's community of countries. These struggles for an identity and role have been dichotomized by Lodge (1992) as 'Internal and External Policies', although she also acknowledges that the distinction is somewhat artificial.

The following part of the book looks at several of the internal and external strands and draws from them a sequence which leads to the logical development of an environmental policy, and the subsequent steps leading to the realization of this policy.

The development of the European Community can be split into several stages which follow this 'internal/external' pattern. The 1960s saw the community struggle with its new identity; the 1970s saw moves towards fuller integration, which, following the slowing of the process in the early 1980s with the expansion of the community, took-up pace again in the late 1980s. It is evident that the 1990s represent another phase, with the European Community establishing not only internal relationships, but also the community's response to international issues, including environmental issues. The community is also spending time trying to resolve its corporate response, *vis-à-vis* those of the individual member states. Thus the focus will continually shift from internal to external discussions and the balance between the two.

The formation of the European Community was the result of several immediate and deeper-rooted concerns of the initial Member States. Similarly, the agenda of the initial Member States was drawn from these and other concerns which set the direction of the community – a direction which was only seriously reviewed and reassessed in the Single European Act of 1987, some 30 years after the initial Treaty of Rome. For this reason it is vital to understand something of where the origins of the European Community are to be found. In these origins lie the foundations of the emergent environmental policy. The next chapter examines some of these background events that led to the formation of the European Community, and how the young community began to address them. From these early stages, the community ultimately found the environmental confidence to declare 1987 the European Year of the Environment (Fairclough, 1986).

The second 'building block' which forms the foundation of Part One is that of an analysis of the administrative and legislative procedures of the community. The means by which the community achieves its policy goals are as important as the goals themselves – a point stressed throughout the text. If the vision is lost in the interpretation or implementation, then it is clearly not going to be realized. Thus, the mechanisms and procedures devised by the Community are critical to an understanding of nature conservation in the Community.

The rest of this part of the book then concentrates upon the environment, first at the community level, then at a world level. The community perspective is given through the various and numerous pieces of legislation which deal with nature conservation, as defined at the start of this book. The global analysis is given by the plethora of surrounding organizations, initiatives and strategies that have been formulated throughout the work. Finally, the European and, as far as is possible, the Community view in this world dimension is given.

It must be stressed at the outset, however, that by analysing and defining these processes it becomes evident that a policy or co-ordinated strategy does not necessarily emerge. On the contrary, this book does not attempt to 'impose' co-ordination where it does not exist. By reviewing the building blocks and assessing how these have been pieced together to meet stated objectives, an objective view of the success of these mechanisms and objectives will be reached. An analysis does not try to impose order and, similarly, simply having a policy does not necessarily imply that this policy is being fulfilled. The chain of events that leads from the formation of the European Community to the delivery of environmental programmes in each individual member state has a lot of links – or a lot of potential points of breakage!

Having made these somewhat negative statements on the development and delivery of policy within the European Community, it must be stressed that in Chapter 5 the emergence of policy becomes evident, and the energy expended by the Commission in attempting to generate and sustain policy rather than a series of independent initiatives is similarly evident. The to and fro of internal and external debate continues in the environmental arena as much as elsewhere, but increasingly the EC has had the strength of will to develop a distinct agenda for environmental policy. This policy takes its direction from the original ideals and priorities of the European Community and thus leads on from general environmental policies to the specific concern of this book – nature conservation and protection. Thus, in any analysis of such policy, the starting point must be the ideals and issues which led to the creation of the European Community. The next chapter looks at these, primarily by drawing upon literature that was contemporaneous with the formation of the EC.

REFERENCES

Fairclough, A.J. (1986) The European Year of the Environment. *European Environmental Review*, **1**, 35–7.
Lodge, J. (1992) The European Community: Internal perspectives, in Lodge, J. *The EC and the Challenge of the Future*, 1st edn, Printer Press, London.

3	# Europe and the environment

In the face of the growing threats to wildlife and natural habitat, most Member States have adopted national or regional policies to protect endangered species and biotopes. These policies however, are far from comprehensive, and vary considerably between different countries in terms of both the administrative structures involved and the extent of land and numbers of animal and plant species afforded protection.

EEC Com (88) 381 Explanatory Memorandum, August 1988

The European Community (EC) is a unique political, legislative and economic system. It provides a framework for many spheres of inter- and intra-national activity, but as the above introductory remark indicates, by providing this framework absolute consistency is not guaranteed. This is in some respects valuable, because each Member State's localized political and environmental circumstances dictate that local solutions to local problems are required. However, where environmental conservation issues cross national boundaries, some degree of consistency is required.

The EC must therefore seek to strike a balance between ensuring this consistency and allowing local flexibility in meeting the wider European and even global objectives for environmental conservation. The EC operates in a series of ways, in co-operation with national government. Where the EC operates, the underlying tenet is laid down in The Treaty of Rome of 1957, which is the constitution of the EEC. Paragraph 4 of Article 130R states that 'the Community shall take action relating to the environment when the objectives can be attained at Community level rather than at the level of the individual Member States'. To this end, European environmental policy has been geared towards meeting three objectives, namely:

Plate 1 The congestion of many modern European cities puts pressure on the natural environment in and around towns.

Plate 2 Poor economic returns from farming have led to the decline of many rural areas and trends of depopulation.

1. Preservation, protection and improvement of the quality of the environment.
2. Contributing towards protecting human health.
3. Ensuring a prudent and rational utilisation of natural resources.

Harris (1989) identifies the environment as one element of the broader concerns of the EC. These broader concerns are not only identified within the Treaty of Rome, but also in the Single European Act of 1987 which represents a series of amendments and additions to the original Treaty. These two enactments identify many areas of interest for the EC, including monetary policy, economic and social cohesion, consumer protection, research and social policy.

In short, therefore, the European Environmental Policy is part of a much wider policy framework. Furthermore, the environmental policy itself is geared towards several broad objectives.

In the context here, it is the 'preservation, protection and improvements of the quality of the environment' that is of most importance. Since the formation of the European Community in 1957 through the Treaty of Rome, several significant initiatives have been started by the community and, as has been intimated each individual member state has also enacted and formulated its own environmental legislation. Details of the legal and administrative power of the European Community and the details of the national and international laws and policies are discussed in Part Two.

By way of a framework, this section seeks to outline some of the changes and processes within Europe which provided the backdrop to the creation of the European Community and its subsequent concern for the environment. These changes and processes cover several areas, specifically: the need for an international planning framework; the growth of environmentalism; and the changes on the socio-political geography of Europe. The references are drawn from sources contemporaneous with these changes so as to show how thinking was developing in the 1950s onwards.

PLANNING IN WESTERN EUROPE

The processes which led to the development of national planning mechanisms within western Europe – particularly in the six countries that originally formed the European Economic Community, were similar across Europe. These are summarized by Hall (1993) as being the result of the industrialization of the respective countries. This industrial development was led by Britain. (Although not an original EC member, the process of industrialization had developed to such an extent that in the early 1950s only 5% of the British population was employed in the agricultural industry, whereas in some mainland European countries this figure was still as high as 70–75% at the same point in time.)

As different countries entered into the complex range of changes that constitute the industrialization process at different times, and progressed at different rates, each country devised its own detailed planning and administrative responses. However, these responses did exhibit similarities, in that most countries identified two areas of concern which resulted directly from the changes brought about by industrialization. Accordingly, planning and policy responses broke down into two broad areas, namely: agricultural policy, and urban and regional planning.

Agricultural issues

In all countries throughout Europe, the agricultural industry has maintained a strong political presence. In most countries such as France, Italy and Germany, this has been because of the sheer size of the rural/agricultural vote. Politicians ignored the farmers at their peril! In Britain, the political power of the farming community appears to be based not on the size of the farming community, but on more historical and subtler lobbying activities (Newby, 1980). For whatever reason, the agriculture industry has held a relatively central position within the political policy making of individual countries. Simplistically, this policy has evolved through two distinct phases, at both national and European Community level.

First, in the 1950s, 1960s and 1970s the main objective was originally to increase agricultural outputs and protect farm prices, thereby ensuring a protected and increasing income for farmers (Clout, 1972). This requirement for increased output was a direct result of the industrialization/urbanization process being witnessed across Europe. Fewer people working on the land were being expected to feed more and more people who were increasingly living in cities.

The second more recent trend has been towards cutting back on agricultural production to reduce the surpluses produced by the first line of policy. This recent requirement for reduced output has resulted from the concern that not only are agricultural surpluses morally and economically unacceptable, but also that on achieving a higher level of output from agricultural land, landscape and natural history quality has been lost from many rural areas due to agricultural intensification (Baldock and Condor, 1986).

Needless to say, the first policy was popular with farmers, while the second has been much less so! Indeed, it has been argued (Heathcote, 1971) that the implementation of any policies which seek to undermine the power base of the farming communities in Europe has been compromised by the political power held by the farmers, which is identified above. In short, the economic and environmental considerations have, to date, been tempered by the political necessity of protecting the farming community.

Interwoven within these policy-making trends are the changes occurring within the rural and agricultural societies of Europe. The changes are complex, but the predominant trend has been of a population drift out of rural areas towards the towns and cities, creating a predominantly urban-based concentrated population. This process was evident across Europe by the 19th century (Organisation for Economic Co-operation and Development, 1965). As we have seen, this shift out of agriculture was partly responsible for the initial demand for greater outputs. But just as the call for greater food output has begun to be reviewed so too has the drift away from rural areas, with some people moving back to the rural areas out of the towns. This brings with it a range of social and physical complexities (Pahl, 1965) that muddy the waters for those seeking simplicity in socio-economic trends.

The demands for more (or less) food from farmland, coupled with the social changes of population movements, have resulted in a series of national and international initiatives aimed at solving the complex web of issues. These have followed four lines of intervention:

1. First, direct support for farm incomes (such as subsidizing hill farmers or other marginal agriculture).
2. Attempting to improve the efficiency of existing farms (capital improvement grants to buy farm machinery or drain land for example).
3. Trying to alter farm sizes and land ownership structures to make farm holdings more economically viable.
4. Aiding lagging regions in a number of ways, such as increasing other industries or helping generate farm diversification.

These initiatives were collectively held in the Mansholt plan for agriculture in Europe which formed the basis for the 1973 Common Agricultural Policy of the European Economic Community. Prior to this, however, individual countries had developed similar internal policies aimed at solving the socio-economic problems of the agricultural industry.

It is difficult to evaluate the success or otherwise of the numerous policies and initiatives. Bowler (1989) suggests that at a European level five conclusions can be drawn.

1. Agricultural policies in Europe have had adverse affects on world trade.
2. Policies have induced unwarranted increase on production.
3. Domestic prices have been distorted.
4. Significant budgetary and other costs result from protectionist policies.
5. The income objective is only reached by a few farmers.

The policies pursued at national levels therefore tried to address problems of levels of food, production, levels of income for farmers, and trends of depopulation of rural areas. This they have tried to do by supporting farm prices, offering direct and indirect grants, helping with farm restructuring and proving other regional infrastructure to help broaden the economic base of rural areas. In trying to solve these problems, however, others were created. The new problems arise in world and local economics over production and, most importantly for our concern, the 'budgetary and other costs resulting from protectionist policies'. The environment has had a price to pay for the drive towards agricultural efficiency and intensification which was felt necessary to protect rural society and farmers incomes. Only in 1986 was this intensification process questioned at a European level (Commission for the European Communities, 1986).

Urban and regional planning

We have seen that one of the main social features of the agriculture industry during the 20th century was the movement of people away from the rural environment into the towns. This movement has been caused by and, in turn is a cause of, technological and industrial development. This led to areas of dynamic growth in all countries being balanced by areas of stagnation in predominantly agricultural and 'peasant' economics (Organisation for Economic Co-operation and Development, 1965). All countries in Europe have witnessed this dichotomy, with each being able to provide examples of areas where the industrial growth has failed to have an impact – the Highlands of Scotland in Britain, the Mezzargiorno in Southern Italy, and the South West of France, for example. This pattern repeats itself at an international level with the points of Europe's 'Golden Triangle' (being Birmingham, Dortmund and Milan or, on a smaller scale, Birmingham, Paris and Dortmund) (Hall, 1993) being balanced by peripheral areas suffering decline and depopulation.

The imbalances of this pattern have been addressed at national level across Europe at both an individual city or conurbation level and at a regional level.

The most developed city-based planning structure exists in Britain (Cullingworth, 1990) and was created initially through the Town and

County Planning Act of 1947. The approach to city-based planning is one of controlling and directing localized development decisions and of initiating some basic infrastructure works such as transport routes or housing areas again at a local level. However, as Europe becomes a more cohesive social and economic whole, the city-based level of planning for urban growth is rapidly becoming replaced by the need for successful regional/sub-national planning. In this context, the French system of regional government and the planning system which it supports is innovative; as Hall (1993) suggests, 'At the National/Regional scale the French have developed a planning apparatus which is unparalleled in its comprehensiveness and its sophistication in the developed world'. Hansen (1968) assesses the strengths of the regional planning approach adopted in France.

All countries within Europe do have a regional/subnational planning structure which varies according to local circumstances. Indeed, as we shall see later, the balance of power between central and regional government is critical not only to the general planning system, but more specifically for nature conservation and landscape protection.

As national and international policy for agriculture has had broad objectives, so too has urban and regional planning policy. Broadly speaking, it has aimed to balance the economic fortunes between the various regions within countries (by offering subsidies to industries locating in peripheral areas or by directly subsidizing transport costs for example). The second objective has been to ensure that the concentration of people, industry and services are both planned properly and operate smoothly. These major conurbation's (called *les agglomerations* in France and *die Ballungsraume* in Germany, for example) increasingly require and generate large skilled workforces, service and transport networks, large areas for building, storage or, less so, manufacturing, and easy access to financial and other services.

There is some concern that, while some agricultural areas are becoming seriously depopulated, Europe's major urban centres are just too big and, no matter how sophisticated the planning machinery, some form of breakdown is inevitable (Thornley, 1992).

The future of Europe is seen by the Community itself, as lying in the continuation of the consolidation of Europe as a 'single market' (Harris, 1989). This will inevitably mean that the regional processes described here will continue and that, within these, the policies of environmental protection will be accommodated within wider economic objectives at the European level in much the same way as they have been at the national level.

To summarize, the various national regional and city planning policies have attempted to direct and control the growth of major conurbations and spread the benefits associated with economic growth, both within regions and between regions. The underlying desirability of the process of conventional economic growth remains unquestioned, certainly within mainstream policy making.

These patterns and concepts were reflected in early (and indeed subsequent) European economic policy. The objective of the European policy is to release the economic potential of regions by contributing to the financing of productive investments, investments in infrastructures and measures for developing the indigenous potential of the areas concerned. In a similar way, European environmental policy has developed as a result of these economic policies, rather than as a separate or leading concept. Thus, for example, pollution control and environmental impact assessment have largely been seen as part of economic development rather than protectionist measures *per se*.

At the urban/regional planning level, however, individual Member States have, prior to and after their membership of the EC, developed their own priorities. With the advent of the Single European Act (SEA) the EC began to assess its corporate role in assisting in the process of urban planning. The Green Paper (for discussion) issued in 1990 entitled *The Urban Environment* (Commission for the European Communities, 1990) suggests that with the SEA, the community has a direct role to play to help alleviate poor design, overcrowding and poor environmental and cultural facilities. In a moment of poetic licence, the turning point has been identified: 'most European cities have stopped growing and, like an individual in middle age, begun to reflect upon their purpose'.

For our purposes here, mid-life crisis or not, the concern for and action on the problems of urban and regional planning formed one of the cornerstones of the original Treaty of Rome (mainly because cities were and still are centres of economic activity) and this action continues to be integral to community thinking.

THE GROWTH OF ENVIRONMENTALISM

Background

While concern for the environment can be plotted in all European countries from the beginning of the 20th century, it was in the United States of America that the first practical steps were taken to protect the flora and fauna particularly of remote, underdeveloped areas. The first National Park in the United States was Yellowstone, which was formed in 1872. The subsequent influence that the United States' concept of National Parks had on the development of nature conservation and land management policies in Europe cannot be overstressed. Cherry (1975), for example, indicates that the American experience was the model for British concepts of National Parks.

Similarly, in the Netherlands for example, we find that, for the Dutch Government, the idea of instituting National Parks originated in the United States and that, like the American model, a National Park 'Is an individual area of land of at least 1,000 hectares, comprising of natural features having a special scientific character and flora and wildlife' (Ministry of Agriculture and Fisheries, 1989). Across Europe, wherever National Parks or other similar types of land designation are used as part of the process of nature conservation, the influence of the United States is acknowledged.

As is usual, however, political initiative did not arise out of a vacuum, and the designation of special protectionist areas, such as National Parks, Regional Parks, Landscape Protection Zones, Forest Parks or Nature Parks arose from a growing *public* demand for protection and conservation of the natural environment. This growing environmental awareness, which preceded and followed the creation of the European Community, is a major force which helped to shape the emerging European environmental policy from the end of the Second World War through the signing of the Treaty of Rome up to the single European Act and beyond.

The growth of environmentalism has both international and local dimensions. Similarly, it is an historic concept, one which many environmentalists would argue is simply witnessing a resurgence in importance (Porritt, 1989). It is indeed true that many ancient cultures, such as the Australian Aborigines, Native North Americans and Ancient Chinese cultures had areas which, for a variety of reasons, were felt to be inviolate (McLuhan, 1972). In modern concepts, the National Park and Nature Reserve can be likened to these former wild areas, protected at the demand of the local community. During the more recent history of Europe, areas of land have also been protected through various mechanisms. One of the strongest was that of ownership by ruling or landed classes; many areas of land in Europe were protected, not least for the hunting that they offered to kings, queens and dukes such as in the forests of Saxony, the Central Massif, La Mancha or England's New Forest.

The concept of protecting land and species of wild animals and plants is therefore not new. What must concern us here, however, is the form that this renewed interest in environmental protection has taken since 1945, from when most environmental legislation has been formulated.

Since the end of the Second World War, environmental concern has followed similar trends to those outlined in the previous section. Attention has tended to focus upon the impact of industrialization, new agricultural techniques, pollution and protectionist policies for land. Prior to this, in the 1950s and early 1960s, at exactly the same time that the concept of the European community was being formulated, a new driving force was identified for all of these environmental concerns: the 'cause' was identified as population growth. In 1963, for example, the Council of Europe examined the potential problems that were being identified (United Nations, 1964).

The estimated population of the world in the year 2000 was set at eight thousand million. Such a huge global population was often referred to in the 1950s and 1960s as a 'population bomb', which would bring with it greater demands for energy, food, work, transport, fresh water and, increasingly, areas of recreation. The talk of the 1950s was therefore of crisis, from which human kind could extricate itself by applying the knowledge accumulated since its relationship with the environment began. As Arvill (1967) suggests, 'Do not 5,000 years of experience suggest that man cannot live on this planet without degrading it, and in any event, would his efforts not be in vain in view of the population explosion? But to survive, man must reject a counsel of despair. He must make his approach simultaneously on three fronts: political; organizational; and professional/scientific.' Here we see all of the issues of the crisis; the population bomb, resolved through the application of knowledge.

The 1960s were marked therefore not only by an increased focus on organizational systems to address the growing environmental problems, and also by an increase in the desire to fully understand the processes involved, such as water pollution, air pollution (Council of Europe, 1964) and wildlife protection (Conservation Foundation, 1964). This process of information gathering still continues, but increasingly the demand is for the political and administrative systems to find methods to use this information.

If we briefly explore the ways in which areas of environmental concern were developing prior to and immediately after the Treaty of Rome was formulated, we can gain a better understanding of the growth of environmentalism. We can identify three significant areas of interest: ecological abuse, environmental protection and popular environmentalism.

Ecological abuse

This rather emotive phrase relates directly to the concerns which were being expressed at the end of the 1950s and the early 1960s. Thomas (1956) plots the growing scientific concern over the impact of human activity on the world's ecosystem. Similar symposia were being held across the globe. The concern was not a new one, but what was being registered was 'a quantum shift in the qualitative impact of man's activities' (Thomas, 1956). The level and type of pollution and destruction was not only growing but also accelerating and, as in the case of radioactivity and DDT, becoming increasingly long-term and irreversible. The situation with DDT, one of the early organo-chlorides to be used in pest control, is a good case in point. Upon entering the food chain, DDT was passed long the chain to end as a residuary deposit in the fatty tissue of the species at the head of the food chain. In many cases this was a bird of prey. (In Britain, the percentage of pairs of golden eagles successfully rearing young fell from 72% to 29% in the late 1950s – a fall due largely to contamination by organo-chlorides.) In other cases, the end part in the food chain was the human species; and once this point had been made, the level of public concern was raised significantly. Of international impact was the book *Silent Spring* (Carson, 1963), which both summarized and led the passionate concern for balance between human activity and the natural environment.

> It is not my contention that chemicals must never be used. I <u>do</u> contend that we have put poisonous and biologically potent chemicals indiscriminately into the hands of persons largely or wholly ignorant of their potential for harm. We have subjected enormous numbers of people of contact with these poisons ... with no advance investigation of their effect on soil, water, wildlife and man himself.

These words of caution were echoing across Europe, indeed across the world. However, as we shall see, in its original conception, the European Community failed to fully grasp the issue of environmentalism in 1957 through the Treaty of Rome.

Environmental protection

The concept of environmental protection, as we have seen, started in the United States of America with the first National Park in 1872. Forms of legislation began appearing within the individual countries of Europe from the early 1900s. In 1916, Spain enacted its first legislation concerned with protecting 'areas of national importance for their natural beauty', and before 1939, Italy designated four National Parks. In both cases, the Parks themselves were to be managed by regional authorities, in a similar way to the United States model. In 1949, Britain passed its 'National Parks' legislation.

The issue then appeared to recede in importance, until the 1970s when several other European countries turned their attentions to conservationist land designation. The conservation of natural resources was therefore a live issue at the outset of the European Community, and is an issue that kept recurring throughout the lifetime of the Community and its Member States.

The other trend of protectionist activity which is worth noting was also alive in the 1960s. Partly as a result of the concern over the impact of human activities, as identified in the previous section, there was a growing demand that any of these activities should pre-empt environmental impact by assessing the environmental impact before the work or the activity commenced. Again, the lead on this particular issue was taken in the United States of America, when this pressure resulted in the National Environmental Policy Act being passed in 1969. This called for Environmental Impact Statements to accompany 'major federal action which significantly affects the quality of the human environment'. Thus, for the first time, it was accepted that environmental protection should form part of the decision-making framework not only in specially designated areas, but also within the wider environment.

Collectively, these two types of environmental protectionist activity form the background against which much of the European framework has been created. It is significant to note that: (1) the impetus for both types of activity has, by and large, come from the United States; (2) while the earliest concerns were for land-use zoning to protect valuable natural areas, it appears to have become quickly apparent that the pressures brought by an energy-hungry and rapidly growing population required a more widespread and general response. This is a theme that can be plotted in the European Community.

Popular environmentalism

Popular environmentalism can be defined as the layperson's increasing desire for knowledge and understanding of the environment, and, in some cases, the desire to become actively involved in its protection. We have already seen how the so-called 'population bomb' became a live issue in the 1960s. Prior to this, and contemporaneously, other concerns and issues were becoming important throughout the world. This world-wide environmental concern has been described elsewhere (McCarmick, 1989). In Europe, as elsewhere, most concerns originated as single or localized issues such as protecting land for the hunt in France, concern over the flow of other countries' pollution along the Rhine as it enters the North Sea through the Netherlands, or concerns for public access to private land in England and Wales. Some of these localized issues have remained and still continue with their own national fervour. Others, such as the problems associated with pollution of the Rhine, have become truly European issues, being resolved at the pan-European level, and popular environmentalism has given way to institutional action. The environmental movement has, however, broadened its horizons and now focuses not only on local problems but also on global problems, such as the destruction of the rainforests, the effects of global warming and the destruction of the ozone layer.

Environmental issues, from the protection of a favourite local woodland to the protection of the earth itself, have their own collection of grassroots champions. Much of this energy is focused upon the political process (Lowe and Goyder, 1983). This was originally at the national level (O'Riordan, 1975) but has increasingly become more sophisticated and international with groups such as Friends of the Earth, Greenpeace, and the World Wide Fund for Nature initiating and sustaining international campaigns on major issues, backed by local groups and popular support. This campaigning is similarly targeted at the international decision makers, mostly the political parties. In some areas, the pressure has been welcomed and action taken (Lowe and Goyder, 1983). In others, the campaigning has been seen as an attack on the political system itself and rejected, if not oppressed (Bulicek, 1990). The growth in popular environmentalism, and the increasing skill with which it has been able to influence political decision making and hence the legislation surrounding environmental protection, has therefore moved in parallel with changes in the political geography of Europe both within individual member states and within the whole European framework, including the former Communist states of Eastern Europe.

However, to summarize, environmentalism was a major force within pre-Community Europe and it manifested itself in several ways. Concerns, such as population growth, were being openly discussed; land designations based solely upon conservationist grounds were becoming more commonplace; increased knowledge and concern were expressed about agricultural and other 'modern' technologies; the demand for solving environmental problems at project design stage was also growing. Public interest in the environment was growing correspondingly, either through organized pressure or lobby groups, or through individual activity such as tourism and public recreation, or indeed through adjustments to personal lifestyles to accommodate environmental protection.

OTHER ISSUES

Political change

The political map of Europe has never been stable, and frontiers to states, countries and alliances have changed almost continually since pre-Christian times (Taylor, 1989). During the course of the 20th century, however, Europe underwent two enormous armed conflicts and witnessed three major political restructurings of the political map, and is now undergoing a fourth at the start of the 21st century. At the end of the 1914–18 war, the European map was redrawn, as too at the end of the

1939–45 war. However, in the latter case, this redefinition also included a distinct ideological boundary emerging between the Eastern Bloc Communist states led by the Soviet Union, and the Western 'Liberal Democratic' States allied to the United States. With the collapse of the Communist bloc in the late 1980s the map was again redrawn; and later still in the mid-late 1990s, with the further redefinition of international boundaries accompanied by armed conflict in Russia, Bosnia, Turkey, Iran and beyond.

At a global level, the Empires of former world powers such as France, Britain, Germany and Spain were beginning to decline. Consequently, the European and Global politico-economy was geared as much towards self protection as it was about an ideological objective of securing free trade and democracy; a process which was inherent in the European political map even prior to 1945 (Taylor, 1974).

The discussion and analysis necessary to fully assess the political dimensions of the establishment of the European Community has already occupied several texts (see Lodge, 1989, for example). It is sufficient here to note that the creation of the European Community was clearly a political response to changing circumstances as much as it was a response to the economic circumstances of the time. Consequently any policies (environmental or otherwise) will inevitably be determined by political agendas and by the continuing internal and external political circumstances of individual member states and of the Community *vis-à-vis* its neighbours.

Social changes

The social environment of Europe in the 1950s was rapidly changing, which in turn added to the overall period of optimism and desire for closer co-operation. Furthermore, it also contributed to the cultural acceptance of closer relationships in a continent which only a decade before had witnessed an appalling war. This cultural change manifested itself in many ways. Tourism, for example, rapidly became a boundary-breaking cultural and economic factor. Dower (1965) defined the leisure industry as 'the fourth wave', likening its cultural and economic impact to that of the three previous waves: urbanization; railway transport; car-based transport. It is true to say that the mass movement of people across Europe did establish a climate of awareness and tolerance unheard of a decade earlier, and this increase in international tourism continues today (World Tourism Organisation, 1992).

Further cultural developments were witnessed in other fields: education, social welfare, public health, for example. Greater access to these benefits also gave rise to the wider desire for a 'better future'. This had a number of effects, not least that it gave a degree of widening support

for the concept of a European Community. The old international
suspicions were partly reduced by a new generation anxious to work
closer together, thereby 'giving development a cultural dimension'
(Berger, 1959).

TOWARDS AN ENVIRONMENTAL POLICY

The foregoing discussion gives some indication of the complex socio-
political activity and processes operating within Europe (and indeed, the
world) immediately prior to and after the time of the formation of the
European Community in 1957. From this constantly changing scenario,
it is possible to see how a truly European environmental policy began to
take shape.

To summarize, individual European countries had begun to witness
disparities in the economic well-being of different regions within them.
The model of densely populated industrially based conurbation set
against intensively farmed agricultural land on the one hand, and
sparsely populated quasi-wilderness areas on the other is clearly an oversimplification, but it does help in understanding the starting point of
European legislation.

This simple model is made more complex by several factors. First, it
is not just rural areas which suffer depopulation and economic decline.
Many former heavy industrial regions are suffering equally dramatic
decline, and these areas are also in need of regional aid packages generated either by national governments or the European Community itself.
A second complicating factor is the interdependence that urban and
rural areas have with each other; their economics (and hence, everything
else) are inextricably linked. For example, urban-based populations buy
their food from rural or wilderness areas or indeed from 'underdeveloped' parts of Europe. On a more localised basis, many choose to
travel to work in towns and cities from more accessible rural areas
(Best, 1981; Clout, 1969; Saville, 1966). Thus, to try to create a single
response to this fluctuating array of issues is clearly difficult if not
impossible. For this reason, as we shall see in more detail later, the
European Community's response has been to create legal and monetary
frameworks, which allow for local circumstances to be taken into
consideration when measures are delivered at the national and regional
level.

If, however, we remain with the model of industrialized conurbations
and relatively sparsely populated agricultural areas we can begin to see
the types of environmental problems that arise under these circumstances.

In agricultural areas, intensive production has led to a land-use
monopoly and a heavy reliance upon chemical, and artificial systems.

This in turn has lead to a marginalization of other issues, such as environmental protection or nature conservation, (Countryside Policy Review Panel, 1987; Shoard, 1980). While there is some evidence that this monopoly is beginning to be readdressed (Baldock and Condor, 1987), the agricultural use of non-developed land is still paramount.

In some larger European countries, it is possible to zone areas specifically for nature or landscape conservation, but in some smaller countries, such as Belgium, the Netherlands or Great Britain almost all land has agricultural pressure upon it. It is a further dichotomy that many areas that are potentially valuable wildlife or natural reserves are also perceived as being underdeveloped and capable of sustaining conventional economic growth, either through service industries such as tourism or through more conventional industrial operations. Such areas might include the Sierra Nevada in Southern Spain (where recent developments include ski-facilities for tourists) and the Prespa National Park in Northern Greece (where land drainage and the development of fish farms took place on land of international ecological importance; Long, 1990). Both of these developments, and others, received financial support from the European Community.

Two broad types of rural situation have therefore developed within Europe: (1) high-production areas, which have tended to force out natural history interests; (2) low-production areas, which are or have reverted to a semi-natural state but are now coming under other pressure.

In the urban context, pressures on the natural environment are somewhat different. Urbanization brings with it demands for land and changes in traditional landscapes (Blatchford, 1990, for example). Thus, semi-natural landscapes are built upon or affected by pollution, noise or visual intrusion associated with urbanization and industrial development. The measures needed to protect the environment are therefore ones of containment and pollution control; hence the nationally based planning mechanisms discussed earlier.

The perceived balance between the need for urbanization, the need to protect semi-wilderness areas and to assist poor rural economics to enter the mainstream economic process varies from country to country. In industrialized nations, the pressure to protect the few remaining areas of natural history value may be great, but in predominantly poor, agricultural countries, the perceived need may be for a broader conventional economic base rather than wildlife protection. In Portugal, for example, 'a viable agriculture is key to the economic and social viability of rural areas, but other concerns such as industrial and service sector/ tourist development are also important' (Organisation for Economic Co-operation and Development, 1988).

The way that these localized and national debates resolve themselves is a function of the political and environmental pressure within each member state; this is discussed in Part Two, when the political and administrative framework for nature conservation in each country is assessed. What must concern us here is the way that the embryonic European Community began to respond to this hugely complex inter- and intra-national set of circumstances. This is the subject of the following chapter.

REFERENCES

Arvill, R. (1967) *Man and the Environment*. Penguin Books, Harmondsworth.

Baldock, D. and Conder, D. (1986) *Can the CAP fit the environment?* CPRE/WWF, London.

Baldock, D. and Conder, D. (1987) *Removing land from agriculture*. CPRE/IEEP, London.

Berger, G. (1959) *Cultural Development*. UNESCO, Paris.

Best, R.H. (1981) *Land-use and Living Space*. Methuen, London.

Blatchford, J. (1990) Village landscapes in Cyprus, *Landscape Design*, 188, 18–23.

Bowler, I. (1989) *Government and Agriculture: A Spatial Perspective*. Longman, London.

Bulicek, J. (1990) The development of the ecological movement in Czechoslovakia. *ECOS,* 11(3). 32–34.

Carson, R. (1963) *Silent Spring*. Hamish Hamilton, London.

Cherry, G.E. (1975) *Environmental Planning: Vol. 2 National Parks*. HMSO, London.

Clout, H.D. (1969) Second homes in France. *Journal of the Town Planning Institute*, 55, 440–443.

Clout, H.D. (1972) *Rural Geography*. Pergamon Press, Oxford.

Commission for the European Community (1986) *Agricultural Policy in the International Context*. European Commission, Brussels.

Commission for the European Community (1988) *Reform of the Structural Funds*. Com (88) 500. European Commission, Brussels.

Commission for the European Community (1990) *Green Paper on the Urban Environment*. European Commission, Brussels.

Conservation Foundation (1964) Wildlife Conservation: *The Ethical and Technical Problems*. Conservation Foundation, New York.

Council of Europe (1963) *Report on the Problems Raised by Population Trends in Europe*. Council of Europe, Strasbourg.

Council of Europe (1964) *Effects of Air Pollution on Animal and Plants*. Council of Europe, Strasbourg.

Countryside Policy Review Panel (1987) *New Opportunities for the Countryside*. CCP 224. Countryside Commission, Cheltenham.

Cullingworth, J.B. (1990) *Town and Country Planning in England and Wales*, Allen & Unwin, London.

Dower, M. (1965) *The Fourth Wave*. Civic Trust, London.

Hall, P. (1993) *Urban and Regional Planning*. Pelican Books, Harmondsworth.

Hansen, N.M. (1968) *French Regional Planning*. Edinburgh University Press, Edinburgh.

Harris, J. (1989) Unity Downs. *Local Government Chronicle*, September, 30–31.

Heathcote, N. (1971) *Agricultural Policies in the EEC*. Occasional Paper No. 7. Australian National University, Canberra.

Lodge, J. (ed.) (1989) *The European Community and the Challenge of the Future*. Printer Press, London.

Long, T. (1990) Structural funds in Europe – the conservation challenge. *ECOS*, **II**(3), 16–21.

Lowe, P. and Goyder, J. (1983) *Environmental Groups in Politics*. Allen & Unwin, London.

McCarmick, J.S. (1989) *The Global Environmental Movement*. Belhaven Press, London.

McLuhan, R. (1972) *Touch the Earth*. Abacus Books, London.

Ministry of Agriculture and Fisheries (1989) *National Parks Policy in the Netherlands*. Commission on National Parks, Den Haagen.

Newby, H. (1980) *Green and Pleasant Land*. Pelican Books, Harmondsworth.

Organisation for Economic Co-operation and Development (1965) *Agriculture and Economic Growth*. OECD, Paris.

Organisation for Economic Co-operation and Development (1988) *New Trends in Rural Policy Making*. OECD, Paris.

O'Riordan, T. (1975) *Environmentalism*. Sion Books, London.

Porrit, J. (1989) *Unity Down Local Government Chronicle*.

Pahl, R.E. (1965) *Urbs in Rure*. Geographical Papers No. 2. London School of Economics.

Saville, J. (1966) Urbanisation and the countryside, in *People in the Countryside* (ed. J. Higg), National Council for Social Services, London.

Shoard, M. (1980) *The Theft of the Countryside*. Temple Smith, London.

Taylor, A.J.P. (1974) *The Struggle for Mastery in Europe*. Penguin Books, Harmondsworth.

Taylor, A.J.P. (1989) *A Brief History of Europe*. Penguin Books, Harmondsworth.

Thomas, W.J. (ed) (1956) *Man's Role in the Changing Face of the Earth*. Symposium Proceedings. University of Chicago.

Thornley, A. (1992) *The Crisis of London*. Routledge, Hampshire.

United Nations (1964) *Report on World Population Prospects*. UN, New York.

World Tourism Organisation (1992) *The Development of Tourism*. WTO, Madrid.

4 | The European Community

The previous chapter dealt with the range of forces which helped to frame the European Community's response to environmental issues and concerns. These were: the growth of environmentalism, national planning policies and the political movements throughout Europe. Furthermore, the move towards some form of European unity was given greater impetus by other, wider economic objectives. The Community which was formed through the Treaty of Rome and which has developed since, is therefore a result of many and continually fluctuating pressures and forces. To speak of the European Community without acknowledging this is to deny the dynamic nature of the organization, and to deny the complexities inherent within the system. Before we can assess the various mechanisms and methods used by the Member States to protect and enhance the natural environment, we must therefore determine how the Community was formed, how it established its own terms of reference and, perhaps of greatest importance, how the Community legislates and seeks to implement its policies through its statutory powers, its relationship with Member States, and its ability to allow individual, national variations within its own broader guidelines.

This chapter deals with the formation of the European Community, and some of its original ideals. It also deals with the subsequent development of the Community and the place that environmental conservation has within this process. The discussion then concentrates upon the *modus operandi* of the Community and how legislation and policy directives are firstly discussed and agreed upon and then how they are implemented across the Member States. This sets the framework for subsequent chapters which deal first with the legislation itself and then with how individual Member States have developed and adapted their land management policies to adopt conservation considerations.

ORIGINS AND FOUNDATIONS

With the end of the Second World War in 1945 came the physical and moral desire to rebuild Europe. This was evident not only on the national level, but also on the international level. We have already seen how this manifested itself at a national and regional level, with individual countries developing planning machinery to deal with economic and agricultural inequalities. It was also evident within the immediate post-war period that these patterns of inequality were found at the international scale, across Europe. There were, however, other pressures and changes in the post-war global economy that influenced events in Europe.

First, other stronger continental economies were developing, notably in Asia and the United States. These areas began to dominate not only their local economic markets, but also began to spread their influence throughout the world. This influence was twofold. On the one hand, these areas were looking for new markets into which they could export their produce, and were also developing potential markets into which other countries could export their own goods. Therefore, it began to become clear that in order to be part of this developing 'global market' a suitably large and strong economy was needed within Europe

The second influence which hastened change within western Europe in the immediate post-war period was the decline of the 'traditional' industries of Europe, notably coal production and steel manufacturing. The European Community was pre-empted by five years when in 1952 six European Countries signed the Treaty of Paris which established the European Coal and Steel Community. The six nations (Belgium, France, the German Federal Republic, Italy, Luxembourg and the Netherlands) sought to manage collectively these critical economic sectors, essential for the success of post-war reconstruction (Hay, 1989).

The Treaty of Rome

Thus, by 1952 major international co-operation was taking place within Europe. This reached a watershed in 1957 with the signing of the Treaty of Rome which effectively signalled the start of the European Community in a form that is recognizable as the one we can see today. The Treaty of Rome extended the scope of the agreements made within the Treaty of Paris, most significantly by heralding the start of the development of the Common Agricultural Policy within the European Community (Articles 38–47).

The Treaty of Rome, which was signed by the six countries who signed the Treaty of Paris, was split into five sections, dealing through a series of over 250 Articles with:

'the underlying problems of economic development and regional inequalities'

Most notably, for our purposes, the Treaty of Rome did not specifically mention environmental protection or nature conservation. The Treaty did, however, identify the need to achieve 'the constant improvement of the living and working conditions of people within the Community'. It is upon this rather tenuous legal foundation that early environmental policy was formulated. Indeed, this was to remain the case well into the 1980s when amendments were finally made to the Treaty of Rome through the Single European Act in 1987.

The Community grew in 1973 from six to nine Members when Denmark, Ireland and the United Kingdom signed the Treaty of Rome. Similarly, in 1981 Greece joined the Community and, in 1986, so too did Spain and Portugal bringing the Membership to 12.

Finally, to date, Sweden, Finland and Austria joined after referenda on 1 January 1995. In that series of referenda, Norway rejected the option to join.

With the growth in the number of Member States, there was also a corresponding growth in the number of objectives set by the Community for its own operations. It is therefore now involved to a greater or lesser extent, in most areas of political, economic, financial, social, cultural and environmental activity. This is reflected by the fact that the Community now has 23 different departments (Directorates-General) which bid for Community funds. (The titles of these Directorates-General are given in Table 4.1).

In order to establish new areas of work and policy direction for itself the Community has to establish its own legal right (termed 'competence') to generate laws and regulations on certain issues. As we have seen, for example, the original basis for much environmental policy was, until 1987, a very flimsy one indeed. This caused some concern, particularly in Denmark, Germany and the United Kingdom who felt that the Community could not set such policy, because it was not legally competent to do so. For this reason, much of the original environmental legislation enacted by the European Community was related directly to economic trade, which still lies at the heart of the Treaty of Rome and which the Community was certainly competent to do. One example of this trade-related environmental policy is the 1982 Regulation which implements the recommendations of the Convention of Trade in Endangered Species. At a different level of environmental protection, pollution control measures were also geared towards monitoring economic production and its impact upon 'living and working conditions'.

Table 4.1 Directorates-General and their staff numbers (1993)

Directorates-General		No. of staff
Cabinets		294
Secretariat-General		335
Legal Service		170
Spokesman's Service		52
Consumer Policy Service		40
Task Force 'Human resources, education, training and youth'		55
Translation Service		1678
Joint Interpretation and Conference Service		506
Statistical Office		352
DGI	– External Relations	613
DGII	– Economic and Financial Affairs	231
DGIII	– Internal Market and Industrial Affairs	430
DGIV	– Competition	309
DGV	– Employment, Industrial Relationships and Social Affairs	295
DGVI	– Agriculture	826
DGVII	– Transport	127
DGVIII	– Development	766
DGIX	– Personnel and Administration	2536
DGX	– Information, Communication and Culture	369
DGXI	– Environment, Nuclear Safety and Civil Protection	119
DGXII	– Science, Research and Development Joint Research Centre	1985
DGXIII	– Telecommunications, Information Industries and Innovation	492
DGXIV	– Fisheries	164
DGXV	– Financial Institutions and Company Law	82
DGXVI	– Regional Policies	196
DGXVII	– Energy	409
DGXVIII	– Credit and Investments	101
DGXIX	– Budgets	260
DGXX	– Financial Control	164
DGXXI	– Customs Union and Indirect Taxation	229
DGXXII	– Co-ordination of Structural Policies	60
DGXXIII	– Enterprises Policy, Distributive Trades, Tourism and Social Economy	56
Euratom Supply Agency		23
Security Office		55

The Single European Act

In order to clear these competence 'blockages', adjustments were needed to the original Treaty of Rome. While, for our purposes, only minor adjustments were made to the Treaty between 1957 and 1987, another watershed was reached in 1987 with the passing of the Single European Act (SEA). The SEA aimed to complete the internal market by the end of December 1992 – the internal market being lengthily defined in Article 8A. The process of completing the market was largely a legal and administrative one, rather than economic, although it clearly carried major economic implications for Europe post-1992, such as the moves towards a single European currency. The completion of the single European Act was seen as being the Maastricht Treaty of 1992, but as the discussion later in this chapter shows, it was at this stage that the process ran into difficulty.

The SEA is not an act in the nationally accepted sense, but is, as is intimated here, a series of amendments to the Treaty of 1957. This process covered several areas of legal and administrative competence. First, it addressed the lack of legal competence for dealing with environmental issues; it also addressed a similar gap in social issues. Second, the Act dealt with the long-contested issue of a lack of democracy in the European Community and introduced the concept of majority ruling, strengthening the role of the European Parliament. Changing the so-called democratic deficit had always been an intention of the European Community, and this was started with the SEA.

The final broad area of intention within the SEA was that of creating an opportunity for common European policy on foreign and security issues. Many of the details of the SEA were only finalized through the Maastricht Treaty but, by way of exemplifying, some of the SEA's new articles are discussed below. However, it is safe to say that, notwithstanding the introduction of environmental and social dimensions to the Treaty of Rome through the Single European Act, the thrust of the Act remained economic.

The most important amendments for our purposes were to Article 130 of the Treaty of Rome, which originally dealt only with the 'foundations, policy and principles' of the Community. This Article had a large number of sub-articles attached to it under the SEA. Most significantly Articles 130R, 130S and 130T deal specifically with the environment. These Articles were introduced not so much to help with the process of integrating European markets, but to clear the problem of competence to deal with environmental issues at Community level (Haigh and Baldock, 1989). The new and attendant Articles were considered so important collectively, that they were given a new title within the Treaty, namely (and not surprisingly) 'Environment'.

The significance (or perhaps lack of) to the Community of the new Environment Articles is shown by the fact that they, and all other Articles not relating directly to economic policy, are referred to as 'flanking policies'.

Other flanking policies have an impact upon the environment and the policies for its protection.

Changes to the Social Policy (Articles 117–122) are designed to broaden the Community's social dimension (in much the same way that the Environment title gave competence to environmental policies). This strengthening of social policies will affect environmental objectives, particularly those geared towards raising or protecting living standards.

Social cohesion (Articles 130A–130E) is aimed at 'reducing disparities between the various regions and the backwardness of the least favoured regions'. Redressing the imbalance between the 'haves' and 'have nots' was one of the issues which led the post-war planning frameworks as discussed in Chapter 3. Therefore, any adjustments to this policy will clearly have a knock-on effect on the environment. In order to bring about a reduction in disparity the European Community offers funds in three main programme areas (Regional, Social and Agricultural Guidance), which seek to reduce disparity. Articles 130A–130E increase the amount of funds available for these three programmes. Although this funding is in principle linked to environmental assessment and protection, in practice the desire to reduce economic disparity often outweighs the environmental considerations, and remote, wild areas will increasingly be subject to greater development pressures as witnessed in the Integrated Mediterranean Programmes, for example. (Baldock, Corrie and Long, 1989).

In order fully to appreciate the economic thrust of the programme funds, we must refer to the wording of the regulation for the reform of the structural fund (Commission of the European Communities, 1988a).

For the reformed regional fund (Economic Regional Development Fund, ERDF) the aim is to 'assist structural adjustments and growth, and to create permanent employment opportunities ... and to contribute to the financing of productive investments, investments in infrastructures and measures for developing the indigenous potential of the other areas concerned.'

Similarly, the European Social Fund (ESF) aims to operate 'in the less developed regions, with measures to help those whose activities contribute to the economic development of the regions, for example re-training.'

Finally, the European Agricultural Guidance and Guarantee Fund (EAGGF) has a 'critical role in promoting the development of rural areas, mainly through measures aimed at the conversion, revitalization and economic stimulation of these areas'. Only in one section of the Reform of Funds Regulation is the environment acknowledged. Within the new EAGGF, the new role 'will also take account of environmental protection needs'.

The significance of the concern over the impact on social, environmental and other 'flanking' issues is that, while the Community was taking the opportunity to review its competence, it took the opportunity to overhaul its mechanism for bringing about change, namely the structural fund. As part of the process of change, the structural funds were reviewed at the end of 1992.

The set of amendments of relevance here are those that covered the democracy deficit. These are dealt with in detail later, but the impact on environmental policy was that, because environment was seen as a flank-ing issue, the need for a unanimous decision in the Council of Ministers was removed and it was replaced with a multiplicity of methods and mechanisms for decision making.

Maastricht Treaty

In Autumn 1991, the heads of the Member States met in Maastricht, Netherlands to finalize the detail and formally agree the conclusion of the lead in to European Union – indeed the Maastricht Treaty has as its full title, 'The Treaty of European Union'. The Treaty therefore repre-sented the formal acceptance of the principles of the Single European Act and, as a piece of legislation in its own right, also made some adjustments.

Most relevant is that Article 2 of the Treaty of Rome, which sets out the objectives of the European Community, was amended so that the new text requires the Community to 'promote sustainable and non-inflation-ary growth respecting the environment'. However, the mention of 'sus-tainable growth' as opposed to 'sustainable development' is seen by some observers as a confirmation to traditional economic values rather than a reassessment of long-term economic growth (Hallo, 1992). Similarly, it is also felt that other opportunities for change to environmental policy were missed, particularly as the Irish Government put the Environment at the top of their agenda when they took the European Presidency in 1990, less than 12 months before the Treaty was finalized.

Notwithstanding these lost (or indeed taken) opportunities, the real importance of the Maastricht Treaty lies in the problems that followed its formal conclusion in February 1992. First, the Danish people were given the opportunity to vote in a referendum to accept or reject the Treaty. In summer 1992 they rejected it. This, to many, signalled the end of the moves towards European Union. In September 1992, the French people also voted in a referendum, and approved the Treaty by a narrow margin. But for several months, between the Danish and French referenda, the Community was unable to decide whether the Treaty was alive or dead. As a result, a severe money crisis developed and the strength of the Community was shaken (Confederation of British Industry, 1993).

Caught up in the middle of this more fundamental debate were the changes in competence and policy blockages on the environment. Thus the moves by the Member States to accept the Treaty at an individual state level, and the accompanying political debate, marked a clear water-shed in the moves towards European Union. As a consequence, the Community's moves towards more integrated environmental policy were also delayed.

Other than the removal of the problem of competence to deal with environmental legislation in general, the debate about the Maastricht Treaty had other spin-offs that also affected the environmental policy in Europe.

The central concerns of the people of Denmark, France and indeed many others in other Member States were not those raised by environmental issues, but those raised by the concept of monetary union and subsidiarity. The perception that Europe was somehow moving towards a large, single super-state which would ultimately have a single currency was the fear that most opponents of the Treaty voiced. Because of these concerns, discussion of the whole process of integration, and the appropriate level of involvement by the Community *vis-à-vis* Member States, was reopened.

As indicated above the most positive aspects of the Maastricht Treaty (which, it must be remembered followed on directly from the Single European Act) were the inclusion of Environmental Principles and Articles, and the promotion of 'sustainable growth'. Four other areas within the Maastricht Treaty are worthy of discussion.

The concept of subsidiarity is that the Commission can only act 'in so far as the objectives of the proposed action cannot be sufficiently achieved by the Member State and can therefore .... be better achieved by the Community'. Far from representing a move towards a 'super-state' the subsidiarity clause moves towards Member State decision making. This could be seen to move away from the more pro-active role that the Commission took on environmental issues prior to Maastricht where the Community was 'to act when objectives can be attained *better* at Community level'. The emphasis is slightly different, but this difference is important.

The second change that had a spin-off effect on environmental policy was that the various programmes in the community were to be integrated better. As a result, environmental issues arose to be an important part of all other policies and programmes such as energy, development, agriculture and research for example.

The third area of change is the decision-making process. This is discussed in more detail later in this chapter, but the terms of the Maastricht Treaty suggest that environmental legislation will be decided upon in a variety of ways notably by qualified majority or unanimous agreement.

Finally, and as a follow on from this, the 'democratization' of the European Community by giving the Parliament more power again has spin-off impact on the environmental policies of the Community. Most 'harmonization' legislation (which by and large refers to bringing economic and trading systems closer together across Europe) will be exposed to increased debate through this new decision process. However, because most environmental legislation is seen as peripheral, this process will not be used automatically in all cases.

Summary

Collectively, the Treaty of Rome, the Single European Act and the Maastricht Treaty represent a chain of legislation and agreements that lead towards levels of harmonization across Europe. The debate continues, however, with further discussions on monetary and political union being undertaken at Community and Member State level (Delors, 1994).

For the environmental policy, the changes have been clear, with moves towards an increased awareness of and desire to influence environmental issues. Including 'the Environment' as a separate series of Articles in the Treaty, and removing competence blockages, represent positive steps in the protection of the environment. The complexity of the process has, however, become clear. Hence the need to 'make haste slowly'.

THE STRUCTURE OF THE COMMUNITY

The European Community is concerned with most aspects of socio-economic development and, through the Articles held within the Treaty of Rome and the Single European Act, has developed its own competence to issue legislation and develop policy in any one of a wide range of topics – including the environment, although, as is already evident, a host of other topic areas inevitably have an influence upon the environment also.

The way that the European Community operates has several layers, as befits any political and executive organization. Indeed, Harris (1989) has quoted the procedures of the Community as 'being of Byzantine Complexity'. The levels relevant to this discussion are:

1. the political process. There is both a direct and an indirect political machinery within the European Community, an understanding of which is important in evaluating Community policy development and its attitude towards the environment.
2. the legislative process. The European Community issues four types of legislation or decision which vary in the degree to which they are legally binding on individuals, Member States or the Community as a whole.
3. the executive process. As with any system of government, the European Community employs a large number of officer or 'civil servants' whose job it is to implement and manage community policy.

While each of these processes clearly interlinks with the others, it would be useful initially to discuss the operational mechanisms of the Community under these three headings.

The political process

The European Parliament consists of over 600 elected representatives from throughout the European Community. The number of representatives that a country returns to the European Parliament is based upon the population of that particular country. Elections are held nationally and, with the exception of the United Kingdom, are held on the basis of proportional representation. Within this system the balance of political parties and viewpoints represented by the Members of European Parliament (MEPs) returned by any country reflect the proportion of votes that each party attracts. It is therefore possible to better reflect the increasing political diversity identified in Chapter 3.

MEPs are elected or re-elected every four years, and operate both as a single body and through a committee and subcommittee system common to most parliamentary systems. Similarly, political allegiances are formed across national boundaries; hence there exist groupings of 'Socialist', 'Conservative' and 'Green' MEPs who seek to operate their own political system to bring about desired change.

The European Parliament can be said to represent the 'voice of the people' at Community level (Commission of the European Communities, 1988b). However, unlike most national situations, it is not the Parliament which has the power to generate and create legislation. The European Parliament, which meets once a month in Strasbourg, has a predominantly advisory and discursive role. Its opinion must be obtained before legislation can proceed or can be adopted by the Council (see below). This power of consultation can and has been used to delay and seek amendments to legislation and raise new issues connected to proposed legislation.

The Single European Act of 1987 increased this consultative role, through Article 149, by introducing the concept of the European Council (which frames European legislation) working 'in co-operation with the Parliament' and the Parliament can propose amendments at a 'second reading'. While this does not give anything like overall legislative control to the Parliament it does strengthen its role. However, this 'co-operation procedure' only operates when a proposed piece of legislation is approved in Council by a 'qualified majority'. Instead of attaining unanimity, therefore, draft proposals can move forward with majority support. In order to understand this process more fully, it is necessary to look at the legislative procedures associated with the European Community.

The Council and the Commission

Before the new, more intricate system is reviewed and the various forms of legislation discussed, it is necessary to look at the nature and the role of both the Council and the Commission.

The Council of Ministers

If the European Parliament can be seen as representing the voice of the people, then the Council of Ministers represents the national interest of the individual member states.

The Council consists of one minister from each of the Member States. Depending upon the issues under discussion, this will vary, so in effect there are several Councils, and these are referred to according to the subject matter: Agriculture Council, Environment Council, Consumer Affairs Council and so on. The European Council *per se*, consisting of Prime Ministers or Heads of State, meets about twice a year to discuss broader policy issues. Presidency of this Council changes from country to country every six months. The President sets an agenda for the period of office and beyond. During its Presidency in 1990, the Irish Prime Minister placed the environment at the top of the Council's agenda (Department of the Environment, 1990).

Each Member State keeps in Brussels, the administrative centre of the European Community, Permanent Representation through a number of officials. This group, and its associated working parties, are effectively civil servants who provide and prepare issues for the Council. The Committee of Permanent Representation (COREPER) is chaired by an official of the Member State that holds the Presidency. In this way, the Council's agenda is set.

The Council is the main decision making-body of the European Commission. On all issues of legislation, it is the Council which finally adopts the prescribed enactments. In order to vote on any issue, the Council now has the ability to support legislation through a qualified majority. The procedure is discussed in more detail below, but the basis of a 'qualified majority' is shown in Table 4.2. In effect, the majority ruling means that if two large countries and one or two smaller ones vote against a piece of legislation it can be blocked. If a piece of legislation only achieves a qualified majority and not unanimity the legislation can proceed only with the co-operation of the Parliament and the Commission. This ruling makes it impossible for a single country to block certain legislation.

Clearly, this makes the situation more uncertain, for not only will different alliances need to be struck in Council to block or support certain legislation, but there is still some confusion over which legislation can proceed with a qualified majority and which still needs unanimity. However, the Single European Act (Article 100A) indicates that the qualified majority system can be used for *most* environmental legislation, as this is seen as an integral part of the 'harmonization measures' needed to attain the internal market and beyond. Increasingly, environmental control legislation at least will be set within the European Community with some democratic input from the Parliament.

Table 4.2 Votes available on qualified majorities

Member state	No. of votes
Germany	10
France	10
Italy	10
UK	10
Spain	8
Belgium	5
Greece	5
Netherlands	5
Portugal	5
Austria	3
Denmark	3
Finland	3
Ireland	3
Luxembourg	3
Sweden	3

Whichever way the Council has to proceed on legislative issues, it still remains the case that the Council of Ministers is a very powerful group at the centre of the European Community. The Single European Act has simply made its work more open, democratic and hence uncertain.

The European Commission

The Commission represents the broad Community Interest, as opposed to the individual interests of the Member States, or those of its individual citizens. Only the Commission can propose legislation.

The Commission comprises 20 individuals, proposed by Member States, who must take an oath that they do not bring to the job as a Commissioner influences from their national government. Because it is the 'powerhouse' of the European Community, the Commission meets weekly and, for legislation to proceed from the Commission, it must be supported with full agreement.

The Commission is supported by the European civil service, the 23 Directorates-General, which provide the Commissioners with support, advice, information and so on. The environment, because it necessarily falls into many areas of concern, is covered by the responsibilities of several Directorates-General; principally DGXI (Environment, Consumer Protection, and Nuclear Safety), DGV (Employment, Social Affairs and Education) DGIII (Internal Markets and Internal Affairs) and DGVI (Agriculture). See Table 4.1 for a description of all the Directorates-General.

Under certain, very specific circumstances, the Commission itself can adopt legislation. This is relevant for environmental legislation where scientific analysis or progress reveals that, for example, a certain animal is endangered. Under these circumstances the list of protected species (usually held in Annexes to the main body of the legislation) can be amended and adopted by the Commission. Normally, however, the Commission must act with the Council and the Parliament in the way outlined above.

The other main responsibility of the Commission is its function as 'guardian of the Treaty' and it is in the name of the Commission that transgressions of Community legislation are brought before the Court of Justice.

The Court of Justice

The final cornerstone of the European Community is the Court of Justice. The Court comprises of Judges appointed by agreement with Member States. As with elsewhere in the organization, the work of the judges is supported by the officers (Advocates-General) who analyse and make recommendations on cases brought before the Court. Four types of case are made to the Court.

1. By European Community institutions against one another – internal rulings.
2. By the Commission against Member States – for non-compliance, for example.
3. By member states against the Commission – against 'illegal' decisions on its part, for example.
4. By individuals against Member States at the Commission – many human rights issues fall into this category.

National courts retain the power to enforce European Community decisions at a national level, including environmental legislation. Before enforcing the decisions, however, the national courts can apply to the Court of Justice for an initial ruling to help their decision-making process.

Where action is taken against Member States, the Court of Justice does not have the power to impose financial or other penalties, but the Member State is required to comply, and generally does so. For the future, the question arises as to whether imposition of financial restrictions on Member States will help to enforce legislation that an individual country might see as restrictive or burdensome. On environment issues, for example, 'conservationists are beginning to look at fiscal sanctions as perhaps the most promising avenue for preventing environmental damage happening' (Commission of the European Communities, 1985). This would represent a departure from existing procedures for the Court of Justice, but one which is certainly on the agenda of environmental lobby groups, and some political groupings.

The first decision to withhold grant-aid for a major infrastructure project (a road) in the European Community on environmental grounds was taken only in 1990 (Long, 1990). A proposed major highway in the Portuguese Algarve was refused grant-aid because insufficient attention had been given to environmental protection. The next steps of actually imposing financial sanctions (in effect, fining) Member States for such action will be the focus of considerable debate.

The legislative process

Until the Single European Act, the legislative procedure of the European Community was:

1. the Commission proposes legislation in a variety of forms: directive, regulations and so on;
2. Parliament debates the issues, giving an opinion (possibly with suggested amendments);
3. the Council adopts the legislation, with or without the amendments.

Table 4.3 Decision-making and environmental policy: Processes after the Maastricht Treaty

Decision-making procedure	Applicability in environment policy
189(a) Consultation Procedure In order to adopt a Commission proposal the Council must support the proposals unanimously.	To be used for (1) provisions primarily of a fiscal nature; (2) measures concerning town and country planning, land use (except waste management) and the management of water resources; (3) measures affecting a Member State's choice between energy sources.
189(b) Co-decision Procedure The Council can adopt a Common Position by a qualified majority. Support of the European Parliament is required then to adopt the Common Position.	Used to adopt general action programmes in the field of the environment.
189(c) Co-operation Procedure The Council can adopt a Common Position by a qualified majority. Support of the European Parliament or Council unanimity is required to adopt the Common Position.	Used for proposals designed to achieve the objectives set out in Article 130r (i.e. the main body of Community environmental proposals).

With the Single European Act, however, this process was split into three different forms of procedures which can be brought to bear on individual pieces of legislation depending upon its subject, status or importance. Much of the post-Maastricht debate has been concerned with which types of legislation should fall under which decision-making procedures, some clearly being easier to pass than others. The features of the three procedures are summarized in Table 4.3. The three procedures are known as 'collective procedures'.

Collective procedures

The Single European Act of 1987 introduced the concept of the qualified majority within the Council of Ministers. The procedure to be followed between the Commission, the Parliament and the Council has changed accordingly, although the overall role of each of these elements within the legislative process has changed only in degree, not in absolute terms. Therefore, the Commission is the only body which can propose legislation, and the Council is the only body which can adopt legislation.

Article 100A of the Single European Act, which permits the use of the qualified majority was aimed at easing the introduction of the internal market and its subsequent operations. Thus whenever environmental legislation is seen as part of this process the co-operation procedure, which is laid down in Article 149, applies (as opposed to the old unanimous adoption required under Articles 130R, and 130S of the Treaty of Rome).

The co-operation procedure is as follows.

1. The Commission proposes legislation.
2. The Parliament debates the legislation, and agrees a position by a simple majority.
3. The Council adopts a 'common position' by a qualified majority.
4. Parliament can now within three months, approve, amend or reject the Councils 'common position'. This is what is referred to as the Parliament's second reading. Any amendments can only be introduced by an absolute majority, that is over half of the votes cast.
5. The Commission may then, within one month, revise its proposals 'taking into account' the amendments proposed by Parliament.
6. Council can then do one of four things:
   • adopt, by qualified majority, the revised proposal;
   • adopt, by absolute agreement (i.e. unanimity) the Parliament amendments not approved by the Commission;
   • amend and adopt, by unanimity, the Commission's proposals;
   • fail to act.
7. If Parliament rejects the original proposal, Council can only adopt it by unanimity.
8. The Commission does, however, retain its own right to amend or withdraw its own proposals prior to it being adopted by Council.

As the Council and the Commission still retain their own original powers, the final decision still rests with the Council of Ministers. However, 'Parliament now has the ability to send a powerful message to the Commission and the Council telling them to think again' (Haigh and Baldock 1989).

Where environmental legislation is not seen as being part of the harmonization process, however, a unanimous vote is still required. The decision-making process was reviewed in 1996.

Types of legislation

The Council of Ministers can adopt four types of legislation, the influence of which have different levels of legal implications on the Member States.

1. Recommendations and resolutions. These are non-binding forms of legislation (if indeed something that is non-binding can be thought of as legislation!). They act simply as suggestions to the Member States, which they in turn can accept or reject as they see fit.
2. Regulations are binding and directly applicable to all Member States. They usually relate to specific financial or administrative procedures. In ensuring that the farming community of Member States is eligible for grant-aid under the Common Agriculture Policy it must adhere to the relevant regulations. A regulation is therefore used only rarely on environment issues, except on very specific issues such as trade in a specific endangered species.
3. Decisions are binding upon the persons or Member State to whom it is addressed. The decisions most relevant to the environment are the ones authorizing the Community to become a party to international wildlife and environmental conventions. Decisions are also relevant for information exchange systems, specific administrative procedures and other detailed operations.
4. Directives are by far the most important form of European Community legislation for environmental issues. A directive is set by the European Community to define limits, targets, objectives and standards which must be adhered to by the Member States, but it does not define the precise mechanism of how this must be achieved. This means that the Community is not faced with the problem of translating the objectives into the legislative framework required by each individual Member State. Each Member State must abide by the standards, objectives and so on, but has some flexibility within its own legal system to do so. As becomes clear later, the directive is the system through which most environmental objectives within the European Community are met. The speed with which Member States respond to achieve the Directive's objectives will clearly vary, being dependent upon several factors. These

include the existing legal framework into which the new legislation must fit, the necessary initial work to introduce the directive and, not least, the Member State's keenness to introduce the legislation. All of this clearly implies that there is a procedure for each Member State to introduce legislation that directly corresponds to a European Community Directive. This is indeed the case.

Formal compliance with legislation

Each Member State clearly has an internal legal and/or parliamentary system within which the European Community legislation must operate. This is discussed in Part Two; any attempt to spend too great a time in assessing these internal requirements would be time consuming. For our purposes, it is sufficient to note the key points and procedures within the adoption or compliance procedures.

Following the proposal of a piece of legislation by the Commission – this is usually referenced by a number preceded by 'COM', such as COM (80) 150 which refers to the 1980 proposal for the regulations controlling the import and export of whales and whale products – the proposal is published in the European Community's *Official Journal* (referenced by a number, preceded by the letters 'OJ'). The proposal then follows its own course within the European Community legislative process, to emerge later as a directive, regulation or whatever. The formally adopted legislation then has an official notification date (the date after which the legislation becomes binding on Member States). As with the original proposal, the final adopted version is published in the *Official Journal*. For directives, the Member States then have a set period of time within which they must comply to the objectives within the directive – this is the formal compliance date.

In order to formally comply with a directive, a Member State must usually refer to the Commission statements of internal, national legislation which, in the Member State's considerations, meets the Directives objectives. This may be accompanied by other information, such as instructions to relevant bodies (regional governments, non-government organizations or statutory undertakers, for example). Should the Commission not feel that Member States efforts go far enough, the Commission will respond with a Reasoned Opinion, which is not a public document.

If on the other hand the Member State wants to enforce more detailed or strict regulations than those proposed by the Directives, this is acceptable to the Commission. Usually, the Commission produces minimum standards or objectives, not bothering itself with 'upper limits'.

In Part Two, the individual pieces of Member State legislation are not tied strictly to the Community legislation; this would also be too time consuming in a discussion concerned with patterns and processes rather than detailed legal hierarchies. However, it is possible to plot in the legislation and mechanisms of all Member States the patterns laid down within the European Community legislation.

ADMINISTRATIVE PROCEDURES

Having established not only its own legislation and the subsequent legislation within Member States, the European Community then has the responsibility for monitoring the implementation of the legislation, and also for pursuing its own objectives. As we saw previously, this was originally concerned almost exclusively with the economic restructuring of the community. For our purposes here there are three important features of the administration of the affairs of the European Community: its financial management; the system of programmes it adopts; and the Civil Service or Directorates-General of the Community, which administer the resources.

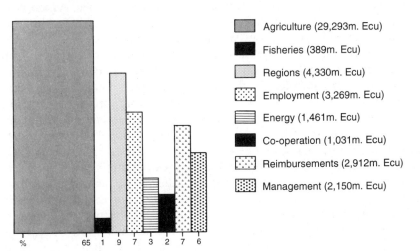

Agriculture (29,293m. Ecu)

Fisheries (389m. Ecu)

Regions (4,330m. Ecu)

Employment (3,269m. Ecu)

Energy (1,461m. Ecu)

Co-operation (1,031m. Ecu)

Reimbursements (2,912m. Ecu)

Management (2,150m. Ecu)

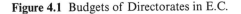

Figure 4.1 Budgets of Directorates in E.C.

Community budgets

The operations of the European community are financed through the central budget which in turn is financed through contributions from Member States and through the financial operation of the Community. The core budget stands at around 45–50 billion ECUs, which represents about 1.1% of the total Gross Domestic Product of the Member States and some 3.3% of the Member States' spending upon public services and administration (Hay, 1989).

Figure 4.1 shows how this central budget is spent. It will be readily seen that by far the greatest proportion of the spending is upon agricultural guaranteed expenditure and structural expenditure – basically supporting the Common Agriculture Policy. Most of this support is aimed at guaranteeing farmers incomes by providing a guaranteed price for farm produce. Only around 10% of this agricultural budget is spent in restructuring the rural and/or farm economy.

The other main budget head is that of regional and transport policy. This is the fund which is used to implement the policy objective of closing the disparity between the prosperous regions within the Community and those that are less prosperous.

Community programmes

In order to pursue its industrial and other objectives, the Community administers its grant-aid through a series of programmes. As we have seen, the bulk of the central grant allocation goes towards funding the common agricultural policy. Within this broad policy, most of the attention is paid towards sustaining the incomes of farmers and producers. This can bring with it the conflicts between conservation and production, as identified in the previous chapter. Shoard (1980) has suggested that the European Community funds that support the costs of the farmers actually contribute towards environmental impoverishment. However, one of the main objectives of the agricultural policy is to support some traditional methods of agricultural production, particularly in hill areas (Commission of the European Communities, 1975). More recently this approach has spread to other areas, which as well as being farmed are also ecologically and visually important (Commission of the European Communities, 1989). The interesting difference in emphasis between the initial 'less-favoured areas initiative' and the more recent 'environmentally sensitive areas' approach is that initially the justification for supporting traditional farming methods was that these areas would be more attractive to tourists and thus the agricultural economy would be broadened and sustained. More recently, the rationale behind the attempt to conserve areas through traditional agricultural techniques has been largely environmental, not tourist-based.

The agricultural programmes, therefore, still have as their central objective the support of the Community's agriculture industry. However, the attendant problems of loss of natural habitats, rural depopulation and poor economic base are increasingly being addressed, particularly as the issue of agricultural overproduction becomes progressively important to the Community.

The other programmes run mainly through the overall policy of 'regional economic restructuring'. The initial concern of the European Community was with compensating for the loss of the traditional heavy industrial base of much of western Europe. Thus, the Coal and Steel Industry was targeted with funds through the European Regional Development Fund (ERDF). This money, usually administered as a grant-aid for basic restructuring works, was available only for strictly economic schemes, such as factory construction, road building and building rehabilitation.

Much of the activity of the European Community is still concentrated upon this type of support. However, notable trends have developed over recent years in the way that these regional aid programmes have developed. First, the monies available have been targeted across a wider range of activities and objectives. For example, the Integrated Development Programme in the Western Isles of Scotland (Commission of the European Communities, 1981) not only had elements of funding from the ERDF, but also funding from the European Social Funds (ESF) and the guidance or strategic element of the agricultural fund. The idea is clearly that a concerted effort will provide more comprehensive results. However, much of the thrust of the programme remains economic, with the environmental protection of the remote and beautiful parts of Europe being largely left to the protection criteria which must be met by all schemes for which grant is sought. The overall co-ordination of the programme was also criticized by the Commission Court of Auditors who suggested that 'the various sub-programmes have not been planned in an integrated manner' (Court of Auditors, 1988).

The second noteworthy trend within the integrated programme mechanisms is 'that the environmental issues are becoming increasingly important'. The thrust for this comes from the Commission itself (Commission of the European Communities, 1989), which states that 'measures financed by the Structural Funds or receiving funds from the European Investment Bank ... shall be in keeping with the provision of the Treaties, including those concerned with environmental protection'. Furthermore, all works must 'be compatible with Community legislation and policies'. Projects must therefore be preceded with a thorough environmental impact assessment. These safeguards are aimed at ensuring that the desire for economic and agricultural restructuring through integrated programmes does not merely pay lip service to environmental protection. The emphasis on environmental protection has been increased not only because of the amendments introduced through the Single European Act, which concentrates upon the environment, but

also because of the controversy surrounding some integrated programmes to the environmental damage caused. In one now infamous
case, funding was withdrawn on a project that was causing damage to
the Prespa National Park in Northern Greece – a project funded
through the Integrated Mediterranean Programme which focused on
Greece, Italy, and France and more latterly Spain (Baldock and Long,
1987).

To summarize, therefore, the European Community reaches its objectives largely through financing works through its integrated programmes.
These are increasingly being subjected to environmental controls and
safeguards, although some question marks still remain about the
compatibility of the goals of economic development and environmental
protection. How these are resolved at Community level is the focus of the
next chapter, and how it is resolved within individual Member States is
addressed in Part Two.

Administrative structure

Table 4.1 shows the list of offices within the core administration of the
European Community. There are 23 Directorates-General (referred to as
DGI, DGII and so on). This administrative staff reports to the
Commission because, as we have seen, the Commission is the legal body
within the Community responsible for safeguarding community interests
per se.

The Directorates-General have increased as the needs of the
Commission have increased. Thus, for example, the Directorates-General
for Agriculture and Fisheries was split into two when it was acknowledged that in order to service the needs of the Community's eight million
or so farmers, a DG with responsibility for agriculture alone was
required.

As is evident elsewhere, the role of managing the environment is
divided between several Directorates-General. Arguably, up to half of the
DGs have an impact on the physical environment. This brings with it the
problems of split responsibilities, predominantly between DGVI, DGXI,
DGIV, DGXXIII (Agriculture; Environment, Nuclear Safety and Civil
Protection; Fisheries; and Tourism respectively). DGXI is by far the most
significant for our purposes.

The principal function of the Directorates-General is to process the
many grant applications to the Commission for funding through the
programmes outlined above, monitoring both the implementation of the
programmes in accordance with the relevant regulations, and also ensuring that the programmes are implemented in keeping with other policies,
including and increasingly, the environmental ones. It is to these safeguards that we can now turn our attention.

Environmental safeguards

In their administrative procedures, and in their dealings with Member States through and in the name of the Commission, the Directorates-General have a number of legally binding safeguards designed to protect the environment. First, Regulation EC2052/88 states that all schemes funded through the European Community must meet the environmental (indeed, all) objectives of the Community. Second, Member States must provide official verification with European Community legislation and policies (Regulation EC4253/88 is a further legally binding requirement on Member States). The third safeguard is the 'contract' drawn up between the Member State and the European Commission whenever a programme is funded or initiated. Finally, at any one time the Commission may be funding up to 300 or more regionally based programmes. The Directorate-General XI (Environment, Nuclear Safety and Civil Protection) will now see all these programmes for comment.

As well as these internal controls, which relate to the European Community's own programmes, DGXI also has a responsibility to monitor the day-to-day activities of Member States, not associated with Community development programmes. This it does through responding to complaints. Table 4.4 shows how the number of complaints received by DGXI has increased dramatically. The procedure in dealing with a complaint is, as to be expected, a relatively lengthy process (European Information Service, 1990). Following a complaint, the Member State is questioned about the event. The Member State has two months to reply, following which DG XI recommends a decision to the European Commission. If the Member State is in breach of legislation, it must cease the relevant operation. If, however the Member State's response is not satisfactory, it records a 'reasoned opinion', and if no satisfactory outcome is then forthcoming, the Commission can take the Member States to the European Court of Justice. These complaints are always taken up with Member State's governments rather than, say, local authorities or quasi-governmental organizations (European Unit Briefing, 1995).

The safeguards are therefore in place to protect the environment, and there is increasing evidence that they are being used to this end. As we have seen, in 1989 the first decision to withhold payment for a project on environmental grounds was taken in relation to a scheme in Portugal's Algarve region. Prior to this, in 1988, the Court of Justice ruled that Denmark had the authority to require that all of its bottles were returnable, and that this did not interfere with the freedom of the internal market. While this does not have a direct implication on nature conservation (a point which will inevitably be disputed by conservationists!) it does indicate the increasing emphasis being placed on broader environmental issues.

Table 4.4 Number of formal complaints to DGXI regarding the environment

Year	No. of complaints
1983	4
1987	57
1988	200
1989	450
1992	1003
1994	2118

SUMMARY

From this broad-brush view of the operations, it is evident that the structure of the European Community and the objectives which it has set itself ensure that the concept of environmental conservation is situated between and within several elements of the system.

The most important issues to note before we assess the environmental legislation of the Community are: (1) monies are administered through the Integrated Development Programmes, and (2) environmental conservation steps are made in those programmes, rather than in specific schemes or projects in their own right. The reason for this is clear. The primary objectives of the European Community remain economic, whether in the rural or built environment. The vast bulk of the budget is spent upon agricultural support or on regional/agricultural restructuring. In developing these programmes, consideration needs to be taken of the environment and its protection but, as we have seen, there are often conflicts between environmental and developmental considerations.

As well as ensuring that the development programmes of the European Community conform to the Commission's regulations and directives, Directorate-General XI must also pursue and monitor, through the Commission, the enactment of the strictly environmental legislation. We can therefore see the situation wherein the Integrated Development Programmes (IDPs) are developing alongside Environmental Programmes *per se*. While we have not reached the stage where environmental programmes are developed and funded to the same extent as the IDPs, they are progressing together. Indeed, in 1993 with the so-called LIFE programme, the Commission started its first programme based entirely on the environment. With the passing of the Single European Act, the European Community is now fully competent to prepare practical environmental programmes and, as we shall see in the next chapter, this has resulted in a more positive position for environmental legislation and programming within the European Community. For the most part, however, the emphasis is still largely with environmental considerations being taken into account when Integrated Development Programmes are being prepared for the regions within the Community.

REFERENCES

Baldock, D., Corrie, H. and Long, T. (1989) *Reform of the Structural Funds*. IEEP, London.

Baldock, D. and Long, T. (1987) *The Mediterranean Under Pressure*. IEEP, London.

Commission of the European Communities (1975) *Farming in Less Favoured Areas*. OJ L128 19.5.75. Brussels.

Commission of the European Communities (1981) *Western Isles I.D.P. Regulations*. OJ L197 20.7.81. Brussels.

Commission of the European Communities (1985) *Regulations on Improving the Efficiency of Agricultural Structures*. OJ L93 30.3.85. Brussels.

Commission of the European Communities (1988a) *Reform of the Structural Funds*. Com (88) 500. Brussels.

Commission of the European Communities (1988b) *European Community Environmental Legislation*. Brussels.

Commission of the European Communities (1989) *Guide to the Reform of the Structural Funds*. Luxembourg.

Confederation of British Industry (1993) Whither Maastricht. *CBI News*.

Court of Auditors (1988) *Special Report: Western Isles I.D.P.* OJ L188 18.7.88. Brussels.

Delors, J. (1994) *Monetary and Political Union: What now?* Proceedings of the CBI Conference, Harrogate, November 1993.

Department of the Environment (1990) *Eire and the Environment*. Dublin.

European Information Service (1990) *Briefing of the Community's Environment Programme*. Report 107. London.

European Unit Briefing (1995) *European Policy and Legislation on the Environment*. European Unit, Doncaster.

Haigh, N. and Baldock , D. (1989) *Environmental Policy and 1992*. IEEP, London.

Hallo, G. (1992) *The Maastricht Treaty and the Environment*. Conference proceedings, University of Utrecht.

Harris, J. (1989) Unity Down *Local Government Chronicle*, September pp. 30–1.

Hay, R. (1989) *The European Commission and the Administration of the Community*. European Commission, Brussels.

Long, T. (1990) *Structural Funds in Europe*. IEEP, London.

Shoard, M. (1980) *The Theft of the Countryside*. Temple Smith, London.

5 | European legislation

The previous chapter indicated that environmental protection was still largely seen as a part of the European Community's principal economic objectives. This was borne out by the European Council of Ministers' Decision in March 1990, following the Western Economic Summit Conference, which stated that 'environmental protection can contribute to improved economic growth and job creation'. However, this situation is understandable given the basis for the creation of the European Community as outlined previously. Notwithstanding the economic priorities that predominate, it is still possible to plot strong environmental policy development within the European Community. This has two aspects: (1) making traditional economic development more sympathetic to the needs for environmental protection, and (2) developing environmental goals which can be pursued separately and/or alongside the economic objectives. These two notions can be distilled into two assumptions which underlie European Community environmental legislation. First, 'prevention is better than cure' and second, 'the polluter pays' principle. These two motifs underlie the development of community environmental policy.

Up to this point, no differentiation has been made between the various types of environmental legislation. The term 'environment' covers many separate and interlinking concepts: waste management, pollution control, hazardous material control, land management, habitat conservation, noise control, world-wide conservation issues and many others are all covered by European legislation. In order to concentrate fully upon the relevant legislations for nature conservation, the following discussion, and Part Two of the book, focuses only upon specific elements of environmental legislation; namely those relating to landscape and nature conservation. These clearly interlink with other environmental issues (is a move to stop pollution of the North Sea a pollution issue or a wildlife issue, for example?) but to make discussions manageable in size some form of filter is required.

Plate 3 The protection of wetlands was one of the first priorities identified by the world environment movement.

This chapter therefore looks at the underlying principles of European Environmental Policy, concentrating upon nature conservation where necessary. The analysis then assesses the development of environmental action programmes within the community. Finally, the individual pieces of legislation which relate specifically to nature conservation are analysed, and their implications discussed. These implications, and their implementation and localized responses at national level, are discussed in Part Two.

UNDERLYING PRINCIPLES

The original Treaty of Rome did not mention the environment except as an element to be considered as part of the overall process of economic development. However, despite the Community's lack of legal sanction for its concern for the environment, as early as 1972 the Heads of the Member States were calling for a Community environmental policy. This was inevitably a new area of debate for the European Community, as only a few fragmented pieces of environmental legislation had been passed at Community level (including a regulation on the management of land in agriculturally less favoured areas – OJ L94 28.4.70) prior to then. As a result very basic principles had to be plotted and primary objectives had to be outlined. In the introduction to the first environmental policy, the following objectives were defined as:

1. to reduce pollution and nuisances;
2. to improve the natural and urban environments;
3. to deal with environmental problems caused by the depletion of certain natural resources;
4. to promote awareness of environmental problems and education.

The method chosen by the Commission was through proposing suitable items of legislation. In an effort to tie together the proposed strands of legislation, 11 underlying principles were framed for the Community's environmental policy.

1. Prevention is better than cure.
2. Environmental effects should be taken into account at the earliest possible stage of decision making.
3. Exploitation of nature and natural resources which cause significant damage to the ecological balance must be avoided. The natural environment can only absorb pollution to a limited extent. It is an asset which may be used, but not abused.
4. Scientific knowledge should be improved to enable action to be taken.
5. The polluter pays: the cost of preventing and eliminating nuisances must be borne by the polluter, although some exceptions are allowed.
6. Activities carried out in one Member State should not cause deterioration of the environment in another.
7. The effects of environmental policy in the Member States must take account of the interests of developing countries.
8. The Community and Member States should act together in international organizations and in promoting international and world-wide environmental policy.
9. The protection of the environment is a matter for everyone. Education is therefore necessary.
10. Establish the appropriate level. In each category, it is necessary to establish the level of action (local, regional, national, Community, international) best suited to the type of pollution and the geographical zone to be protected.
11. National environmental policies must be co-ordinated at national level. This is to be achieved by the implementation of the action programmes and of the environment information agreement.

These initial principles and the first steps towards an environmental policy are laid out in Commission of the European Communities, (1973a).

ENVIRONMENTAL ACTION PROGRAMMES

In order to co-ordinate the environmental legislation and pursue in a logical fashion the objectives and principles outlined above, the European Community began in 1973 a series of Environmental Action Programmes. Up to 1992, four of these had been formulated, with the fifth commencing in 1993. Each Environmental Action Programme operates for between three and six years; Table 5.1 shows the operational dates for the first five programmes. The progress of these programmes has been reviewed by the Community itself (Commission of the European Communities, 1984b; 1993a).

Table 5.1 Environmental action programmes

Programme	Period	Approval date	Official Journal reference
1	1973–76	22.11.73	C112 20.12.73
2	1977–81	17.5.77	C139 13.6.77
3	1982–86	7.2.83	C46 17.2.83
4	1987–92	19.10.87	C328 2.17.87
5	1993–2000	1.2.93	C138 17.5.93

The Environmental Action Programmes do not fall into the acknowledged categories of legislation, and therefore do not represent a legally binding policy. The Council of Ministers, for example, does not approve the detailed implications of each general approach. However, the action programmes provide an opportunity to assess the direction of the Community's environmental legislation.

Two functions are performed by the Environmental Action Programmes (Haigh, 1989). First, they present a broad discussion on environmental issues, and an overall assessment of the direction that the Community should be taking over the forthcoming years. The second function is to identify specific areas of concern which the Community feels warrant legislation, and which should be forthcoming. As suggested above, in agreeing each Environmental Action Programme the Council of Ministers does not necessarily agree to each proposed piece of environmental legislation; these are assessed on their individual merits as they are introduced through the legislative process.

The first Environmental Action Programme was a relatively lengthy affair, being the first attempt by the European Community not only to draw together existing legislation, but also to give long-term direction to the work of the Community in protecting the environment. The underlying principles are mentioned above. In order to achieve these broad aims, the action areas proposed by the Community were, to reiterate:

1. to reduce pollution and nuisances;
2. to improve the natural and urban environments;
3. to deal with environmental problems caused by the depletion of certain natural resources;
4. to promote awareness of environmental problems and education.

The first Environmental Action Programme also indicated that the objectives would be met mostly by drafting and enacting suitable pieces of legislation. The progress of the first programme was monitored by the Community itself (Commission of the European Communities, 1980).

The second Environmental Action Programme followed similar lines to the first, concentrating upon pollution control measures and the more obvious areas of abuse of land of conservation importance. It must be remembered that, at the time the second and indeed the third Environmental Action Programmes were being formulated, there was still some debate within the Member States as to whether the Community had the legal authority ('competence') to generate environmental legislation. None the less, the second Environmental Action Programme did begin tentatively to explore some of the more proactive environmental legislation which was to appear much later, such as Environmental Impact Assessments, for example.

It was the third Environmental Action Programme, however, which changed the focus from 'curing' environmental problems to preventing them. The third programme contained a section entitled 'developing an overall strategy' which sought to create an overview of the work of the Community. It is for this reason that the third Environmental Action Programme marks a watershed in the evolution of the programmes. This point is actually emphasized in the introduction to the fourth programme, the creation of which coincided with the enactment of the Single European Act and its subsequent amendments to the Treaty of Rome. It is with the fourth programme, therefore, that the Community entered its most recent phase of operations, having become competent, through the Single European Act, of legislating for environmental protection and conservation; a phase continued through the fifth Action Programme.

The fourth Environmental Action Programme called for environmental policy to be integrated fully into the other policy areas of the

European Community, particularly the Common Agricultural Policy (which was itself being reviewed) and the Regional, Social and Integrated Development policies and programmes (Commission of the European Communities, 1987a). While this objective had been established in the third programme, 'rather little had been achieved, except in the field of agriculture' (Commission of the European Communities, 1987).

The second underlying concern of the fourth programme was that of effective implementation of Community policy and legislation within Member States. The consistency of implementation throughout the European Community depends as much upon the mechanisms through which policy is ultimately delivered as upon the capacity of the Community itself to monitor implementation.

The issues of integration and implementation are discussed within the fourth programme under the general heading of 'general policy orientations'. Other than these objectives, the fourth programme identifies the priority areas.

1. Implementation and monitoring through Community environment inspectors, and monitoring through non-government organizations (NGOs) and organizing workshops to exchange Member states experiences of implementation.
2. Source-orientated control, which re-emphasizes the Community's commitment to prevention of problems rather than control.
3. Job creation, which aims not only to integrate the environmental legislation with the economic objectives of the community, but also seeks to examine the employment potential of environmental investment.
4. Information about the environment being readily available. This not only entails allowing individual citizens to have access to information about the environment, but it also emphasizes the need for Member States to exchange information.

This latter point is a reaffirmation of an earlier priority identified by the Community in 1973 (Commission of the European Communities, 1973b), the Environment Information Agreement.

The information agreement, which was formulated at Community level in 1973, was not envisaged as being a legally binding agreement. It requires Member States to inform the European Community (specifically, the Commission) of any impending legislative or administrative changes. The Commission then has two months to decide whether or not the issues raised by the changes need to be addressed at Community level. The objective of this agreement is not to control Member States legislation and administration, but to enable the individual Member States to initiate Community legislation. This has been an important mechanism of initiating environmental legislation, particularly for the Member States that have been at the forefront of developing environmental legislation, such as the Netherlands and Denmark. The agreement is discussed in more detail later.

While the initial 1973 arrangement was intended to be entirely voluntary, the fourth Environmental Action Programme suggested that the agreement should become binding legislation, which indeed became the case.

To summarize, the Environmental Action Programmes have changed over the years since their inception of 1973. Initially they attempted to identify and suggest cures for the environmental problems caused by economic progress. Latterly, the Programmes concentrated upon proactive prevention of these problems. Consistently, however, the Programmes have both summarized environmental issues of the day and projected the Community's legislative programme to deal with and address the issues. As a broad guide, therefore, the Programmes represent a clear indication of the corporate view on environmental issues.

Consequently, the fifth Environmental Action Programme continues this pattern and indicates a clear progression on the part of the European Community towards broader-based environmental protection. The fourth programme, described at some length above, represented a logical conclusion to the thought processes that led to the creation of the first three Action Programmes. However, in much the same way that the Rio Summit represented a progression from previous environmental conventions, so the fifth Environmental Action Programme marks a similar quantum shift. The Action Programme continued with the 11 underlying principles mentioned above, but advocated a new approach to environmental protection. This included a number of specific observations as to how this new approach might come about. These were:

1. a deep-rooted integration of environmental issues into all Community decision making, rather than a timetable or list of specifically 'environmental' legislation or proposed directives;
2. a broader cultural approach to environmental issues;
3. the need for a range of policy options and instruments rather than the usual legislative 'we tell, you do' approach to implementation;
4. a need for shared responsibility between governments, the private sector and the voluntary and non-governmental organizations.

This general policy was adopted in October 1992, prior to amendments to procedure introduced post-Maastricht. The policy has been both welcomed and criticized by environmentalists. Welcomed because it does seek to broaden the influence and impact of environmental thinking, but criticised that, by so doing, the targeted role of legislation could be lost – by spreading the message, the overall effectiveness of a more singular and traditionally legislative approach could be weakened.

The public statement of the fifth Environmental Action Programme is the most comprehensive summary of EC environmental policy to date. The document, *Towards Sustainability: A European Community Programme of Policy and Action in Relation to the Environment and Sustainable Development* (Commission of the European Communities, 1992), identifies four features which changed the emphasis of the entire programme for environmental protection, namely: sustainability; pro-activity; integration; and more mechanisms for implementation.

Several subsequent initiatives and discussion papers have built upon this new, broader environmental agenda. For example, the Commission's White Paper (for discussion) on *Growth and Competitiveness* (Commission of the European Communities, 1993a) considers the impact on the environment of so called 'linear development', which relies upon an 'insufficient use of labour resources and an excessive use of natural resources'. Furthermore, it also advocates the creation of jobs directly as a result of environmental protection.

An initiative which follows up the agenda set out by the fifth Action Programme is that of voluntary participation in eco-audit and monitoring by private sector industries (Commission of the European Communities, 1993b). Whereas prior to 1992 greater emphasis would have been placed upon legislation, with the fifth Action Programme, partnership and co-operation became recognized as a valuable way to make progress.

OTHER PRINCIPLES

The foregoing analysis assesses the environmental programmes of the Community, but it is worth emphasizing the context within which the environmental policy has developed.

The overriding concern of the European Community is for economic development, and the changes brought about by the Single European Act and the fourth Environmental Action Programme do not change this. Fairclough (1987) records the European Community's decision following the 1985 Bonn economic summit that environmental protection can contribute to improved economic growth and job creation.

Also, the European concept of the environment is very broad. This broad-based approach can be traced back to the systems for environmental protection which were in place in the original Member States, particularly France and Germany. The all-embracing nature of environmental agencies such as the *Haute Comité de la Qualité de la vie* in France can be noted within the remit of the Directorate-General XI, which addresses issues ranging from water pollution, waste disposal, air pollution and chemical safety, to countryside and wildlife protection and noise control.

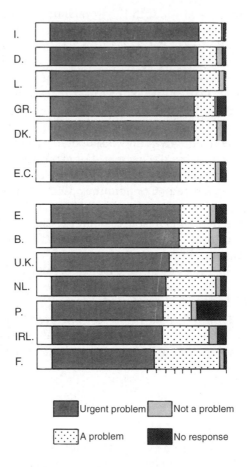

Legend:
- Urgent problem
- A problem
- Not a problem
- No response

Figure 5.1 Environmental concerns in E.C. Member States.

This raises two particular points of relevance here. First, it is important to appreciate in the following analysis that environmental legislation *is* wide reaching and that this itself may cause administrative repercussions with the Member States. A broad environmental policy, for example, may cut across the departmental responsibilities of some Member States. The second issue of relevance is that in focusing upon one specific area of environmental policy – nature conservation – it is inevitable that divisions will be created and some policy areas will be seen in isolation. This is necessary in order to concentrate upon nature conservation across the European Community. While one area of interest is explored, the broader environmental consideration must be acknowledged, yet at the same time discussed in much less detail.

ENVIRONMENTAL LEGISLATION

This section deals with the items of environmental legislation generated by the European Community which relate directly to nature or landscape conservation. The definition of this is difficult, in that the Community itself does not delineate between one form of environmental legislation and another. Furthermore, it is arguable that almost all legislation will, in one way or another, have an impact on wildlife and the natural history of an area.

Notwithstanding these difficulties, it is possible to follow a line of legislative development within the European Community, from which a number of areas of continued interests can be identified. In short, there are certain types of legislation which preoccupy the Community. This is determined not only by the attitudes and ideas about nature conservation held by the Member States, but is also determined by the 'competence' of the Community to create environmental legislation. This competence blockage has been resolved to some extent by the Single European Act, and this in turn has been reflected in the new legislative direction taken by the Community.

The legislation covered is from several programme areas – agriculture, environment and information, for example. Furthermore, the legislation is of different types - regulations, directives and decisions. All in all, therefore, the series of environmental legislation enacted by the European Community is in itself varied. The legislation identified in each case is the key piece of legislation: in each case this may have been preceded or followed by other decisions or amendments, but the discussion concentrates on the single most important piece of legislation, with other supporting legislation being mentioned in the discussion.

Environmental Information Agreement, 1973

The so-called 'gentleman's agreement' is not strictly a piece of legislation, being simply an agreement or promise by individual Member States to inform the European Commission when draft environmental legislation is being prepared within those states (Commission of the European Communities 1973b). This allows the Commission the opportunity to decide whether it feels that a European initiative is required. Member States also agreed to transfer information about international environmental initiatives which may affect the functioning of the Community.

The Commission must then, in turn, inform all other Member States of the proposed legislation.

The agreement of 1973 also commits Member States to 'co-ordinate their views on any international initiative in respect of the environment likely to affect the functioning of the common market or the implementation of those parts of the Communities programmes for the reduction of pollution and nuisances and the protection of the natural environment' (Commission of the European Communities, 1973b).

The 1973 agreement was followed up in 1979 by a further supplementary agreement. This was as result of the first Environmental Action Programme having been produced in 1973. The result of the supplementary document was that the original agreement extended to 'measures liable to affect the implementation of the Environmental Action Programme' (Commission of the European Communities, 1974).

The importance of this two-part agreement is that it placed some onus upon Member States to co-ordinate their individual legislative proposals and also on the Community to co-ordinate its views on international initiatives. It is on this basis that the European Community responds collectively to international conventions, proposals and the like.

Polluter Pays Principle, 1975

While the greatest direct relevance to pollution control measures, this Recommendation of March 1975 (Commission of the European Communities, 1975a) reinforces the principle outlined in the first Environmental Action Programme and defines a polluter as 'someone who directly or indirectly damages the environment'. The critical issue here is that damage is defined by relevant local standards, specific usually to each Member State.

Countryside protection in agriculturally less favoured areas, 1975

While often quoted as being the initiating piece of legislation in a long line of environmental initiatives, the concept of countryside protection in agricultural areas as part of the common agricultural policy is contained within the Directive in mountain and hill farming, and farming in less favoured areas (Commission of the European Communities, 1975b). The objective of the Directive is not conservation *per se*, but 'the continuation of farming thereby maintaining a minimum population level or conserving the countryside'.

This Directive is the first attempt to link environmental (and specifically, conservation) policy to other policy areas within the Community. This was identified within the first Environmental Action Programme, which also specifically isolated the links between agriculture and conservation as being important.

The original Directive of 1975 has subsequently been amended on several occasions (OJ L108 26.4.76; OJ L180 14.7.80; OJ L327 24.11.82) but the central thrust remains the same, that by protecting agriculture in these less favoured areas, the countryside would also be protected. This view has been criticized (see Smith, 1985, for example) and it has become apparent that the objectives of protecting the environment and protecting farming are not necessarily compatible. None the less, the Directive of 1975 did mark an attempt at integration of policies. Equally importantly, it also laid some of the foundation for a later European Regulation for environmentally sensitive areas in 1985.

The Directive operates by offering additional aid to farmers who work in mountain areas, depopulated areas or areas with 'specific handicaps'. These specific handicaps are principally permanent, natural limitation. However, in 1985 this definition was changed in the 1985 Regulation to incorporate 'man-made' specific handicaps, which included constraints or limitation imposed by conservation legislation. It is through this mechanism that additional support can be channelled to farmers to help protect the environment in specific areas, as we shall see later.

Decision on an Inventory of Information of the Environment, 1975

As part of the Community's drive towards an understanding of the various knowledge and initiatives within each Member States, in 1975 a further Directive was adopted which re-emphasized the commitment to information exchange (Commission of the European Communities, 1976). The decision made in 1975 established a common procedure for establishing an environmental inventory and constantly keeping it up to date. The inventory was to include: 'scientific and technical information and documentation centres and services; specialist centres and independent experts; current or scheduled research projects'. The seven Articles within the Decision outline how the inventory is to be established and updated. Included within this procedure is the automatic referral of any information to the International Referral System of the United Nations Environment Programme. This indicates the European Community's Commitment to maintaining its environmental action within a global framework.

Recommendation following the Convention on Wetlands of International Importance, 1975

Following the International Wetlands Convention (usually known, like all conventions, after the place in which is was held – hence the Ramsar

Convention) of 1971, the European Community raised a recommendation (Commission of the European Communities, 1975a) which suggested that the Member States became party to the Convention agreement. The Community itself is not a member.

Plate 4 The coast has long been a pressure point for tourist development. This can
cause severe damage to the environment.

The significance of the Convention is detailed in the following
chapter. It is sufficient to note here that the Convention aims to stem the
increasing destruction of wetland habitats. Parties to the Convention
undertake to designate at least one international site, and establish
wetland reserves.

Birds and their habitats, 1979

The Directive on the Conservation of Wild Birds marks a turning point
in European environmental legislation. Prior to this, the Community had
concentrated upon pollution control measures, information exchange or
amendments to existing major policy areas, such as the Common
Agricultural Policy. The Birds Directive was specifically targeted at nature
conservation. The Decision was aimed at 'the conservation of all species
of naturally occurring birds in the wild state in the European territory of
the Member States to which the Treaty (of Rome) applies. It covers the

protection, management and control of these species, and lays down rules for the exploitation. The Directive shall apply to birds, their eggs, nests and habitats.'

The perceived need for this arose out of the annual slaughter of birds (particularly migratory birds) in Europe. This was most evident in countries with a strong tradition of hunting of birds, such as Spain and France.

The Directive sought not only to protect specific species (which were named in a series of Annexes at the end of the Directive) but also the protection of 'biotopes and habitats ... by the creation of protected areas, upkeep and management in accordance with the ecological needs of habitats, the re-establishment of destroyed biotopes, the creation of biotopes' (Commission of the European Communities, 1979).

The hunting lobby of each Member State did gain some recognition within the framing of the Decision. First, the bird populations were to be maintained at a 'level which corresponds in particular to ecological, scientific and cultural requirements'. Second, the necessary control of hunting is to rest with the Member States which were to draw up the necessary legislation.

The Annex (later supplemented by amendment/additions in OJ L233 30.8.85) is in five parts. The birds listed in Annex 1 are particularly vulnerable, and they and their habitats are the subject of special control measures (140 species are named in all). Annex 2/1 lists 24 species which can be hunted anywhere, but under licence, and Annex 2/2 lists 48 species that can only be hunted in specific countries, again under licence. Further restrictions are placed on the killing of birds in the other Annexes, and the need for research into certain species is also raised.

General controls include 'prohibiting the use of all means, arrangements or methods used for the large-scale or non-selective capture or killing of birds or capable of causing the local disappearance of a species'.

Overall the objective of the Directive was to protect specific species, control the killing and methods of hunting used against a wider group of species, but also curb excessive hunting of all species of birds, and go some way towards ensuring the protection of their natural habitats. As indicated already, this marked a turning point of European legislation, because it was a piece of legislation that specifically dealt with nature conservation and also had a broader focus (i.e. habitats) beyond its initial concern for migratory birds. It laid a foundation that later helped to create the 1992 Habitats Directive.

Import of whales and other cetacean products, 1981

The Regulation of January 1981 is aimed at controlling the importation by Member States by ensuring that all products listed in the Annex to the

Regulation 'shall be subject to an import licence. No such licence shall be issued in respect of products to be used for commercial purposes'. This was a reaction to the killing of whales (particularly sperm whales and baleen whales) for the oils. In 1979, the International Whaling Commission banned all commercial whaling by factory ships. Some Member States, particularly Britain, sought to strengthen this ban by introducing restrictions at Community level. Thus, in just over one year, the International Whaling Commission ban was translated into Community action (Commission of the European Communities, 1981a).

Further inclusion within the Annex were also brought about by combined lobby group pressure and political requirements. Fur skins, for example, appear in the Annex attached to the original Regulation, and the skins of seal pups (harp seals and hooded seals) are mentioned in the Amendment to the original regulation that was brought in when Spain and Portugal entered the European Community in 1985 (OJ L302 15.11.85).

Decision following the Convention of Antarctica Marine Living Resources, 1981

The Canberra Convention, prepared in 1980, seeks to regulate the harvesting of marine organisms in Antarctica. The European Community's decision of 1981, following the Convention, approves the Convention, although it does not make the Community a party nor does it enforce Member States to become parties (Commission of the European Communities, 1981b). The details of the Convention are given in the next chapter.

Decision on the Conclusion of the Convention on the Conservation of European Wildlife and Natural Habitats, 1982

The Berne Convention was drawn up in 1979 by the Council of Europe (a body older, and separate from the European Community). The Convention seeks to conserve wildlife in its natural habitats, particularly in cases where the protection requires the co-operation of more than one country. The Community decision (Commission of the European Communities, 1982a) simply approves the Convention, as is the usual case.

Decision on the Conclusion of the Convention on the Conservation of Migratory Species of Wild Animals, 1982

The Bonn Convention (drawn up in 1979, like the Berne Convention) was similarly approved by the European Community in 1982 (Commission of the European Communities, 1982b). As with the Berne and the Canberra conventions, the Community decision approves the Bonn Convention, which seeks to promote concerted effort to protect migratory species, although it does not enforce any Member States to become party to the convention.

Regulation on the Implementation in the Community of the Convention or International Trade in Endangered Species, 1982

The Washington Convention (or, as it is usually known, CITES) was held in 1973, and the regulation of 1982 enforces 'Member States to notify the Commission of the provision which it adopts for the implementation of this regulation ... wherein the Convention shall apply throughout the Community' (Commission of the European Communities, 1982c). The Convention itself is accompanied by a complex and lengthy listing of species which includes mammals, birds, reptiles, fish, molluscs, plants and so on. The Community regulation enforces a uniformed system of documentation and licensing to cover trade in the listed flora and fauna, and actually progresses the ideas within the Convention by, for example, imposing a ban on certain species within the Community which the Convention does not. (The Convention itself is discussed more fully in the next chapter.)

The Community did not agree to become a party to the Convention in 1982, but will do so when an amendment to the Convention is agreed by a sufficient number of existing parties. One side-effect of the Community's regulation and subsequent future status within the Convention is that individual Member States do not have to produce individual annual reports about trade in the species; an overall report is submitted to the Secretariat of the Convention by the Community. This clearly does not report in too much detail about trade within the Community. In order to overcome this shortfall in information, the European Commission has requested that an independent body prepare reports on the implementation of the regulation in Member States.

Directive Concerning the Importation of Skins of Certain Seal Pups, 1983

Following the Whales Directive of 1981, the Seals Directives (Commission of the European Communities, 1983) was a contribution of the widespread condemnation of the annual slaughter of certain species of seals, particularly seal pups. The European Community initiated the Directive following a petition sent to the European Parliament containing three million signatures (Van Moltke, 1983). The resulting Directive took steps to stop skins of harp and hooded seals (and their by-products) being imported. The Directive 'shall only apply to products not resulting from traditional hunting by Inuit people'.

Regulation on Action by the Community concerning the Environment, 1984

The Regulation (Commission of the European Communities, 1984a), usually referred to by its acronym ACE, is a piece of financial legislation through which Community monies are made available for environmental projects in three areas of work: measuring the quality of the environment; 'clean technologies'; and protecting habitats for endangered species.

For our purposes, the most important are the projects to protect habitats of endangered species, for which financial support is available for up to 50% of costs. The legislation was to run for three years. In 1986, the Commission proposed a further regulation which would extend the three areas of support to six, and would remove all time constraints on the financial support (OJ C18 24.1.87). This proposal identified: recycling projects; restoring sites contaminated by hazardous wastes; and restoring or conserving population of species in danger of extinction. This regulation, in effect, establishes a broadly based environmental fund within the European Community.

From the first Regulations, financial support was provided for 28 habitat projects.

The Regulation is a landmark in European legislation in that, prior to this, environmental legislation was haphazard, but ACE regulations sought to put the funding of environmental projects as part of the mainstream activities of the Community. The Regulation was not without controversy, because there were still some Member States which felt that the European Community was still not legally competent to create such an 'Environment Fund'. Indeed, the British Government was at pains to stress, for example, that it was assuredly not an environmental fund. As a compromise, the legislation was time-limited, and the total allocation was reduced (Haigh, 1989). None the less, the Regulation and its subsequent legislation and proposals was a very significant point in the development of a Community environmental policy.

Environmental Impact Assessment, 1985

While the concept of Environmental Impact Assessments is similar in its application to the planning controls and legislation of some of the Member States, Environmental Impact Assessments also have roots in American legislation (Roberts and Roberts, 1984). The Directive

(Commission of the European Communities, 1985a) is concerned with assessing the overall effect on the environment of projects which, because of their size, type and/or location, are felt to have a potentially significant impact. The effects are to be assessed under six different headings: human beings; flora and fauna; soil, water, air and climate; landscape; interface between the first two groups; physical and cultural environment.

The Directive has three Annexes; the first one listing the types of project which should be the subject of an assessment, and the second one containing projects which may be the subject of an assessment. As with all Directives, the application of the legislation is left to the individual Member States, and the vigour with which locally based enforcement agencies apply the conditions clearly varies from one Member State to the other, particularly on Annex II projects.

The third Annex lists the information which must be provided by the project developer. Much of this is based upon an assessment of the present state of the environment, a projection of the likely state of the environment after the development, and an assessment of how ongoing monitoring will take place.

As an indication of the varying degrees of acceptance of the Directive across Europe, the Netherlands and Germany introduced legislation to meet the Directive in 1985, while Britain waited until the time limit for complying with the Directive had almost expired in 1988.

Information on the State of the Environment, 1985

One of the main concerns of the European Community throughout its development of an environmental policy has been that of creating networks and consistent methods of gathering and transferring information. The 1985 legislation (Commission of the European Communities, 1985b), known usually as CORINE, was concerned with information collection. The CORINE legislation established a specialist project which was to collate information on four areas of environmental priority: acid deposition; protection of the Mediterranean environment; the improvement in compatibility of data and environmental analysis techniques; biotopes worthy of conservation.

It is with this last area of information gathering that we are principally concerned here. A four-year programme was started in January 1985, aimed at identifying and describing the habitats within the Community worthy of protection and conservation. This collation of information was to be undertaken in close co-operation with the Council of Europe.

This particular element of the Decision has had two longer-term impacts upon the Community environmental policy. First, the fourth

Environmental Action Programme continued the drive towards comparable data and collective information started by CORINE. Second, the European Community is in the process of using the information gathered on habitats through CORINE. This is through the development of a Community-wide network of habitat protection, the aim of which is to establish a series of sites across Europe, designated on common natural history and landscape criteria. This particular development is discussed later, as Natura 2000.

The complexity of the information gathering process has been modified since the concept of truly international compatibility was first mooted. From 1974 until 1985, therefore, the techniques used to assemble the information have become less complex, although none the less far reaching. The impetus started by CORINE was, to a large extent, continued through the creation of the European Environmental Agency (see later).

Environmentally Sensitive Areas, 1985

The Environmentally Sensitive Areas (ESA) Regulation (Commission of the European Communities, 1985c) takes its lead predominantly from the agricultural policy of the European Community. The Directives and Regulations associated with farming in less favoured areas is directly linked to the 1985 Regulation. Primarily the ESA Regulations aims at assisting the restructuring of the farming economy, but with the conservation of natural wildlife and habitats linked directly to agricultural policies.

The Regulation allows for agricultural grants to be paid for 'the protection and improvement of the environment', although this is still part of the broader, agricultural objective of assisting farmers to improve their incomes and living and working conditions.

The Regulation further permits Member States to introduce their own schemes to support 'appropriate agricultural practices in environmentally sensitive areas'. This part of the Regulation, in Article 19 of the legislation, defines ESAs as 'being of recognised importance from an ecological and landscape point of view'. Grant-aid is permitted for farming techniques which 'preserve or improve the environment ... and are compatible with conserving the natural habitat'.

The sting in the tail of the Regulation is that the environmentally sensitive farming practices are not, in themselves, eligible for European grant-aid, and any support for ESAs must, at least initially, come from within the resources of the Member States.

However, the 1985 Regulation was followed by a further amending Regulation in 1987 (Commission of the European Communities, 1987b). Some of the amendments relate to Article 19, which link farming in

Environmentally Sensitive Areas with reduced agricultural output, but also indicate that where this is the case the European Community can provide a contribution towards the grant-aid paid to farmers.

Council Directive on the Protection of Natural and Semi-natural Habitats and of Wild Flora and Fauna, 1992

The European Community's Habitats Directive (Commission of the European Communities, 1988b) is the culmination of several different areas of policy development within the Community. The concept of protecting specific species (particularly birds) has been long established within the Community. Similarly, with the creation of the fourth Environmental Action Programme (EAP), the need for proactive protection became paramount.

The fourth EAP stated that:

Such a framework should ensure that, throughout the Community, positive measures are taken to protect all forms of wildlife and their habitats; such measures should be aimed at the three main objectives of the World Conservation Strategy:

 i) the maintenance of essential ecological processes and life support systems
 ii) the preservation of genetic diversity
 iii) the sustainable utilisation of species and ecosystems.

The Environmental Action Programme takes these strands of policy development and boldly states that 'the Commission will make appropriate proposals on these lines'. Because of the far-reaching nature of the proposed Directives, it is worth spending some time plotting its development.

The first draft of this powerful proposal emerged in 1988 (Commission of the European Communities, 1988b), only nine months after the fourth EAP was published. However, after this rapid start the proposed legislation ran into some stormy debate. Initially some members of the Environment Council demanded that it be rejected unanimously. Two particular aspects of the proposal caused concern. First, the Commission would, under the draft Directive, have power to intervene if some countries were slow in designating Special Protection Areas (SPAs). This was seen as a deviation towards centralized authority. Second, the 11 technical Annexes were viewed as too numerous by some Member States. Only three of the suggested 11 Annexes were prepared with the draft document, but even these were seen as over-burdensome by certain Council members .

For their part, the Conservation lobby felt that the outline Annexes were not too long, but the Directive did not mention any financial support for the proposals. Thus, they felt on that side of the debate that the proposals would be simply cosmetic.

These apparent blockages were released in 1990 when not only were the final eight Annexes prepared in draft form (Commission of the European Communities, 1990a) but funding regulations were also prepared, again in draft form (Commission of the European Communities, 1990b). With these difficulties at least partially addressed, the document could be progressed towards a final form.

The Annexes contain lists of threatened species, species which could be 'exploited' (i.e. hunted) under SPA Management Plans, and lists of endangered habitats. The initial lists were to be agreed as part of the final Directive. As the proposal is not critical to the creation of a Single European Market, the Directive was agreed on a unanimous basis. However, it is indicated within the draft proposals that subsequent additions and amendments to the Annexes would only need to be approved by a qualified majority.

The original proposals of 1988 were updated in 1991 (Commission of the European Communities, 1992). The update was prefixed by the explanatory memorandum which gives a brief resumé of the progress of the original draft proposal. The explanatory memorandum indicates that:

1. the original document was submitted in 1998, with supportive annexes submitted in 1990; from the Commission to the Council;
2. the European Parliament proposed 53 amendments with a large majority;
3. 29 of these amendments were acceptable to the Commission;
4. the draft was amended accordingly.

This brief summary indicates not only the way that the relationships between the Commission, the Parliament and the Council has been developed, but also the opportunities which exist for the Parliament, and hence lobby groups, to influence the process.

Many of the amendments cover details of specific species and taxa to be protected by the Directive. However, Article 2 of the Directive was also significantly amended. The original Article covered only the general principle of 'maintaining diversity and abundance'. Some 10 amendments that are included in the 1990 Directive however, expanded this to include definitions of 'conservation status', 'extent of satisfactory protection' and 'special protection areas'.

Finally, an accompanying note summarizes the potential effect of the Directive upon 'competitiveness and employment' as if to re-emphasize the underlying rationale for environmental competence in the European Community.

It is worth noting the difficulties met by the Habitats Directive because in many ways it reflects the friction between the Commission and Member States. The very great detail contained within the Habitats Directive was seen by many Member States as a direct challenge to their own ability to legislate and was seen by many agriculturists, developers and hunting organizations as a threat to their own interests.

Notwithstanding these problems, the Habitats Directive was adopted in 1992 with a deadline set for formal compliance of June 1994. From this point, up to 2005, the process of designation of sites, reporting on progress and final designations would take place. The Habitats Directive is a culmination of the processes that are analysed in the foregoing analysis: the two components of the Directive seek to protect a strategic network of European Habitats, and to protect the most threatened species in Europe. The two annexes list the habitat types, and the species concerned.

One innovative element to some out of the Directive is the concept of a 'coherent European ecological network' of sites across the Community. This is known as Natura 2000. The concept of Natura 2000 is discussed in Chapter 6 where conservation strategies are discussed more fully. A framework of Natura 2000 has been produced (Institute of European Environmental Policy, 1991) which suggests that the objectives for such a network should help to refocus concern for nature conservation 'from species to habitats; from sites to ecosystems; and from national to international measures'.

Proposed legislation

Having suggested that the fifth Environmental Action Programme was not concerned exclusively with specific pieces of legislation, there are none the less pieces of environmental legislation within the Community's system which, as we have seen with the Habitats Directive, can take a long time to emerge from the process. The only way to monitor or register these is to record the definite proposals that have been made by the Commission. In 1994, there were over 50 proposals relating to the environment in general, with three specifically relating to wildlife and the countryside, and a further four relating to Community decisions on international convention.

The nature conservation proposals referred to zoos (the management and capture of natural species in zoos and other collections), CITES (amendments to the endangered species directive arising originally from the Washington Convention in Trade in Endangered Species) and amendments to the Birds and their Habitats directive originally legislated in 1979.

COMMUNITY AGRICULTURAL POLICY

It is impossible to examine the policies of the European Community relating to nature conservation without addressing at least the broad framework of the Common Agricultural Policy (CAP). Indeed some of the Directives and Regulations already examined are, strictly speaking, part of the agricultural policy rather than any environmental policy within the Community.

Plate 5 The demand for more intensive agriculture in southern Euorpe has led to large areas devoted to plastic-covered 'greenhouses', as here in Portugal.

We saw in the previous chapters that the protection of agricultural production and the safeguarding of farmers' livelihoods has always formed an integral part of Community objectives; so much that in 1986 some 65% of the Community budget was spent funding the CAP.

Community Agricultural funds are split into two very unequal parts: the guarantee fund and the structural fund. The former supports the prices that farmers receive for their produce and hence supports agricultural income, while the latter is used to restructure the farming industry and guide farmers towards broader Community objectives. It is usually through this latter, much smaller element of guidance-funding that environmental measures have been attempted. However, from the beginning of the 1990s the much larger, guarantee funds have been viewed as providing a possible mechanism for bringing conservation and agriculture closer together (Potter and Lobley, 1990).

The Common Agricultural Policy is usually held to have been framed through the Mansholt Report (Mansholt, 1969) although CAP actually started some seven years earlier in 1962. Through the Mansholt Plan, the various problems identified in Chapter 1 were addressed: unpredictable farm incomes; farm structures; population drift away from rural areas; low or non-existent alternative employment opportunities in rural areas and so on. The CAP was, and still is, an economic response to these issues.

The principal mechanism for attempting to solve these problems was one of guaranteed farm incomes. Through this process, it was felt that farms would remain viable, and therefore the social, political and environmental system associated with them would also remain viable.

However, it became apparent through the 1980s that the policy of producing costly food surpluses was also damaging to the environment. As a result, structural adjustments were made to the Common Agricultural Policy which began to resolve the growing conflict between it and the environment. This debate was initiated through a Commission document of 1985 (Commission of the European Communities, 1985d).

The review of CAP was still to be largely based upon economic rationale, but within the priorities outlined by the document. There were several which referred to 'supporting agriculture in place where it is essential for the protection of the environment and landscape' and 'making farmers more aware of environmental issues'.

The paper also contained the first proposals to establish new priorities for the agricultural funds (collectively known as FEOFA, the French acronym) which at the time was relatively innovative. Up until 1995 about 95% of the agricultural funds within FEOFA were targeted on guaranteed farm prices, with only 5% targeted upon guidance or structural reform. Within this 5%, however, were found the funds for the ESAs and the Less Favoured Areas Directives.

In the mid-1980s therefore, the European Community began to address the criticisms and obvious shortcomings of the Common Agricultural Policy.

The mechanisms for achieving restructuring were based, to some extent, on German legislation of April 1986: within this 'Marktentlastungs programm', several restructuring measures were identified.

1. The search for alternatives to traditionally produced goods in areas of deficit, i.e. grain, legumes and so on.
2. The search for new uses for agricultural commodities.
3. Qualitative restrictions and quotas on production of some commodities.
4. Voluntary schemes to take whole farms or acreages out of production.
5. Farm diversification and the Environmentally Sensitive Areas proposals identified above.

However, it should be stressed that the driving force behind all of these proposals, especially at European level, remained economic not environmental. Despite the changes made to the Structural Funds brought about through the Single European Act (which, as we have already seen, sought to better integrate the funding and development programmes of the European Community) this remains the case. Indeed it has been suggested (Baldock, 1990) that in linking FEOGA to the Regional Development Fund (ERDF) and the Social Fund (ESF), the environment will continue to be disadvantaged because major economic and infrastructure proposals will be targeted on many remoter rural areas, such as the priority areas of Greece, Italy, Spain, Portugal, Corsica and Ireland.

The mechanisms for achieving a reduction in production and in restructuring the agriculture industry still, therefore, have the economic objectives as their prime concern. As a result, opportunities to improve the environment which arise through the restructuring process, either as part of an integrated development programme or as a separate individual measure, can be missed. One such example is that of agricultural set-aside, which is worth assessing in greater detail.

The basic principle of removing land from agricultural production (either permanently or temporarily) is one that has been on various political agendas for several years. Initially, it began to become part of the European debate around the time of the review of the Common Agricultural Policy. At that time, is was suggested that set-aside could be used to create environmentally valuable farm landscapes (Commission of the European Communities, 1985c). However, as the ideas developed, this notion was dropped for a more socio-economic rationale (Commission of European Communities, 1985a)

At this point set-aside had many possible means of implementation. Pre-pension plans, for example, were envisaged which could remove whole farms out of production where the owners were aged 55–65. Again, however, this was later amended so that land was not necessarily taken out of production, but that farm ownerships would transfer to keep younger people employed in agriculture.

A further addition to the debate surrounding set-aside was gained from experiences within the United States, where environmental set-aside was formulated under the Conservation Reserve Scheme (Ervin, 1987).

Despite this broad-based debate, the regulation which ultimately framed the European legislation rejected the environmental objectives and concentrated upon the economic objectives. Land which is set-aside will simply be removed from production for a short period: alternative, ecological land uses and valid ecological timescales are all ignored. As one observer commented, 'It calls into question the ability of agricultural policy makers to move towards a more integrated approach in which the needs of rural communities and the environment are given adequate consideration. In this sense the present set-aside proposals represent a clear step backwards' (Baldock, 1987).

Perhaps this is an extreme view, but the view of many conservationists at present is that adjusting the peripheral issues of agricultural guidance policy is not acceptable, and that what is required is a reassessment of the agricultural guarantee structure so that the environment (natural, cultural, landscape and heritage) is adequately evaluated through the funding process. In this context, Environmentally Sensitive Areas represent a clear step forward, in that they represent a 'shift away from compensatory payments for sacrificed profits, and towards more direct environmental remuneration' (Potter, 1987).

As a result of this desire to establish the environment as part of the broad agricultural decision-making process, many Member States as well as the Commission have begun to look at the longer term implications of the restructuring of the Common Agricultural Policy. Following the Council of Ministers agreement, reached in May 1992, additional regulations were developed to review both the agricultural, forestry and environmental implications of the broader proposals.

The objectives of what have come to be known as the 'Agri-Environmental Measures' are to reduce the polluting effect of agriculture, to encourage environmentally favourable extensification of crops and livestock, to protect the countryside, to recover abandoned land, to set up environmentally beneficial long-term set-aside; to facilitate public access to land; and to educate farmers and landowners on agri-environmental matters.

Several Member States reviewed the impact that these fundamental policy changes would have on their own agriculture industries. Britain, for example, initiated a House of Lords Select Committee review (Her Majesty's Stationery Office, 1992) which broadly welcomed the proposals but raised several questions about resources, missed opportunities for more proactive conservation, the need for targeting of vulnerable areas and the need for longer-term farm plans which incorporated a wide range of economic, agricultural and environmental objectives.

The Dutch Authorities similarly reviewed how the CAP actually made an impact upon their agricultural methods and, equally importantly, how any adjustments made to CAP could be influenced to bring about advantages for wildlife conservation (Baldock and Beaufoy, 1993).

From the reforms set in motion in May 1992, which concentrated upon arable production, sheep, beef, milk and tobacco, the study concluded that, even in the areas of production that had some degree of policy discussion, the future is uncertain. This uncertainty is brought about by global trade agreements (the so-called Uruguay round of the General Agreement on Tariffs and Trade Talks – GATT) and the uncertainty over other world producers and hence prices. Consequently, agreements made within the EC over levels of production and prices may need to be revised in the light of

GATT. Hence the uncertainty. It is suggested in the Dutch study, however, that the mechanics of control (such as intervention prices, quotas, headage prices for animals and capital grants, for example) will remain the same. The potential changes will come through prices and export/import control.

The implications of this on the natural environment are numerous and varied, but there are several areas in which change could be witnessed: the continued intensification of agricultural methods; or conversely the extensification of some types of production; agricultural set-aside; increased ability to blend conservation and agricultural needs through, for example, farm management plans; abandonment; land-use change of a more permanent nature.

The 1992 reforms could point the way towards greater integration of the rural landusers alongside agriculture. This greater integration, if managed properly, could have an advantage for wildlife. If not a great opportunity will have been missed. For this to happen, both farmers and conservationists should become more realistic about what can be achieved (Green, 1987). Central to this realism must be the integrated rural strategies discussed in Chapter 23, but in the shorter term the opportunities presented by the 1992 McSharry reforms must be taken, even in the uncertainty that surrounds the current CAP programme.

EUROPEAN ENVIRONMENTAL AGENCY

A further environmental initiative which is worthy of note is that of the European Environmental Agency. The management and handling of information has always been a priority of the European Community. In 1989, the Commission agreed to establish the Agency, the objectives of which were set out at the time (Commission of the European Communities, 1989) and in its subsequent constitution when it was formally established in 1990. These objectives are:

1. to provide the Community, Member States and participating third countries with objective information with which to formulate and implement environmental policies;
2. to provide technical and scientific information requested by the Commission to implement and monitor environmental legislation;
3. to stimulate the development of modelling and forecasting techniques;
4. to harmonize and improve comparability of environmental data across the Community, and help integrate European information into international information and monitoring programmes.

The information network (entitled EIONET: European Environmental Information and Observation Network) will be established as a matter of priority for the Agency. Its primary areas of interest are air quality, water quality, flora and fauna protection, natural resources, waste management, noise emissions, chemical substances and coastal protection.

After a great degree of debate within the Community, the Agency found a permanent home in Copenhagen in 1993, and only then was it able to tackle its mission properly. Its initial aim is to establish a series of 'State of the Environment' Reports, although this will take some time to develop, as the Agency only moved into its new Headquarters in 1994, with a few key members of staff (European Community Committee of the American Chamber of Commerce, 1995).

A SUMMARY OF EUROPEAN NATURE CONSERVATION POLICY

The foregoing discussion has made clear at least one main point; that Community environmental policy is far from clear-cut. This is particularly the case for nature conservation. The reasons for this are evident: there has, up until the 1987 Single European Act, been no identifiable legal basis for nature conservation legislation; the nature conservation legislation has developed as part of broader policy areas, including agriculture and regional development; and as a result of this latter situation nature conservation has progressed along a number of avenues which, at times, have appeared disparate.

The fifth Environmental Action Programme has served to bring many of these strands together. Furthermore, with the Single European Act, the Community has also identified the 'policy gap' and has started to look towards being more proactive in its nature conservation legislation.

Prior to 1987, the Community had gone through several stages of legislating for nature conservation. Initially, steps concentrated upon assembling information, which was and still remains one of the cornerstones of conservation policy. A first watershed was the 1979 Birds Directive. With this legislation, the Community first directly addressed the issue of protection of the natural environment. About the same time, the Community also began to take its place amongst the other international players within the sphere of nature conservation by endorsing international conventions, the first of which being the Decision in 1975 following the Ramsar Convention on Wetlands. This pattern continued until the Single European Act, with nature conservation legislation as much following outside influences as pursuing its own internal direction.

The fourth Environmental Action Programme identified the need for internal direction, by listing six areas of general policy orientation; including integration with other Community policies and the development of information networks. On nature conservation in particular, the

Community identifies the need for 'important developments' particularly full integration into all policies to protect 'not just birds, but all species of flora and fauna, and not just the habitats of birds, but the habitats of wildlife more generally (Commission of the European Communities, 1987c). This debate was further expanded by the fifth Environmental Action Programme which, as we saw earlier, expands the concept of environmental protection beyond legislative mechanism towards a more holistic concept of sustainability, within which nature conservation plays its part.

The Environmental Directorate-General (DG XI) has therefore assumed a much more central role within the Community's machinery, being responsible for monitoring policy integration and a nature conservation policy *per se*.

There is no doubt however that this theoretical path will be littered with practical obstructions, most critically, the enthusiasm, methods and priorities of the Member States in implementing Community environmental policy. On this issue the Commission states that 'we have in the past identified a considerable number of omissions and deviations in national laws ... complete and effective implementation of the Community environment acts by all Member States is a matter of priority concern'.

The second area of concern to many conservationists is the continued, if slightly adjusted, emphasis on economic development (Haigh, 1994). On this, this Community suggest that 'the challenge is to find a way of making progress in environmental policy in such a way that economic and employment benefits foreseen by the European Council can also be achieved' (Commission of the European Communities, 1994). For the 21st century, this surely is the greatest challenge of all.

REFERENCES

Baldock, D. (1987) *Set-aside: Some Observations in Removing Land from Agriculture.* IEEP, London.

Baldock, D. (1990) *The EC Structural Funds – Environmental Briefing.* WWF/IEEP, Surrey.

Baldock, D. and Beaufoy, G. (1993) *Nature Conservation and New Directions in the EC Common Agricultural Policy in the Netherlands.* IEEP, London.

Commission of the European Communities (1973a) *The First Environmental Action Programme.* OJ C112 20.12.73. Brussels.

Commission of the European Communities (1973b) *Environmental Information Agreement.* OJ C9 15.3.73. Brussels.

Commission of the European Communities (1974) *Agreement Supplementing the Agreement of 5 March 1973.* OJ C86 20.7.74. Brussels.

Commission of the European Communities (1975a) *Recommendation on Cost Allocation and Action by Public Authorities on Environmental Matters.* OJ

L194 25.7.75. Brussels.

Commission of the European Communities (1975b) *Directive on Mountain and Hill Farming in Certain Less Favoured Areas.* OJ L128 19.5.75. Brussels.

Commission of the European Communities (1976) *Decision Establishing a Common Procedure for Setting Up and Constantly Updating of an Inventory of Sources of Information on the Environment.* OJ C21 6.1.76. Brussels.

Commission of the European Communities (1979) *Directive on the Conservation of Wild Birds.* OJ L103 25.4.79. Brussels.

Commission of the European Communities (1980) *Progress Made in Connection with the Environmental Action Programme and Assessment of the Work Done to Implement it.* COM (80) 222. Brussels.

Commission of the European Communities (1981a) *Regulation on Common Rules for Imports of Whales or Other Cetacean Products.* OJ L39 12.2.81. Brussels.

Commission of the European Communities (1981b) *Decision on the Conclusion of the Convention on the Conservation of Antartic Marine Living Resources.* OJ L252 5.9.81. Brussels.

Commission of the European Communities (1982a) *Decision on the Conclusion of the Convention on the Conservation of European Wildlife and Natural Reserves.* OJ L38 10.2.82. Brussels.

Commission of the European Communities (1982b) *Decision on the Conclusion of the Convention on the Conservation of Migratory Species of Wild Animals.* OJ L210 19.7.82. Brussels.

Commission of the European Communities (1982c) *Regulation on the Implementation in the Community of the Convention on International Trade in Endangered Species.* OJ L384 13.12.82. Brussels.

Commission of the European Communities (1983) *Directive Concerning the Importation into Member States of Skins of Certain Seal Pups and Products Derived Therefrom.* OJ L91 9.4.83. Brussels.

Commission of the European Communities (1984a) *Regulation on Action by the Community Concerning the Environment.* OJ L176 3.7.84. Brussels.

Commission of the European Communities (1984b) *Ten Years of Community Environmental Policy.* European Commission. Brussels.

Commission of the European Communities (1985a) *Directive on the Assessment of the Effects of Certain Public and Private Projects on the Environment.* OJ L175 5.7.85. Brussels.

Commission of the European Communities (1985b) *Decision on the Adoption of the Commission Work Programme Concerning an Experimental Project for Gathering, Co-ordinating and Ensuring the Consistency of Information on the State of the Environment and Natural Resources in the Community.* OJ L176 6.7.85. Brussels.

Commission of the European Communities (1985c) *Regulation on Improving the Efficiency of Agricultural Structures.* OJ L93 30.3.85. Brussels.

Commission of the European Communities (1985d) *Perspective on the Common Agricultural Policy.* COM (85) 333 20.5.85. Brussels.

Commission of the European Communities (1987a) *European Community Environmental Legislation.* European Commission, Brussels.

Commission of the European Communities (1987b) *Regulation amending Regulations EEC Nos 797/85; 270/79; 1360/78 and 355/77.* OJ L167 26.6.87. Brussels.

Commission of the European Communities (1987c) *Fourth Environmental Action Programme.* OJ C328 7.12.87. Brussels.

Commission of the European Communities (1988a) *Agricultural Set-aside.* OJ L106 27.4.88, OJ L121 11.5.88, OJ L121 11.5.88. Brussels.

Commission of the European Communities (1988b) *Directive on the Protection of Natural and Semi-natural Habitats.* OJ 247 21.9.88. Brussels.

Commission of the European Communities (1989) *European Environmental Agency.* OJ C217 5.5.89. Brussels.

Commission of the European Communities (1990a) *Supplementary Annexes to the Proposals for a Council Directive on the Protection of Natural and Semi-natural Habitats of Wild Flora and Fauna.* Com (90) 59 30.3.90. Brussels.

Commission of the European Communities (1990b) *Proposals for a Regulation on Action by the Community Relating to Nature Conservation.* Com (90) 125 15.4.90. Brussels.

Commission of the European Communities (1992) *Towards Sustainability: The 5th Environmental Action Programme.* Com (92) 23. Brussels.

Commission of the European Communities (1993a) *Growth, Competitiveness and Employment.* COM (93) 700. Brussels.

Commission of the European Communities (1993b) *Voluntary Participation by Companies in the Industrial Sector in a Community Eco-audit and Management System.* OJ 168 15.7.93. Brussels.

Commission of the European Communities (1994) *Review of the 5th Action Programme.* European Commission, Brussels.

Ervin, D. (1987) *Cropland Diversification in the US: Lessons for Set-aside in Removing Land from Agriculture.* IEEP, London.

European Community Committee of American Chambers of Commerce (1995) *EU Environmental Guide.* ECCACC, Brussels.

Fairclough, J.A. (1987) EC Environmental Policy, in *European Environmental Yearbook.* DocTer, Milan.

Green, B. (1987) *Environmental Opportunities Offered by Surplus Production in Removing Land from Agriculture.* IEEP, London.

Haigh, N. (1989) *EEC Environmental Policy and Britain.* Longman, London.

Haigh, N. (1994) *Manual of Environmental Policy and Britain.* Longman, London.

Her Majesty's Stationery Office (1992) *Environmental Aspects of the Reform of the CAP.* House of Lords Select Committee Session 1992/93. HMSO, London.

IEEP (1991) Natura 2000: *A report for the Department of the Environment.* Den Haag, The Netherlands.

Mansholt, S. (1969) *Le Plan Mansholt: le Rapport.* Seclaf, Paris.

Potter, S. (1987) Set-aside: Friend or foe? *ECOS,* **8**(1), 36–39.

Potter, S. and Lobley, D. (1990) Adapting to Europe. *ECOS,* **11**(3), 3–9.

Roberts, R.D. and Roberts, T.M. (eds) (1984) *Ecology and Planning.* Chapman & Hall, London.

Smith, M. (1985) *Agriculture and Nature Conservation in Conflict: The Less Favoured Areas of France and the UK.* Arkleton Trust, Devon.

Van Moltke, K. (1983) *Influences on Environmental Policy in the EEC in Britain, Europe and the Environment.* Centre for Environmental Technology, London.

The environment, Europe and the world | 6

One of the underlying principles of the European Community has been the view that Europe is only part of a world-wide network of organizations, political structures, problems, opportunities and economic markets. For this reason, if no other, it is necessary to examine this global environment within which the European Community operates. However, the rationale clearly does not stop there. The environment has no notion of political or ownership boundaries, and similarly many wildlife or environmental organizations operate at an international level.

Given the desire of the European Community to be an integral part of a global environmental network, and also the very characteristics of the environment itself, it is clearly worthwhile discussing the world-wide environmental movement. But where is this movement to be found? As becomes evident later in this book, even in individual Member States the political and management structures which deal with nature conservation are complex. The foregoing discussion has identified the complexity of the European perspective. If we therefore extend this to the global scale, the picture inevitably becomes even more complicated.

In order to rationalize this complexity to some extent, it is necessary to simplify and select the organizations and structures discussed; in short, many things will be left out. The starting point for such a filtering process must be the opinion of the European Community itself, and the organizations, conventions and issues that it perceives as important.

The following analysis therefore addresses several separate components which, collectively, make up the world wide conservation movement with which the EC has most contact.

Plate 6 Recreational and tourist pressure is now felt all over Europe, even in the most remote or inaccessible places.

ORGANIZATIONS

There is an enormous number of organizations which operate at the international level, and to list them all would clearly be impossible. Furthermore, some organizations also shift their activities and emphasis from time to time. For these reasons, the following organizations represent the more permanent and easily definable examples of those operating on the international circuit.

Some of these organizations are collections or associations of national governments, others are umbrella organizations for the voluntary or non-government sector. Others are single voluntary or non-government organizations which because of their size have taken an important role within the world network independently from umbrella groupings.

A further consideration is that the relationship between these individual and grouped agencies varies. On some occasions, the non-government organizations act as lobbyists, on others they are an official part of the consultation or discursive stage of decision making. Similarly, some national governments may disagree with the stated policy of some of their own umbrella groupings and may, on occasions, show greater or lesser support for the views of the voluntary and non-government organizations. This complex interaction between public, private and voluntary organizations is a characteristic of the network within nature conservation both at the national and international level.

The parameters used to analyse European legislation for nature conservation and land management are used to analyse the world-wide network of environmental organizations. In short, if an organization's primary function is with nature conservation, it is clearly relevant to the discussion here, if it is sufficiently large or influential to warrant our attention. Other organizations, on the other hand, may not have nature conservation as their primary objective, but may be involved as a tangential or recent concern. In these cases, the importance of the organization is judged not by its overall policies, but its specific policies and impact on nature conservation.

A specific case in point is the United Nations Environment Programme. The overall remit of the United Nations is as large as the member states wish to make it (or alternatively as large as some member states are prepared to allow it). There are several subgroups and specific agendas which operate within the United Nations, such as the United National Educational Scientific and Cultural Organisation (UNESCO) or the Food and Agriculture Organisation of the United Nations (FAO). One such group is the United Nations Environment Programme (UNEP). UNEP is influential largely because of its programmes and its funding of the work of others. Its contribution to world conservation and land management tends to be through its assistance and forward thinking on strategies. For this reason, it is discussed in greater detail later in this chapter. The World Wide Fund for Nature, on the other hand, has sufficient impact at a global level in a number of areas of work that it is best discussed as an organization.

While this method of determining the relevance of each particular organization or world conservation strategy is not, perhaps, as cut and dried as might be thought best, it does in part reflect the diverse and organic way in which the world conservation movement has developed from the bottom up.

Council of Europe

The Council of Europe was founded in 1949, and is therefore the longest standing organization with a pan-European remit. It consists of representatives from 21 countries: Austria, Belgium, Cyprus, Denmark, France, Germany, Greece, Iceland, Ireland, Italy, Liechtenstein, Luxembourg, Malta, Netherlands, Norway, Portugal, Spain, Sweden, Switzerland, Turkey and the United Kingdom.

The Council of Europe is not a legislative or executive body, and operates through the processes of negotiation and diplomacy. Its original and principle objective consists of two elements: to uphold parliamentary democracy and to improve the quality of life. The Council operates in a similar way to national government and has a Main Council, which is served by several subcommittees, and employs a number of administrative staff who are all based in Strasbourg. The secretary-general is responsible for drawing up the agenda of the Council which is then debated by Council members and, following any agreements, the Council then acts as an agent of encouragement for the member countries.

In 1961, an Environment Committee was founded, which set its objectives as 'establishing a permanent system of co-operation on questions concerning the protection of nature in Europe'. In 1961 this was a far-sighted step, and since then the Council of Europe has played a leading role in guiding the progress of nature conservation not just in Europe, but world wide.

The fully developed mandate of the 1961 Committee is:

> To promote the conservation of nature and natural resources to protect the natural environment, the countryside and particular locations, especially areas of scientific value or of outstanding beauty, also to created new nature reserves and national and international parks within Europe.

In order to achieve this the Council of Europe has, among other initiatives, instigated several important Conventions in Europe to discuss global issues. The Council also disseminates large amounts of information on environmental matters and operates an award system – the European Diploma – for countries or organizations that achieve high standards in nature conservation or wildlife protection. The European Diploma was introduced in 1966, and by 1988 some 28 sites across Europe had been awarded the Diploma for effective management and protection of conservation areas.

Another initiative of the Council of Europe is the establishment, in 1967, of the European Information Centre for Nature Conservation. The centre generates a range of scientific information not only for politicians in Member States, but also for the general public.

Finally, in 1976, the Council of Europe adopted a resolution to establish 'A network of Biogenetic Reserves'. This network was intended to link into the world strategy being developed by the International Union for Conservation of Nature and Natural Resources (IUCN; see below). However, the council of Europe has chosen to define its own system of classification for protected areas:

Category A: For the protection of flora and fauna, where human activity is strictly limited.
Category B: For the protection of landscapes and natural features. Public access is permitted to a level which will not jeopardize the site.
Category C: For areas where recreational and/or educational use co-exists with natural history or landscape protection.

To summarize, it is fair to say that for a non-executive organization the Council of Europe has had considerable success in concentrating the collective mind of Europe on nature conservation and subsequently by encouraging positive action by individual members of the Council (Orme, 1989).

International Union for the Conservation of Nature and Natural Resources

The International Union for the Conservation of Nature and Natural Resources (IUCN) was established in 1948. It is a model of co-operation between governmental, non-governmental and national organizations; some 600 organizations currently contribute to the work of IUCN.

It is not a funding organization, nor an executive organization, but works with its partners by providing information, technical advice and policy frameworks. Collectively, the IUCN tries to ensure that nature conservation and related issues do not slip through the net of national and international decision making.

In order to provide this policy and information service, the IUCN draws upon a network of specialists, which in turn service six subcommittees of the General Assembly. The General Assembly meets every three years. The six commissions are: Environmental Policy, Law and Administration; Sustainable Development; Education; National Parks and Protected Areas; Ecology; and Species Survival. The six commissions and the General Assembly are serviced by a secretariat and by three specialist centres. The three centres are spread across western Europe: the Centre for Conservation for Development is in Switzerland (as too is the IUCN Headquarters); the Environmental Law Centre is in Germany; and the Conservation Monitoring Centre is in the United Kingdom.

Each of these centres provides an international and local data base on each specialist area. The framework within which the IUCN operates is provided by the World Conservation Strategy and the World Charter for Nature. The works of the IUCN is funded from a variety of sources, including National Government, the United Nations, the World Wide Fund for Nature and its own commercial activities.

Because of the sheer size of the organization of IUCN, it is inevitable that the day-to-day management of its programmes and projects should be regionalized. Similarly, some countries have developed their own sub-committees at a national level, so that the exchange of information, ideas and strategy implementation is broadened and made two-way. One such example is the United Kingdom. The idea for a UK committee of IUCN was formed in 1975, and the constitution of the group was amended in 1980 to accommodate the creation and implications of the IUCN World Conservation Strategy. This UK committee meets three times a year, with the Chairmanship and Secretariat being provided by English Nature. This government agency is, in turn, a member of the IUCN General Assembly (Nature Conservancy Council, 1987). At the European level, the IUCN Western European

Regional Committee was formed in 1984, and meets every three years, in part to feed from National Committees and into the General Assembly.

The IUCN is in a unique position because it represents a combination of types of organization which have come together to form a large agency which not only has direct access to government decision makers, but can also draw upon many of the worlds finest specialist advisers. It can therefore choose from a combination of lobbying, consultative, advisory and proactive work methods to achieve its objectives.

The IUCN objectives are laid out clearly in two documents discussed later in this chapter, namely the World Conservation Strategy and the World Charter for Nature. Other than this level of activity, the IUCN plays an active role in monitoring numerous international conventions on nature conservation, species or ecosystem protection or education/information exchange. At a more local level, IUCN assists and/or advises upon specific projects, particularly in countries and areas where such environmental advice may not be readily available. These projects may include irrigation schemes, designation of national parks or other protected areas or the development of national strategies.

Organisation for Economic Co-operation and Development

The Organisation for Economic Co-operation and Development (OECD) was formed in 1960 as part of the global desire for economic restructuring and co-ordination which was prevalent at the start of the 1960s. There are around 30 countries which participate at some level within the OECD system. The Paris convention, which was originally signed by 19 countries on 14 December 1960, stated that the aims of the OECD are:

to promote policies designed:

- to achieve the highest sustainable economic growth and employment and a rising standard of living in Member countries, while maintaining financial stability and thus to contribute to the development of the world economy;
- to contribute to sound economic expansion in Member as well as non-Member countries in the process of economic development; and
- to contribute to the expansion of world trade on a multilateral, non-discriminatory basis in accordance with international obligations.

(Organisation for Economic Co-operation and Development, 1961)

It is evident, therefore, that the OECD, like the European Community, is first and foremost an economic organization. However, unlike the European

Community, OECD has no executive or legal powers. It develops its policies through discussion, agreements and co-operation.

As with other economic groupings, however, OECD has come to accept that the development of and expansion of Member countries' economies have implications for the environment. This was first formally acknowledged around the close of the 1980s, when it was accepted that 'the economic and social structures of the OECD area's rural regions have changed considerably' (Organisation for Economic Co-operation and Development, 1988). While this does not go a long way towards altering the economic focus of the OECD, it does mark the beginning of an acceptance that in some of the more rural areas of the OECD (such as Turkey, Spain, New Zealand or Pakistan) economic development may not always be easily defined in terms of simple economic parameters. As a result the 'need for new institutional frameworks through which policies are generated and implemented has arisen' (Organisation for Economic Co-operation and Development, 1988). Sectorally based departments (such as forestry, agriculture or trade and industry) no longer meet the integrated needs of rural areas or indeed urban areas.

It is through the discursive process at the heart of the economic policy making that OECD is likely to have its greatest impact on protecting the natural environment. Practically, OECD's contribution is minimal, but as a source of policy making and as an influence on economic thinking, it is a potent force. As a result, it is in a strong position to assist (or, indeed otherwise) in the process of environmental protection.

The particular problems of developing new institutional frameworks is one that will arise time and again in Part Two of this book, when the process of nature conservation in Member States of the European Community is discussed.

United Nations

In common with the Organisation of Economic Co-operation and Development, the United Nations was established for one particular reason and, in its development, has become involved with the processes of nature conservation.

The United Nations was formed in 1945, after the end of the 1939–45 World War, in a spirit both of reconciliation, and of forward thinking. The attitude at the time was that if nations could talk openly, then the need for war would be reduced. It is this centrally diplomatic function that still dominates the activities of the UN, although in some types of work its activity is becoming more interventionist.

Outside its main activities, the UN has also developed specific programmes of action. These it undertakes either by employing its own research and/or project staff or, more usually, by funding work through other international, multigovernmental or non-governmental organizations.

Two programme areas of the United Nations are of particular relevance here. First, the United Nations Environment Programme (UNEP) assists with and leads policy developments specifically on environmental issues. (See later in this chapter for an analysis of some of its programmes and strategies.) The second important group is the United Nations Educational, Scientific and Cultural Organisation (UNESCO), which develops policy and programmes aimed not only at raising global education standards, but also protecting the cultural environment of the world. This links with the objectives of the UNEP in that both programmes seek to develop policies to protect specific sites, and many sites contain natural and cultural points of importance. Thus, some sites may be covered by both programmes.

As well as leading discussion/policy development and funding other agencies to create global strategies, UNEP and UNESCO also directly contribute to the management of sites of world importance, either natural, cultural or both.

One of the most important events of the latter part of the 20th century was organized by the United Nations. The Earth Summit in Rio in 1992 was a landmark for the environmental movement, and is detailed later in this chapter. UNCED (United National Conference on Environment and Development) was significant not only for the scale of its agenda, but for its proactive nature. This positive role is evident elsewhere in the United Nations' increasingly proactive peace-keeping and humanitarian work. UNCED reflected this new approach on environmental issues.

Non-governmental organizations

Non-governmental organizations (NGOs) refer to the voluntary or 'not-for-profit' sector, sometimes also referred to as the third sector to distinguish it from public and private organizations. Traditionally, the environment has been the focus for a large amount of voluntary activity. People use the environment for their spare time and, at a more organized level, NGOs have developed to lobby, become active and participate in environmental debate and work, often at an international level.

In conjunction with other NGO sectors, environmental organizations will take on several roles (Raine *et al.*, 1992), including: service-providing function; pressure group function; resource co-ordinating function; self-help and networking function; fund-raising function.

At a general level, it has been argued that the European environmental NGOs do not currently support the European Community as currently constituted (Baine, Falk and Webster, 1992). This is largely because of the overriding emphasis on sustained growth rather than sustainable development that lies at the heart of EC policy.

The overall network for European environmental groups is the European Environmental Bureau (EEB) based in Brussels. Every six months, the EEB produces a memorandum for the incoming President of the Community (European Environmental Bureau, various years). This has, over the years, included a wide variety of issues, including: financial contribution to global environmental problems; amendments to the General Agreement on Trade and Tariffs (GATT) to control trade that is dangerous to the environment; a revision of the Treaty of Rome to accommodate more positive environmental rights; the improvement to EC structures to ease the passing of environmental regulations; and the creation of an EC Inspectorate of the Environment.

EEB was formed in 1974 with EC support. The original 25 members have grown to over 125. Over the years it has developed a valuable and important role and has direct access to the Commission through Directorate-General XI.

Individual groups within EEB are free to pursue their own policies and continue with their own particular areas of concern. Some of these, such as the World Wide Fund for Nature, are large enough to have an impact on their own. Other assemble themselves into other issue-specific alliances (Harvey, 1992). These include:

1. The Euro group for the Conservation of Birds and Habitats (ECBH) which concentrates on the protection of birds and the control of hunting.
2. International Conservation Action Network (ICAN) which focuses upon the exchange of information and training and the networking opportunities for active conservation.
3. International Fund for Animal Welfare (IFAW) which is a powerful lobby group which seeks to ensure that legislation and policy is enacted to protect species and illegal trade.

Given the strength of these groups and alliances, it is little wonder that the environmental NGOs represents some of the most powerful groupings in politics of the EC (Harvey, 1992).

The future for the non-governmental organizations appears to be becoming clearer. The role of NGOs has increasingly been seen as integral to the overall process of change, and consequently the numerous agencies have been brought into the formal decision-making process. Most Member States, for example, have developed mechanisms for including the voluntary sector in debate. Similarly, at a global level, the Rio Summit involved the voluntary sector in its programming and deliberations, albeit at a 'fringe' or parallel conference.

Within the EC, the objectives of the environmental NGOs, as expressed through the European Environmental Bureau, are to make the environment a more integral component of EC policy, and consequently make changes to existing policy to accommodate this (Raine *et al.*, 1992). Despite the recent moves made around the Single European Act and consecutive moves to ensure that the EC is legally competent to legislate on environmental issues, less than 1% of the EC budget is spent directly on the environment. Hence, the role of NGOs will continue to be relevant in lobbying, direct action and practical conservation.

At the broader level, Falk (1994) has identified five roles that the NGOs perform in European environmental politics and initiatives. These are as campaigners, visionaries, promoters/animateurs, environmental managers and developers.

Following this analysis, it is evident that some organizations fall into just one category, whilst others fall into several. At a European level, organizations such as Greenpeace or Friends of the Earth are predominantly campaigning organizations, while the Royal Society for the Protection of Birds (RSPB) is first and foremost an environmental manager that is becoming more adept at campaigning and providing a vision for how the conservation ethic can be interwoven into other land-use planning. At a national level, NGOs operate in a variety of ways similar to those at the international level. Ranging from very localized organizations to national branches of international organizations, NGOs at the level of the individual Member States are not only gaining in confidence but also developing very strong networks. Some of these organizations are discussed in the chapters on individual Member States in Part Two.

INTERNATIONAL CONVENTIONS

Given the plethora of agencies, only a few of which are identified individually in the previous section, it is an amazing feat of determination on the part of the key environmental organizations that, since 1971, there has been a consistent, if not overwhelming, succession of environmental conventions aimed at promoting wildlife and countryside protection. These conventions have been called by a number of agencies, and through various degrees of intergovernmental agreement. The purpose of each one has, however, been relatively consistent. The governments attending the conventions are called upon to sign up to the final statement of intent. The government then must implement the convention through their own management and administrative procedures.

Throughout this process of discussion, framing the final agreement and implementation the governments are subject to lobbying and open discussion with the environmental voluntary groups and pressure groups. Increasingly, the voluntary sector has become an important player in the main discussion and forum in conventions. For example, in the first convention to be discussed here, the voluntary sector non-governmental organizations were barely present.

In the most recent convention discussed here, at Rio in 1992, they were important contributors, with over 2000 NGOs represented as delegates.

The importance of the conventions is many fold. First, they seek to co-ordinate a genuine response and commitment to action from a wide range of governments. Second, they also allow governments and NGOs to come together to discuss and analyse specific issues. The conventions do not always end with intergovernmental agreement, and similarly they do not always end (or indeed start) with governmental/NGO agreement. However, they do provide a forum for debate.

The conventions also allow a major event to focus world attention onto the environment. The lead-in to the convention, the event itself and the subsequent promotion of the results allow an opportunity for the environment to take centre-stage in media and general debate.

The significance for the discussion here is that the European Community Member States have mostly signed up to the conventions as individual governments. Furthermore, the European Community itself has increasingly sought to develop a corporate response to the conventions. The final convention that is discussed here formed a turning point in the Community's response to international conventions, in that at Rio in 1992 the Community was, for the first time, debating a response at the corporate level which would supersede the individual responses. As it eventually turned out, this joint response did not materialize, but in itself the intention was significant.

The following discussion therefore highlights seven international conventions which are relevant to wildlife conservation. There have been other conventions which have had some sort of impact upon wildlife issues (such as the Convention for the Protection of the Mediterranean Sea against Pollution, held in Barcelona in 1975). However, the same criteria for determining a cut-off point for the debate has been used here; where the principal concern of the convention is wildlife conservation, it is included here.

Table 6.1 Timetable of international flora/fauna conventions

Date	Location	Subject
1971	Ramsar, Iran	Protection of wetlands and waterfowl
1972	Paris, France	Protection of world cultural and natural heritage
1973	Washington, USA	International trade in endangered species
1974	Paris, France	Marine pollution from land-based sources
1979	Bonn, Germany	Conservation of migratory species
1979	Berne, Switzerland	Conservation of European wildlife and habitats
1992	Rio, Brazil	Sustainability and development

The protocol of conventions

International conventions (which are usually referred to by the city or location in which the discussion takes place) are the means through which governments place some obligations upon themselves and each other. The wording of the final agreement is usually a result of diplomatic and secretive negotiations. However, the growing need to provide complex administrative support and back-up for the conventions has meant that the convention and subsequent agreements are now increasingly promoted and drafted by international agencies who have access to full-time paid staff and secretariat support (such as the Council of Europe or the United Nations).

Conventions are formally agreements between the sovereigns or leaders of nation states, and as a result the 'signing' of an agreement at the end of a convention is in fact a precursor to the formal acceptance through parliamentary and 'sovereign' ratification.

Thus, the European Community's role is ultimately reliant upon this independent ratification, but in all instances the Community has attempted to be party to the final agreements. This has inevitably been dependent upon the competence of the Community, which as stressed elsewhere in this text is a complex issue. However, where it has been impossible, the community has sought to encourage joint participation by Member States, and as has been explained above, at Community level.

This also causes problems, because of the issues of loss of sovereignty, lack of 'competence' and the relevance of the Convention to all Member States. Should all those issues be resolved, the route for Community-level participation is that the Commission asks the Council for the authority to discuss and enter negotiation on behalf of the Community. However, it is not unknown for the Council to affirm its own authority and competence and give the Commission authority to enter into discussions and negotiation, but for individual member states to ratify the convention, 'and the Community position ends in a sort of a limbo; a Council decision, which does no more than authorise a conclusion' (Haigh, 1989).

Thus, the European Community is, as elsewhere, striving to find its internal and external relationship with each other and with the following conventions. Notwithstanding, these conventions remain landmarks on the world movement towards a better protected and promoted environment.

Wildlife conventions

The discussion about each convention follows a similar pattern, and includes issues such as the contents of the convention, its date and location and the Community response to its formal conclusion. As suggested above, the response varies according to the Community's perception of its own competence, the relevance of the convention and its own internal problems of individual ratification. Thus, for example, the Bonn Convention on migratory species warranted a Council Decision, whereas the Washington Convention on trade in endangered species warranted a Council Regulation – specifically because the latter is a trade issue and therefore relates directly to the community's original economic remit.

Ramsar Convention

The convention on Wetlands of International Importance especially Waterfowl Habitats was held in Ramsar, Iran in 1971 and came into force in 1975. The convention was significant in that it was the first to be concerned exclusively with the protection of a specific habitat type, namely wetlands. Protection was to be through the 'wide use' of the habitats.

The method for implementations of the convention was for each signatory to designate sites that they considered to be suitable for designation and submit these unilaterally to the International Union for Conservation of Nature and Natural Resources (IUCN) for recording in their capacity as secretariat. Parties undertook to designate at least one site.

The other thrust of the convention was for research and information exchange into all wetlands, including estuaries, tidal flats, lakes, peak bogs, fens and marshes and mangrove swamps.

In its role as secretariat, the IUCN co-ordinates regular meetings, at intervals of less than three years where signatories do not have to submit reports on progressing the convention but do have to submit reports on changes to the ecological characteristics of 'Ramsar sites'.

The European Community has not responded corporately, except to recommend to member states that they become party to the convention; this indeed is what most have done, but as usual with varying degrees of speed. Italy, for example, ratified in 1976, while France ratified in 1986.

World Heritage Convention

In 1972, the United Nations Educational, Scientific and Cultural Organisation (UNESCO) adopted the convention concerning the Protection of the World Cultural and Natural Heritage. The convention is open to all member of UNESCO, and indeed non-members through UNESCO's General Conference.

The convention, which came into effect in 1975, seeks to establish a list of World Heritage sites and a similar list of World Heritage in danger.

Sites potentially of World Heritage status are submitted by Governments to the UNESCO World Heritage Committee who evaluate submissions for both lists. The selected sites cover a wide range of habitats and areas, and indeed buildings and artefacts, such as the breadth of the convention and concept of World Heritage site.

Many European Community Member States have ratified the convention but, as with the Ramsar Convention, the European Community itself has not ratified. This is a result of the Community's lack of competence not only in dealing with issues of natural heritage (of which it was acutely aware in 1972) but also in dealing with issues of the artificial environment. Consequently, no recommendation for ratification of the convention by Member States was felt appropriate by the Community.

Paris Convention

The Council of Europe first began to address the subject of water pollution in 1969 when it began to draft a European Convention for the Protection of International Watercourses against Pollution in Strasbourg. This met with many problems and sadly, despite several attempts between the Council of Europe and the European Community to finalize the draft, it remains uncompleted and consequently remains unadopted.

However, in 1974, the Council of Europe turned its attention to water pollution of another sort, happily with better results. The convention for the Prevention of Marine Pollution from land-based sources was held in Paris. Its original target was to draw attention to and ultimately prevent pollution of the north-east Atlantic and the North Sea from land-based sources. It is a landmark because, like the Ramsar convention, it reflects an early and relatively successful convention not only aimed at environmental protection *per se* but also at wildlife conservation. The original pressure for the convention and subsequent resolutions came mostly from countries with an economic as well as an ecological reliance upon the north-east Atlantic.

The European Community's role was initially that of observer, at the time when most of the signatories were states which bordered the Atlantic/North Sea. As other land-based states began to sign the convention, the Council of Ministers took the decision to take full negotiation, and finally took several Council Decisions (at the formal level) to adopt the relevant measures.

While this convention does not fit tidily into the broader criteria discussed above and does not concern itself solely with wildlife or nature conservation, it is included here because it is significant as a milestone in the development of international conventions and it was initiated partly as a response to concern about pollution from rivers such as the Rhine, the Seine and the Tees affecting the wildlife of the north Atlantic/North Sea.

Washington Convention

The Convention on International Trade in Endangered Species (usually referred to by its acronym, CITES) marks another turning point in the development of international convention. Opened for signature in 1973, the convention not only directly links wildlife conservation with economic trade, but also marks the European Community's first 'full' response to any international convention.

The function of the convention is to regulate international trade in wild animals and plants that are faced with or could be faced with extinction, or that individual countries have registered as 'endangered'.

The three appendices of the report cover the three grades of categorization. Appendix I carries a list of flora and fauna which are 'all species currently threatened with extinction', while Appendix II covers species not included in Appendix I but which would, if not regulated, very soon face extinction. Finally, Appendix III lists species which individual states wish to protect (and which are covered by national legislation) but which have not been registered by the international community. The parties to the convention fund a permanent secretariat which operates the permit system used to regulate the trade.

The European Community has responded to CITES by issuing over 10 Regulations which aim to ensure uniform application of the convention. The key regulation is Council Regulation 3626/82, notified in December 1982; subsequent regulations have responded to the changes in the original convention, where new species have been included in the Appendices for example.

Article 1 of the Regulations 3625/82 states, 'The Convention shall apply throughout the Community under the conditions laid down in the following articles. The objectives and principles of the Convention shall be respected in the application of this Regulation.'

This regulation, and the others that pre- and postdate it, represent the most comprehensive response that the community has made to an international convention. Because of the legal constraints identified above, however, the community itself is not a party to the convention, but has required all of its Member States to become parties. However, as part of the monitoring process of CITES, the European Community submits reports to the secretariat on behalf of the whole Community; a move which could be criticized because its masks the trade between Member States.

The Community response, at individual and corporate level, has been possible because the competence of the Community clearly and unequivocally covers trade issues. Any measure which might jeopardize fair and equal trade can legitimately be part of the European Community's legal procedures, at least to set the base-line. Should Member States wish to proceed further than this, and impose stricter internal laws, they are still free to do this.

Bonn Convention

The 1979 Convention of the Conservation of Migratory Species of Wild Animals was called as a consequence of the United Nations conference on the Human Environment in Stockholm in 1972. The convention acknowledges, and takes as its starting premise, that 'conservation and effective management of migratory species of wild animals require the concerted action of all States within the national jurisdictional boundaries of which such species spend any part of the lifecycle'.

The convention outlines the principles by which the 'Range States' must operate, namely by joint research, by offering immediate protection to species named in Appendix 1 of the report, and work towards agreements to protect, conserve and manage migratory species named in Appendix 2.

The concerted effort to protect threatened migratory and mobile species of animals does not match the Community's perceived measure of its own legal competence, so its response has been to issue a Community Decision which 'approves' the convention and accesses to the Treaty as a non-signatory state.

Any addition to the Appendices is undertaken through the usual procedure – the regular meetings of the convention organized through the Secretariat, namely the United Nations Environment Programme.

Berne Convention

The Council of Europe drew up the conventions on the Conservation of European Wildlife and Natural Habitats in 1979 to 'conserve wild flora and fauna and their natural habitats especially those species and habitats whose conservation requires the co-operation of several states'; furthermore 'particular emphasis is given to endangered and vulnerable species, including endangered and vulnerable migratory species'.

At first sight, therefore, there are many similarities between the Bonn and the Berne conventions, particularly their emphasis on migratory species. This is also true of the format of the convention, because the Appendices also specify particular species of flora and fauna that require 'strict protection' and 'protection'. However, the Berne convention does contain some significant developments. Most importantly the Berne convention addresses the issues of habitats as well as specific species of flora and fauna. Also while the convention names species requiring prioritization, it does not identify any similar priorities for natural habitats except to say 'those habitats of all wild flora and fauna, but particularly those specified in Appendices 1 and 2'. Instead it requires contracting states to 'take requisite measures to maintain the population of wild flora and fauna at, current levels or adapt it to a level which corresponds in particular to ecological, scientific and recreation requirements and the needs of sub-species, varieties or forms at risk locally'.

Within this statement, the Council of Europe broadened the whole debate about wildlife considerations to a level approaching that of conventional and contemporary understanding. As a general principle it is important and it is also important within the context of cultural, recreational and other considerations, because of the broad definition it puts on environmental protection; area based not site specific.

Not surprisingly, the European Community, in its Decision of 1981, did not consider itself competent to issue a recommendation, but as with several preceding conventions 'approved' the convention, and deposited the instrument of approach accordingly; i.e. it told the Secretariat that it approved the convention.

Canberra Convention

The Canberra Convention was drawn up in 1980 and is relatively unique in the relationships between Europe and International Convention, in that the convention on the Conservation of Antarctic Marine Living Resources specifically covers a set of resources outside the European context. Notwithstanding this apparent anomaly, the European Community responded to the Convention with a Decision in 1981.

The ratifying parties agreed to establish a Commission, and maintain this Commission to monitor and service the requirement of the Convention, the objective of which is the conservation of Antarctic Marine Living Resources, including rational use. The conservation process starts in the eyes of the Convention, with the need to restrict harvesting of krill and other similar species.

The relevance of the Convention to the European Community is somewhat hazy, but the Community's commitment chose to make the necessary decision.

Rio Summit

Strictly speaking the discussions at Rio amount to several separate conventions, so the Rio Summit is perhaps a better description for the proceedings at the assembly in Rio in Summer 1992. The five key elements of the Summit covered: Agenda 21 (an agreement on sustainable world development); the Biological Diversity Convention (aimed at maintaining a sustainable diversity and spread of flora and fauna across the world); the climate convention (aimed at controlling global climate change particularly global warming); the Forest Principle (aimed at moving towards world-wide environmentally sympathetic management of world forests, particularly rain forests); and the Rio Declaration (previously known as the Earth Charter, which identifies 27 principles for sustainable growth). The Rio Declaration is reproduced in Appendix A of this book.

The Rio Summit is a watershed in the progress of global environmental policy and agreement. This is for a number of reasons. First, the preceding publicity was so intense that the Rio Summit can be seen as the first such convention that received truly global attention. Second, the non-governmental organizations were not actually involved in the Summit, but did participate in a parallel event – the Global Forum. Thus, the links between the 'official' process and the lobbying process were brought closer together, but did not actually coincide. Also the European Community was grappling with its own competence to agree common foreign policies. The Rio Summit was the first opportunity for the Community to test this competence. Finally, the Summit was conceived at a time when the world economy was in a positive state, but convened at a time of world-wide recession. Therefore, the Summit tested the world's commitment at a time of economic hardship.

The five components of the Summit, which was called by the United Nations under the title of 'A Conference on Environment and Development', required different responses from the states attending the Summit. However, as an overall assessment of the success of the Summit, it has been commonly accepted that the initial publicity was not matched by the output from the conference. For example, the United States did not sign the Biodiversity Convention, and 'developing' nations such as Malaysia and India opposed the Forest Principles because they threatened their national and economic sovereignty.

As individual nation states, the Members of the European Community signed the elements of the Summit, but as an organization, the Community did not, largely because the Maastricht Treaty had, at the time, not resolved the issues of competence.

A full assessment of the outputs of the Rio Summit can be found elsewhere (UNESCO, 1992). Arrangements were made to monitor and implement the proposals from the Summit, particularly the Rio Declaration and the Agenda 21. This was achieved through the Autumn session of the United Nations in 1992, when the Sustainable Development Commission was created.

The European Community responded formally to the Rio Summit (Commission of the European Communities, 1992) principally by identifying how the EC legislation and policies echoed and reflected many of the issues raised at Rio, and sought to add detail to how implementation could take place (and indeed was already taking place).

The response also pointed out that the EC had, for several years prior to Rio, been meeting regularly with the African Caribbean and Pacific States (ACP), of which there were 69. These meetings had included the environment as a specific focus for discussion and the topic for several written agreements. For example, the Fourth Summit of 1989 stated 'the enhancement of the environment and natural resources, the halting of the deterioration of land and forests, the restoration of ecological balances, the preservation of natural resources and their rational exploitation are basic objectives that the ACP States concerned shall strive to achieve with Community Support' (Commission of the European Communities, 1989).

Not only do these subjects mirror some of those raised at Rio, but also we see some of the potential conflict raised at Rio. A perception of the ACP nations was that Europe and the US were demanding conservation measures from them while not 'putting their own house in order'.

Notwithstanding these views, the Rio Summit and its various agreements, documents and action programmes marked a significant part in environmental thinking. Agenda 21 showed commitment to integration and local actions and the agreement on biodiversity and climate changes showed how global understanding could be reached on the enormous danger faced from global issues. Many countries, including many EC Member States, now frame their own environmental performance measures against this global background (Department of the Environment, 1994).

Summary

There are several strands of progress that can be plotted through the international conventions discussed here. First, the most obvious conclusion is that progress is relatively slow. The logistics of staging, managing and monitoring world-wide conventions is clearly prohibitive for rapid progress. Thus, over 20 years, some eight conventions have been generated. Similarly, finding a wording to suit all parties is difficult and time consuming.

A further point is that the conventions have, until the Rio Summit, concentrated upon specific issues, and have therefore been able to meet with some degree of success. The exception to this was the Rio Summit, where general principles and, in retrospect, an overburdening agenda, in the end led to problems.

Finally, the European Community has grappled with the problems of competence, and has therefore been limited in their response to community decisions with the exception of CITES. In this case, the concerns were clearly related to trade, and thus the Community was more confident of its own competence and responded with a full regulation. As we have seen, the series of world conventions, the development of the Community's environmental policy and the progress of the community's legal framework have all developed consecutively and have therefore led to interesting juggling with the Community responses and progress.

WORLD CONSERVATION STRATEGIES

There is no doubt that the plethora of international conventions has helped to shape the progress of the world-wide environmental movement. Partly as a consequence of this, and also partly as a consequence of the wide range of international agencies, there is similarly a large number of international conservation strategies.

Just as the European Community has both a collective and an individual response, the international strategies also elicit varied responses from the community. The main determinant of this response is not so much the nature of the strategy, but more the need to be seen as promoting specific initiatives. Indeed, the Community supports the principle of all of the key strategies.

This is not as repetitive as it might first seem, because the individual strategies, several of which are discussed here, cover different areas or concepts within the broad definitions of environment. For example, the 'Man and Biosphere' programme is primarily research based, while the 'United Nations list of National Parks and Protected Areas' is, as the title suggests, a collection of protected and important sites.

Furthermore, the various strategies are now beginning to be pulled together and co-ordinated by the organizations mentioned earlier in this chapter, particularly the International Union for Conservation of Nature and Natural Resources (IUCN) and the United Nations.

The following analysis therefore looks at the individual elements of what is becoming a widely based framework for world-wide conservation. It must be stressed, however, that strategies are implemented at the level of the nation states, and are necessarily inconsistently applied across the world. As with the international conventions, progress is measured and slow.

Man and the Biosphere

The Man and the Biosphere (MAB) Programme was launched by the United Nations Education, Science and Culture Organisation (UNESCO) in 1970. Its main thrust is as a research, educational and networking initiative that has as its aims 'to predict the consequences of today's actions on tomorrow's world, and thereby to increase man's ability to manage efficiently the natural resources of the biosphere'.

The programme is managed through a series of individual projects which cover geographic areas (such as mountain regions, polar regions and so on) or specific items or issues (such as the control of pests, or the conservation of energy). For the nature conservation movement, the most important project is MAB Project 8, which has as its objective, the creation of a world-wide network of biosphere reserves which represent all major ecosystems.

A significant feature of the programme is the emphasis that it places upon the human use made of the environment. The zoning concept is threaded by the role of man in the environment; either as land manager, as scientist or as recreationalist (Table 6.2).

Table 6.2 Zoning of biosphere reserves under the MAB Programme

Zone	Details
1. Natural or core zone	Consisting of examples of minimally disturbed ecosystems. These areas have legal protection, e.g. as a strict nature reserve. Only activities that do not adversely affect natural ecosystem processes are allowed, although in some ecosystems human intervention, such as controlled grazing, may be needed to maintain natural characteristics.
2. Manipulative or buffer zone	Adjoining or surrounding the core. It's area is legally set out and often corresponds to that of other protected areas, such as a National Park. Activities are diverse and can include research and training, environmental monitoring, traditional land use, recreation and tourism.
3. Transition zone	Is not a demarcated area but represents an expanding co-operation zone where the work of the biosphere reserve is applied directly to the needs of the local communities. The zone may contain settlements, fields and forests and other activities that are in harmony with the natural environment. The zone is useful in helping the biosphere reserve integrate into the planning process of the surrounding region.

An interesting comparison can be made with the French system of national parks, for example, where this method of zoning is also used.

The process of building up the network is managed by an International Co-ordinating Council which in turn manages a series of national committees in participating countries. Decision over designation, approval and monitoring are made initially at the national level. Most MAB reserves cover sites already designated within the host nation, but on rare occasions, the sites have been specifically designated for the MAB programme.

World Conservation Strategy

The World Conservation Strategy (WCS) was drawn together and launched in 1980 by the International Union for the Conservation of Nature and Natural Resources (IUCN, 1980). The IUCN was assisted in the World Conservation Strategy by the United Nations Environment Programme (UNEP) and the World Wide Fund for Nature (WWF), which provided advice, funding and information for the work.

The WCS is themed around several programme areas, in much the same way as the MAB Programme. Overall, the WCS provided guidance for governmental and non-governmental organizations throughout the 1980s (IUCN, 1985). The programme areas covered data collection and analysis, sustainable development, conservation of habitat, education and training. Many countries, including several within the European Community endorsed the WCS and established their own responses to it. Indeed, the Council of Europe prepared its collective contribution to the WCS by pro-ducing a European Conservation Strategy, and the European Community's response has been less focused and has been covered by the Habitats Directive and the Environment Programmes (Chapter 5) among other initiatives (IUCN, 1987).

To a large extent, the World Conservation Strategy has been followed by the Rio Summit which has raised the profile of many of the issues in the strategy. As a result, the World Conservation Strategy, while still operative has become part of a greater drive towards world-wide co-operation. None the less, the WCS did provide a framework for may other strategies across the world.

United Nations list of National Parks and Protected Areas

The IUCN (International Union for the Conservation of Nature and Natural Resources) compiles for the United Nation list of National Parks and Protected Areas. The purpose of the list is to provide an international framework for protected areas throughout the world. This framework cate-gorizes sites according to the purpose for which they are designated. For example, Table 6.3 shows the classification categories; Spanish National Parks would normally fall into category A II (National Parks) whereas British National Parks or French Regional Parks would, if nominated, fall into category AIV (Protected Landscapes).

Table 6.3 United Nations designation categories for internationally important sites

Category	Name	Details
A		
I	Scientific Reserve/ Strict Nature Reserve	An area where nature is protected with minimum human interference.
II	National Park	A large area of wild land where resource use is generally prohibited, but with provision for appropriate public use and enjoyment
III	Natural Monument/ Natural Landmark	An area with similar qualities and protection as a national park, but with less diversity.
IV	Nature Conservation Reserve/ Managed Nature Reserve/ Wildlife Sanctuary	A protected area where habitat may be manipulated to achieve conservation goals.
V	Protected Landscape or Seascape	Defined as (1) an area with landscapes with special aesthetic qualities resulting from human interaction with land and, (2) an area that is primarily natural, but is managed intensively for recreation and tourism.
B		
VI	Resource reserve	An area of wild land awaiting evaluation as to its potential for production and/or protection.
VII	Anthropological Reserve/ Natural Biotic Area	A predominantly natural area where inhabitants maintain traditional ways of life
VIII	Multiple Use Management Area/Managed Resource Area	An area managed on a sustained yield basis for production and recreation.
C		
IX	Biosphere Reserves	See Table 6.2.
X	World Heritage Sites	Natural sites or mixed natural and cultural sites.

The cross-linkages with other UN initiatives come within the categorization, with Biosphere Reserves as defined under the MAB Programme falling into category CIX, and World Heritage Sites as defined through the 1972 Convention filling category CX.

Agenda 21

Agenda 21 marks a departure from the preceding series of convention strategies, in much the same way that the Rio Summit marked a departure from the conferences which preceded it. An unusual conference produced an unusual strategy. The full title of the Agenda 21 is the Rio Declaration on Environment and Development. The Declaration contains 21 principles, the action points of which are contained in the 800-page document of Agenda 21.

The Declaration and the Agenda do not cover nature conservation as defined in this book in a specific way; they deal with it in the generality of the term 'environment'. Furthermore, the protection of the environment is linked explicitly with development, international law, women's rights, indigenous population and education. This is where the Declaration differs so much from previous strategies. Rather than define a geographical area to be protected, the Declaration indicates that sustainable development stretches across the whole spectrum of human activity and geographical impact.

Appendix A to this book gives the 27 principles which form the Rio Declaration. In strict terms, it cannot be said to be a conservation strategy. However, it does form an important component of the continuing activity towards a protected environment. For this reason alone, it merits inclusion here.

Natura 2000

Natura 2000 is not a world-wide conservation strategy, but is a European Community initiative which seeks to identify a network of nature conservation sites across the Member States and, it is to be hoped, beyond. So, while it is not a global initiative, it does follow the pattern set by many of the foregoing strategies (site based) and clearly complements them.

Natura 2000 follows on from the concepts defined within the Birds Directive of 1979 which came into operation in 1981. Here, the concept of Special Protection Areas (SPAs) was identified as the most suitable mechanism for protecting the habitats of birds. Following the passing of the Habitats Directive in 1992, the concept of SPAs was extended to encompass a wider range of habitats and semi-natural areas. These areas, known as Special Areas of Conservation (SACs), will be identified by Member States, corresponding to a list of both species and habitats listed in the Directive's Annexes (Chapter 5). A timetable has been set for registering relevant sites with the Commission, stretching from 1994 until 2004.

The Directive and the subsequent Natura 2000 Network is the 'most important EC measure on habitat and countryside protection for many years' (Bennett, 1991). The network that is proposed will take shape through a series of interlinking measures.

1. Natura 2000 will be established through nominated sites from Member States.
2. The Community will draw up the first 'full' list of sites in 2000.
3. Member States and the Community then have a further six years to fill any gaps in the network. These gaps could be geographic or habitat-types.
4. The sites (Special Areas of Conservation) will be afforded tight protection measures in the Member States.
5. Additional work will be obliged, where necessary, to strengthen the coherence of the network.

It is this last stage, that is causing a lot of interest amongst the conservation movement, because it allows the opportunity to protect and enhance habitats outside the network in order to support and enhance Natura 2000. Therefore, habitats such as hedgerows, water courses, semi-natural woodland or scrub, which would not fall into the higher category necessary for inclusion in Natura 2000, could still be statutorily protected as an enhancement of the Network. Pressure is already growing in some Member States for this last phase to be taken more seriously (*Sunday Times*, 1994).

Natura 2000 therefore represents a major breakthrough for Community legislation, and a contribution to the already existing pattern of conservation strategies across the world.

As an initiative it has its roots in the Habitats Directive, but it is paralleled by an initiative from the Dutch Government, entitled Econet (Bennett, 1991). The rationale for the proposals is similar to that of Natura 2000: 'In the 1950s, species loss at a global level was between five and ten species a year ... by the end of the century it will be 50,000.'

The concept of Econet is however more far reaching than Natura 2000, because it seeks not only to identify key conservation sites, but also to link these sites by wildlife corridors, sympathetic forestry and agricultural managements and extend them across non-EC countries.

The emphasis for the EC is that of collecting information to create Natura 2000, but the logical conclusion of that process is the creation of a broader network along the lines of Econet which builds upon vegetation and species research of the late 1980s, and not just key sites (Council of Europe, 1987). Given the EC desire for integrated and comprehensive policies, this progression is becoming increasingly likely (Commission of the European Communities, 1993).

SUMMARY

The contents of this chapter quite literally cover the whole world. Any summary, therefore, can only hope to identify very broad patterns and trends. Notwithstanding this fact, there are a number of clear points that emerge. Furthermore, these points are ones which will be echoed later in the book when we examine patterns of nature conservation management specifically within the European Community.

An initial point to note is that all of the non-governmental organizations discussed here have progressively taken the environment as part of their overall remit. Essentially political or economic organizations, such as the OECD or the Council of Europe, have increasingly acknowledged that the environment should be part of their work. The acceptance of the environment as an integral part of the overall agenda has not shifted to any great extent the main objectives of these organizations. It has, however, meant that they have had to develop a new language and a new dimension to their discussions. The OECD in particular has begun to take a significant leading role in the debate about integrated rural strategies and rural economics.

Inherent within this debate is the need to protect the natural qualities of the rural environment which need to be balanced against the local demand for development. As is evident from the discussions about the European Community in Chapters 2 and 3 this balance is sometimes tipped in favour of economic development rather than the natural environment. However, it is also worth noting that even as late as the mid-1980s, the natural environment was not even part of the discussion within many of these organizations. A second trend worthy of note is that the organizations, and indeed the outcomes of the international conventions, have recently moved away from specific issues (such as the protection of wetlands, or the protection of certain species of animals) to the broader-based concept of sustainability. The Rio Summit of 1992 finalized this process, thereby opening the way for greater integration of the natural environment into the process of sustainable development.

The speed with which various organizations including the European Community and individual countries take up this difficult challenge is already varying, and will continue to do so in the future. Agenda 21 places the onus for progress back onto individual countries.

It is also worth highlighting the fact that there has been, and continues to be, a variety of definitions of sites that are worthy of protection. The United Nations, for example, links human heritage and natural heritage in their list of protected sites. Natura 2000 however, concentrates upon purely natural history resources. The effect of this disparity is that the numerous systems of designations do not provide a consistent set of criteria with which to compare sites. Consequently, sites often have several overlapping designations, covering two or three of the systems of land designation. If the same sites are also designated differently within each country (which is usually the case), the result is a complex array of designations within other designations. This issue repeats itself throughout the world, and manifests itself at national and international levels. This is a complicated enough process for professional environmentalists to fully appreciate; for members of the 'general public' it must appear overwhelmingly daunting. This does not help in the broader process of conservation, because, as a native North American saying points out, 'You will only protect that which you love, and you can only love that which you understand'; our understanding of the importance of sites, species and habitats is sometimes not helped by the complexities of the designation systems used to define them.

REFERENCES

Bennett, G. (1991) *Towards a European Ecological Network*. IEEP, Arnhem, Netherlands.

Commission of the European Communities (1989) *Report on the proceedings of the 4th Lome Summit*. European Commission, Brussels.

Commission of the European Communities (1992) *Report of the Commission of the European Communities to the United Nations Conference on Environment and Development*. European Commission, Luxembourg.

Commission of the European Communities (1993) *Protecting Our Environment: Europe on the Move*. European Commission, Luxembourg.

Council of Europe (1987) *Map of Natural Vegetation of the Member States of Europe*. Council of Europe, Strasbourg.

Department of the Environment (1994) *This Common Inheritance: Annual Report*. Her Majesty's Stationery Office, London.

European Environment Bureau (various years) *Memorandum to the Presidency*. EEB, Rue de Luxembourg, Brussels.

Falk, N. (1993) *Voluntary Sector Networks in Europe*. National Council for Voluntary Organisations, London.

Falk, N. (1994) *Voluntary Work and the Environment*. European Foundation for the Improvement of Living and Working Conditions. Dublin.

Haigh, N. (1989) *European Environmental Policy and Britain*. Longman, London.

Harvey, B. (1992) *Networks in Europe*. National Council for Voluntary Organisations, London.

International Union for the Conservation of Nature and Natural Resources (1980) *World Conservation Strategy*. IUCN, London.

International Union for the Conservation of Nature and Natural Resources (1985) *Implementing the World Conservation Strategy*. IUCN, London.

International Union for the Conservation of Nature and Natural Resources (1987) *Protected Landscapes: Proceedings of the International Symposium*. IUCN, London.

Nature Conservancy Council (1987) *The British Contribution to IUCN's Conservation Programme*. NCC, Peterborough.

Organisation for Economic Co-operation and Development (1961) The *Paris Convention Terms of Reference*. OECD, Paris.

Organisation for Economic Co-operation and Development (1988) *Trends in Rural Policy Making*. OECD, Paris.

Orme, E. (1989) *The Role of the Land Manager in Nature Conservation*. University of Reading, England.

Orme, E. (1989) *Nature Conservation and the Role of the Land Manager*. College Estate Management, Reading.

Baine, S., Falk, N., Webster, J. (1992) *Changing Europe: The Challenges Facing the Voluntary and Community Sectors*. National Council for Voluntary Organisations, London.

Sunday Times (September 15th, 1994) Hedgerow protection supported.

UNESCO (1992) The Rio Summit. *UNESCO Newsletter Connect*, Vol. 2. United Nations, New York.

PART TWO

The European Member States

An introduction

This part of the book deals with the individual Member States of the European Community. More specifically, it deals with their land management policies which aim at protecting their national landscape and natural history integrity. It will become clear, however, that individual nations' policies have developed much further than the guidelines created by the European Community itself. Indeed, in many respects several countries have created a more comprehensive policy framework than the Community has been able. Therefore, the national policies discussed in the following chapters represent a mix of community guidelines and independently developed policies.

We saw previously that Community legislation requires 'formal compliance'. Within the constraints of this book however, it is not possible to link national policies and legislation directly to the Community legislation through this formal compliance procedure. This would not only be time consuming, but also misleading, because as has been suggested, most countries have developed their policy far further than that created centrally through the Community. In most cases, Member States have nominated their existing policies as their 'formal compliance'.

The following analysis therefore takes the Community legislation beyond the specific Regulations and Directives, and discusses the national policies in as broad a context as is possible, with community legislation forming only part of this overall context. Indeed the greater part of this 'overall context' is created by national objectives and legislations as well as Member States' own characteristics. Whenever necessary, however, Member States' policies are related back to Community legislation. Haigh (1992) has identified the monumental task of following Community Environmental legislation throughout the various legislative processes identified in the previous chapter to their ultimate enactment through national legislation.

In order to achieve a broader overview, this level of detailed investigation is sacrificed.

Levels of information are confused, and consequently the analysis here can only reflect this available information. Clearly, the amount of information is, in itself, an indication of the level of commitment that a country attaches to the dissemination of environmental information. In part, this can be seen as a reflection of the wider concern for the environment (Bennett, 1991).

POLICIES INTO PRACTICE

The review of conservation in the countries of the European Community is not intended to be a detailed discussion of types of vegetation, habitats or landscape zones. This is covered adequately elsewhere. What the text is designed to do is provide a discussion on how this knowledge is translated into action. As has been indicated elsewhere in this book, the framework within which environmental conservation takes place is not simply provided by the available environmental information. The mechanisms of practical land management and conservation are as much a product of political, governmental and managerial systems as they are of knowledge of the natural environment. It is political pressure, for example, which frames legislation for landscape conservation in the National Parks of England, Wales or the Regional Parks of France. Similarly, the practical management of National Parks or Nature Reserves is carried out in Europe by a wide variety of agencies: central government employees in several government departments, government sponsored semi-autonomous agencies, local government employees, private landowners or volunteer groups. The operational considerations of land management therefore dramatically influence the practical implementation of conservation policy. This influence can either constrain or assist the process of conservation; this it does in one of three ways.

1. By altering the European guidelines generated at community level. This could be done by national governments putting different interpretations on community directives, for example.
2. By implementing the policies in different ways, through direct control or through voluntary agreements with landowners or developers, for example.
3. By delegating the management of the process of implementation to one of a number of organizations or departments. A conservation policy implemented under the management of a government Department of Forestry, for example, would have a different emphasis if it was managed through a Department of Agriculture, or indeed a Department of Conservation.

Many of the initiatives of the individual countries were developed prior to the European policies and international agreements. Consequently, many of the newer ideas have been implemented through planning and management systems already in place. Consequently, in those countries which have devised a conservation policy only relatively recently (perhaps, partly in response to European directives and legislation) the opportunity has existed to create new models for implementation. The picture that emerges is, however, broadly speaking one of compromise. While the policies and aims behind them have been almost universally accepted, the conservation ethic is often managed through government departments which have other more powerful areas of responsibility, such as economic development or forestry.

A further aspect of management which is covered only tangentially in the discussion is that of the appreciation of natural environments, particularly by members of the public. The links between public appreciation of natural history and the protection of the landscapes are clear and well documented; popular and well-loved sites will usually command a greater degree of protection than less respected sites. Appreciation, in turn, derives from many influences which shape public perception of beauty. These may include artistic influence (Watson, 1976), the age of the landscape or, indeed, the person perceiving the natural environmental (Lowenthal, 1985) or conventional wisdom inherent within a country (Bourne, 1990). Within each of the countries of Europe, this model of public perception and appreciation will inevitably be different. What may be considered as of great value in one country may not be considered as such in another for purely subjective reasons. While methods of scientific analysis and international co-operation will subsequently reduce this level to a certain extent, individual and national value judgements will influence conservation policy. This must be accepted, and the references for each country indicate only part of the overall debate over the aesthetics of the natural environment.

The following discussion therefore concentrates on the management, political and legislative mechanisms which are used to protect the natural environment. This includes relevant Acts of Parliament, land-use zones, special designations of conservation areas and, equally important, any accepted omissions from the management framework which affect the objectives of conservation.

The discussion about each country is arranged in a similar way: a broad brush introduction leads into an analysis of the political structure of the country's government, and an analysis of its ministerial areas of responsibility. Following this, specific methods of landscape and wildlife protection are discussed: types of land designation, methods of management and so on. Finally, other key environmental issues are discussed, as too are areas which are perceived as weaknesses within each country's legislative framework, as well as its strengths. The focus throughout is the protection of wildlife, landscape and the natural environment. While this definition will clearly fade into other issues, such as pollution control or trade in endangered species, it is important to remember that the discussion is specifically targeted on certain issues – otherwise the analysis would become far too cumbersome and far too complex.

AN OVERVIEW

There are many ways in which an overview of the European Member States could be presented. The objective within this section can be no more than to provide a framework within which some common parameters can be compared. But which parameters? Number of endangered species; levels of public awareness of environmental issues; per capita spending upon environmental work?

The parameters presented here are, in the interests of clarity, simple and common. Table 7.1 shows a variety of statistics for the Member States which, together, give a very brief snapshot of the country. The measurements of area, population and density of population give some indication of the pressure on land from sheer weight of the people in the country.

A further indicator of 'pressure' on land is the amount of land that is managed for economic agriculture and forestry. Together with the population pressure, the demand for land for agriculture and forestry gives a broad picture of what land 'might' be 'available' for conservation. Clearly, however, the detail is much more subtle than this, and analysis given for each country goes into this detail. Notwithstanding this detail, however, there are some trends which are revealed even through this crude analysis.

The Gross Domestic Product (GDP) per head of population gives a measure of the level of economic activity within each Member State, and also gives some indication of the affluence of the country. As with the foregoing statistics, there is no simple correlation between wealth and conservation, but it does provide part of the backdrop against which conservation must be viewed. For example, while it may be easy to criticize some countries for putting economic growth before nature conservation the reality could be (as with a number of the Mediterranean countries) that their GDP is considerably lower than other Member States. Conservation does not exist in isolation from economics or other land-based pressures.

Finally, by way of background, Table 7.1 gives a percentage of land that is designated for nature conservation in each country.

The statistics are drawn from various reports and analyses prepared by the Organisation for Economic Co-operation and Development (OECD). Other parameters do exist, but it is felt that these provide a baseline from which to measure each Member State's environmental performance.

Table 7.1 Key statistics for Member States (Environmental Indicators, Organisation for Economic Co-operation and Development, 1994)

	Area ('000 km²)	Population ('000)	Density ('000/km²)	Agriculture and Forestry ('000km²)	(%)	Protected (%)	GDP per capita ('000 US$)
Austria	83	7 884	95	74	89	19.0	17.4
Belgium	30	10 025	334	20	67	2.4	17.6
Denmark	42	5 170	123	33	79	9.8	17.7
Finland	305	5 042	16	260	85	2.6	14.8
France	549	57 372	104	458	83	8.7	18.3
Germany	349	80 058	229	284	81	13.9	19.7
Greece	129	10 300	79	70	54	0.8	7.8
Ireland	69	3 547	51	60	87	0.4	12.3
Italy	294	56 859	193	237	80	4.3	17.0
Luxembourg	3	390	130	2.5	85	20.0	21.1
Netherlands	34	15 178	446	23	68	9.5	16.6
Portugal	92	9 858	107	72	78	4.9	9.3
Spain	499	39 085	78	465	93	7.0	12.8
Sweden	412	8 678	21	314	76	3.9	16.4
UK	241	57 848	240	197	81	18.9	15.5
EU	3 131	367 294	117	2 569.5	85	8.4	15.6

All figures are from 1993/94 data.

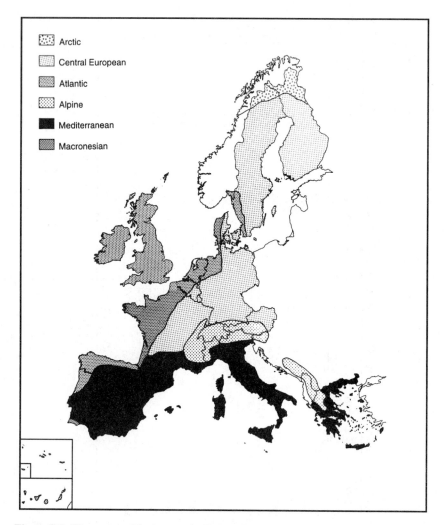

Figure 7.1 Bio-geographical zones in Europe.

In terms of biogeographical zones within Europe, there are four dominant zones and two lesser ones. These are shown in Figure 7.1. The biogeographical zone for each country is defined in the introduction for each Member State. However the six zonal types are:

1. Atlantic. Stretching along the western margin of Europe, from Norway to Portugal. It is characterized by low fluctuations in temperature and relatively high precipitation.

2. Central Europe. Inland in Northern Europe, from Norway/Sweden to mid-France and Austria. Similar to Atlantic, but with less precipitation and more extreme annual variations in temperature.
3. Mediterranean. Reaching across Southern Europe from Portugal to the Caspian Sea. The low precipitation and high mean temperature leads to semi-arid environments providing some of Europe's best 'wilderness areas'.
4. Alpine. As the name suggests is concentrated around the mid-European high mountain belt, from Switzerland, Northern Croatia to the Pyrenees. It is characterized by short growing seasons, extreme cold and high precipitation. This leads to very specialized and vulnerable habitats.
5. Macronesian. A relatively poorly represented zone, it is found only in south-west Iberia and the Spanish Canary Islands. Very high mean temperatures and low precipitations. Also, given the island nature of much Macronesian biogeography, a relatively high proportion of species are unique to the zone.
6. Arctic. With the entry to the EC of Sweden and Finland, there is now small representation of Arctic zonal characterization. Similar to Alpine, the low mean temperature and short growing season leads to specialized and delicate species and environments.

REFERENCES

Bennett, G. (1991) Habitats in Western Europe, in *Towards a European Ecological Network*. Institute for European Environmental Policy, Arnhem, Netherlands.
Bourne, I. (1990) Landscape architects in France. *Landscape Design*, 186, 25–29.
Haigh, N. (1992) E.C. Policy and Implementation in Britain, in *European Environment Year Book*, Doc Ter, Milan.
Lowenthal, D. (1985) *The Past is a Foreign Country*. Oxford University Press, Oxford.
Watson, J.R. (1976) Literature and Landscape, in *Aesthetics of Landscape*. Rural Planning Services, Oxford.

8   Austria

Austria is one of the most recent additions to the EC, having joined on 1 January 1995 along with Finland and Sweden (Norway rejected membership in the referenda held during 1994). Austria has one of the highest GDP per capita in the EC, and entry to the EC has already brought about dramatic changes, most notably in the cost of some products (Confederation of British Industry, 1995).

The Austrian record on nature conservation is good, particularly through designation of protected areas which stood at 19.3% in 1989, with a dramatic increase occurring between 1985 and 1989. This is a remarkable achievement in such a short space of time, and was part of a wider upgrading of environmental legislation to meet the necessary convergence standards for EC membership.

Over 65% of Austria's 83 000 km² are under arable or forestry land use, with by far the greatest proportion being under forestry. Together with the more inaccessible mountainous areas over 90% of the country is of non-urban land use giving a population density of 91 per km².

The dominant biogeographical zonings are 'Alpine' and 'Central European'. This reflects the fact that a large proportion of the land (relative to other European countries) is at over 2000 m above sea level.

POLITICAL STRUCTURES

Austria is a Federal State, with nine self-governing provinces or Lander. These are Burgenland, Carinthia, Lower Austria, Salzburg, Tyrol, Vienna, Stynia, Upper Austria and Verbegen. These Lander are very powerful in that most powers, unless otherwise decreed, are their responsibility rather than of the Federal or National Government. This situation is similar to that found in Germany.

The appointment of elected representatives to both levels of government is through universal suffrage and proportional representation. At the national level there are two houses of elected representatives, while at the regional level there is just one.

The organizational structure has many similarities with other European countries, with elected Ministers heading Departments or Ministries of State and, increasingly, these Departments managing their affairs through agencies which have a relatively large degree of autonomy from the government.

Plate 7 Provision for tourism and camping in the Nockberge National park in Austria.

There do appear to be several potential areas of overlap between the Federal and Provincial governments which because of the very strong position of the Provinces can lead to some large-scale disagreements between the various levels of government (*The European*, 1995).

Other levels of government

The only other level of government that is significant within Austrian politics is the community of Municipalities. While there is a layer of government which corresponds to the German or United Kingdom counties, to all intents and purposes the levels of responsibility are concentrated either at the Provincial level or the city community level. Each of the Lander tends to be dominated by a large conurbation, and any responsibilities not undertaken by the Lander are passed to the Community or Municipality. These are mostly the day to day operations of government work, ranging from waste collection and small project management, to the issuing of hunting licences and local planning.

ENVIRONMENTAL RESPONSIBILITIES

The environmental concerns of the Austrian Government have been for many years closely linked with the broader issue of quality of life. Indeed, the link made between the environment and social issues at ministerial level is unique within the European Community. More often than not, if the environment is linked to any other ministerial responsibilities it is with agriculture, forestry or a similar land-based concern. This link in Austria, however, has repercussions with environmental management throughout all levels of governments and with other non-governmental agencies, but is most evident at the national level.

National government

The Austrian Constitution states that the responsibility of nature conservation is with the provincial governments. However, the national government has become increasingly involved in the process of nature conservation and environmental management for a number of reasons. The main reasons are that the need for co-ordination and the setting of standards between the Lander has increased, and also the fact that Austria has begun to be more involved in the international environmental arena (of which process, membership of the European Community is part) has meant that a national voice is needed more and more. The authority for this voice does, however, still come from the Lander in large part (Federal Environmental Agency, 1994).

    The most important ministry for environmental issues is the Federal Ministry for Environment, Youth and Family Affairs. As is suggested above, the combination is unique within Europe and reflects not only the relationship that the Austrians see between the quality of life and the environment, but also that because the Lander undertake much of the practical environmental work, the national role is restricted more to the setting of standards, monitoring and co-ordination.

Federal environmental agency

The function of data collection, monitoring and researching into environmental issues is undertaken by the Federal Environmental Agency, which is an agency managed through the Ministry for Environment, Youth and Family Affairs but which has a large degree of autonomy. The Federal Environmental Agency, formed in 1991, mirrors the European Environmental Protection Agency and similar agencies elsewhere in European Member States. The rationale behind the creation of these agencies is that a large degree of autonomy from government is needed to allow objective and sometimes critical information to the presented (Federal Environmental Agency, 1993). The Agency is not directly involved with land management, other than through experimental or research-based work. However, they do collect the relevant case information from the Lander and recommend policy to the Federal Agency.

Provincial and local government

The Austrian constitution is clear that most of the responsibility and authority for environmental action rests with the Lander. Any transfer or delegation of the responsibility either to the Municipalities or to the Federal agencies must be with the agreement and formal approval of the Provincial governments. The responsibilities of the Lander cover nature conservation, animal and species protection, physical and land-use planning, waste disposal and recycling. The Lander have transferred to the Federal agencies responsibility for environmental research, hazardous substances, environmental impact assessments, and international policy and issues across the whole environmental spectrum (European Community Committee of the American Chambers of Commerce, 1995).

The Lander are mainly preoccupied with the process of physical planning and through this process the management of the demands of an increasing population and the consequent requirements for more intensive agriculture in the more accessible lowland areas.

Policy initiatives

The Austrian government has recently taken a more holistic stance on the environment and in 1992 launched its new strategic approach to environmental planning and policy. The Austrian National Environmental Policy (NUP) seeks to integrate the objective of environmental quality improvement into all policy sections, e.g. industry, energy, transport, forestry, consumer affairs and agriculture (Ministry for the Environment, Youth and Family Affairs, 1992). This new initiative has meant that the Federal agencies, particularly the Federal Environment Agency, have begun to become more important because many of the central issues in the National Environmental Policy either require a national overview (such as the response to the biodiversity programme from the Rio Summit) or are of an international dimension (air pollution or the reduction of carbon dioxide emissions). One of the key areas within the National Policy of direct relevance here is the protection of the 'unique Austrian natural and cultural heritage' (Ministry for the Environment, Youth and Family Affairs, 1992). This has resulted in a new impetus on the process of land designations, particularly National Parks.

Non-governmental organizations

The non-governmental organizational structure within Austria is not as advanced as it is in, say, Italy or the United Kingdom. None the less, there are several important large organizations and a number of smaller, locally based organizations. Indeed, the most significant group that represents the environment is an association of many of these local, smaller organizations. The Austrian Association for Nature and Environment Protection (OGNU) is a grouping of over 100 locally based environmental agencies. Their individual interests range from land-based or species-based protection to broader environmental protection such as recycling. In many ways this reflects the Austrian link between the environment and quality of life that is made at the federal level.

Another significant NGO has an equally broad remit; the ECO-Office is first and foremost an organization that collects and disseminates data on the environment, and does nor confine itself to any single environmental issue. ECO-Office also acts as a lobbying organization.

Finally, many of the international NGOs such as Greenpeace, Friends of the Earth and the World Wide Fund for Nature all have Austrian branches.

LAND DESIGNATIONS

The National Environmental Policy of 1992 gave new impetus to the process of land designation. As is evident from Table 8.1, the rate of designation has been maintained over recent years, and more designations are planned, particularly for National Parks.

Table 8.1 Land designation in Austria

'000 km²			
1980	1985	1990	1990 (%) of total area
2.6	3.0	15.9	19.0

There are three significant categories of designation on Austria, namely National Parks, Nature Reserves and Landscape Protection Areas.

National Parks

Prior to 1994, there were three National Parks in Austria, with a further four planned for designation between 1995 and 2000. Table 8.2 shows the areas of these National Parks and, as is evident, they vary considerably in size; more so than in many other European countries. Indeed, the smallest National Park is of a similar size to many Nature Reserves.

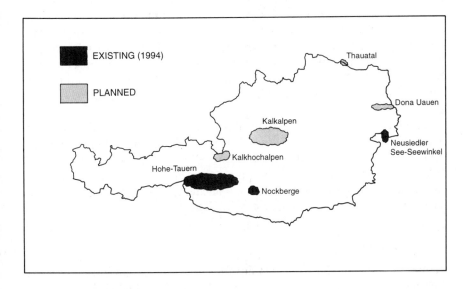

Figure 8.1 National Parks in Austria.

Table 8.2 National parks in Austria (1994)

Name	Area (km²)	Status
Hohe Tavern	1 787	Existing
Nockberge	184	Existing
Neusiedlersee-Seewinked	58	Existing
Kalkalpen	750	Planned
Donau-Auen	110	Planned
Thayatal	7	Planned
Kalkhochalpen	200	Planned

The principal aim of National Park designation, of which two only came into being relatively recently in 1991 and 1992, is to protect the natural habitats of the area. To this end, the National Parks are organized along similar lines to Belgian and French National Parks. A central zone is surrounded by a peripheral zone, with very tight restrictions being imposed on the central zone, but some development and recreational/tourist activity being permitted in the peripheral area. It is usual that around half of the total area of the National Park is designated as the central zone.

It is the policy of the Federal Government that, through agreements and partnerships with the Lander, the National Parks are accepted by the local populations and that designation should also be sought under the IUCN classification. The role of the Federal Government in both these contexts is critical, first because of the international significance of the designations and second because in several cases the National Parks cross Provincial boundaries. In one instance (Neusiedlersee-Seewinked National Park) the boundary actually crosses over into the Republic of Hungary; an initiative that has only been possible since the decline of communism in Eastern Europe.

The planning and management of the National Parks is done through a Park Management Plan, which is a guiding document containing not only the land-based proposals but also the detailed arrangements for funding and management. These plans are prepared or commissioned by the Federal Environmental Agency (Federal Environmental Agency, 1992).

Nature Reserves

As the majority of the responsibility for nature conservation lies with the Lander, it is evident that 'there is no uniform nature protection law, but nine provincial nature protection laws' (Federal Environmental Agency, 1994). Nowhere is this best seen than in the designation of Nature Reserves. In Upper Austria, for example, the number of nature reserves rose from 30 to 50 from 1980 to 1993. Over the same period, the number in Styria rose from 20 to 105.

It must be stressed, however, that progress in terms of numbers and area covered has been made in all nine Lander, with the exception of Vienna where the tight boundary around the built-up area precludes further desig-nation of nature reserves.

It is also worth noting that, while there is the potential for incon-sistency in the criteria used for designation of Nature Reserves, the Lander and the Federal Government have co-operated to ensure com-monality between the various areas. Nature reserves are therefore by-and-large small (less than 800 hectares on average) and designed to protect specific habitats or in some instances species. At the end of 1993, there were over 300 Nature Reserves in Austria, of which 33 were designated after 1991, again reflecting the recent commitment to nature protection (Table 8.3).

Table 8.3 Designations of protected land in Austria (1994)

Designation	Number	Area (hectares)
National Parks	5	202 956
Nature Reserves	324	283 449
Landscape Protection Areas	242	1 370 901
Plant Protection Areas	14	27 901
Others	7	130 743
Total	592	2 015 950

Landscape Protection Areas

By far the largest category of designations are the Landscape Protection Areas. There are over 230 in Austria (Table 8.3) with a coverage over 1.25 million hectares. There is some degree of uniformity in the basis of their designations, a fact that is due largely to the efforts of the Federal Environmental Agency. The purpose of the designation is to safeguard the landscape through support for the traditional methods of land management, most usually agriculture and forestry. The legislation, made at Provincial level, specifically relates to landscape rather than species or habitat protection, but clearly one has a bearing on the other.

There is wide variation between the Lander and how big an area is designated and consequently how much money is spent on supporting traditional land management techniques. At one end of the scale, Lower Austria had no Landscape Protection Areas in 1993, but upper Austria had over 400 hectares so designated. Similarly, Styria spent 30.2 million Schillings on nature protection in 1993 while Vienna spent 3.1 million (Federal Environmental Agency, 1994).

Other designations

There are a few other, less important land designations within Austria, most of which relate to only one or two Lander. This is because the Lander are responsible for their own legislation and designations. Plant protection areas, nature areas and rest areas are all forms of designation used in one or more of the Lander.

It is worth emphasizing here the rapid and recent increase in land designated for protection within Austria which includes these 'lesser' designations. Similarly, the rate of loss of many of the designated areas is enviably small. In the period from 1991 to 1993, for example, only one nature reserve was lost 'since the grey herons in need of protection no longer nested there' (Federal Environmental Agency, 1994). Such a small rate of lost designations is admirable.

OTHER ISSUES

Three significant environmental issues have begun to command the attention of both the Federal and Provincial governments. While these issues are not unique to Austria, they are none the less important, namely: agricultural intensification; urbanization; and international issues such as acid rain and ozone depletion.

Agriculture

The pressures on agricultural land are pushing in two ways in Austria. First, the overall area of agricultural land has fallen by 10% between 1980 and 1990 (in the corresponding period, the area of forestry rose by 3%). There has, however, been an increase in the use of chemicals over the same period due to the intensification of agricultural techniques. This has meant that the pressure of agriculture on the natural environment has similarly increased. It was largely as a result of this pressure that the 1992 Act came into effect, the objective of which was to integrate nature conservation into all aspects of the Austrian economy, including agriculture.

A social trend that is worthy of note is the gradual reduction in the number of agricultural enterprises, which is common across Europe. The drift of people away from farming and the subsequent increase in farm sizes is particularly evident in the more rural Lander of Austria where the tradition of dividing a farm between sons is rapidly dying out (Organisation for Economic Co-operation and Development, 1994). Consequently, there is an increasing problem of rural unemployment which drives the search for other economic opportunities for rural areas.

Urbanization

One of the overriding reasons for the loss of agricultural land mentioned above is the growth of the urban centres in Austria. Austria has one of the highest standards of living in Europe and the subsequent demand for land for development is great. For example, the rate of growth of the motorway network was higher in Austria between 1980 and 1992 than anywhere else in Europe with the exception of Portugal. Similarly, the rate of urban growth was higher than in most other European countries.

International concerns

Austria's position in the heart of Europe and, significantly, adjoining the former East European bloc, has increased the Austrian concern for the effects of international pollution, e.g. the poor record of many former Communist countries on pollution control and waste emission. The

Austrian government has been active in seeking wider control of emissions. Indeed, part of the reason that Austria sought to join the European Community was to increase its potential influence on this wider agenda.

Signing of conventions

Austria has signed all of the international conventions mentioned in Chapter 6 and is an avid supporter of international action.

Implementation of EC Directives

Being a relative newcomer to the European Community, it would be expected that there would be some inconsistencies between European and Austrian policy and legislation. However, like the other countries that joined in 1995, Austria began the process of alignment several years previously, and the Act of 1992 mentioned above can be seen as part of this process. Consequently, Austria has a good record of implementation of European Directives, given that it is one of the most recent members of the Community.

SUMMARY

Austria has one of the highest amounts of land designated for nature conservation in Europe. This will be increased significantly again in the late 1990s when the new proposed National Parks actually become formally designated. Notwithstanding this, Austria's record is laudable. Between 1985 and 1990 Austria increased the amount of designated land by over 12%, to 19% of the land surface.

Austria has also become committed, like an increasing number of its European neighbours, to integrating nature conservation and environmental protection into all elements of the modern socio-economic process. For this reason, and unique to Austria, at the national level the environment is linked to Family and Youth Affairs, rather than agriculture or economic development as is the norm elsewhere.

REFERENCES

Confederation of British Industry (1995) Austria back in circulation. *CBI News,* February.

Federal Environmental Agency (1992) *National Parks in Austria.* FEA, Vienna.

Federal Environmental Agency (1993) *Report of Activity: 1991–1993.* FEA, Vienna.

Federal Environmental Agency (1994) *State of the Environment in Austria.* FEA, Vienna.

Ministry for the Environment, Youth and Family Affairs (1992) *National Environmental Policy*. Vienna.

Organisation for Economic Co-operation and Development (1994) *Integrated Rural Development*. OECD, Paris.

The European (1995) Getting in knots. 17 August.

Belgium

Belgium is the second smallest country in the European Community with an area of 30 000 km², and a population of 10 million. The country is therefore relatively densely populated, but not withstanding this, there is still, within Belgium, a discernible rural–urban divide with many of the associated issues of imbalance between the relative prosperity of some regions as against others. This imbalance is partly increased by the fact that Belgium, and particularly Brussels, lies at the heart not only of Europe but also at the heart of the European Community itself. Brussels forms one corner of the so-called golden triangle of prosperity within the community.

With 76% of land use in Belgium being agricultural, the rural coverage is one of the lowest in Europe, and so too is percentage of land protected for nature conservation (2.4%).

Belgium, like all of its neighbours on the Western seaboard, has both 'Atlantic' and 'Central European' biogeographical zones. The eastern edge of the country rises in parts to over 300 m but for the most part the country is low lying.

POLITICAL STRUCTURE

Of all the countries within the European Community, Belgium has perhaps one of the most complex political structures. This is because Belgium is not only following the same path of regionalization as many of its European partners, but also the provinces and communes have traditionally been strong, similar to France or Germany. This in itself leads to a multi-tiered system, but the picture is further complicated by the fact that Belgium also has three officially recognized communities, based on their cultural and linguistic heritage; these are the French, the Flemish and the German

communities. These culturally based communities have powers and functions parallel to those of the more geographical-based regions, except in
the Flemish region, where Community Powers and Regional Powers have
been merged. Even in this brief analysis, therefore, it can be appreciated
where the complexity of Belgium's political organizational structure has its
roots. As we shall see later in the chapter, this has its repercussions in land
use and conservation.

Plate 8 Commercially managed woodland as a nature reserve and recreational site
on the outskirts of Brussels.

National and regional administration

Of the five categories of public/political structures within Belgium
(National, Community, Regional, Provincial and Municipal) by far the
greatest amount of power lies with and between the National and Regional
tiers. This balance, which was first significantly changed in 1980 and subsequently in 1988, 1989 and 1992, is still being amended.

The national state has two elected houses, the Chamber and the Senate.
Both of these houses are elected by universal suffrage. Between them they
have the necessary legislative power to enact binding laws, but only in those
areas of responsibility for which power has not been transferred to the
regions. The four dates mentioned above mark points at which specific areas

of responsibility were changed to the Regions. Where there has been no specific hand-over of responsibility, this remains with the state rather than the regions.

The second element of the state authority is the executive organization which is effectively the civil service or government which is nationally appointed by the Sovereign. This means that the executive arm of government is politically separate from the elected representatives.

As is explained here, the transfer of power has been spread over several years. A measure of this transfer can be gained, however, from the fact that prior to 1980, less that 10% of public expenditure was made by the Regions, but by 1990 this figure was almost 40% (Centre d'études juridiques des problemes regionaux, 1991).

The authority and responsibility of the Regions is handled in very specific blocks from the central government. The Regional governments themselves are elected by universal suffrage, and appoint their own executives. The three regions (Walloon Region, Flemish Region and Brussels Region) not only therefore have their own internal responsibilities, but also have to take account of those powers and responsibilities still held by central government.

The laws that have transferred power and responsibility to the regions have been far from clear in their definitions. As a result, confusion still arises about which level of government holds the final responsibility. None the less, large areas of control have been acceded, including town and country planning, land use planning, waste management, transport policy and so on.

In the areas of responsibility that lie with the regions, the central government does not involve itself in the local implementation of policies. Thus, there are no regional offices that apply local solutions from national governmental departments. The main confusion does not lie, therefore, between competition for responsibility, but in the lack of clarity of the legal framework.

As elsewhere, in Europe, it is usually the national government which represents the country in international initiatives. As a result, European policy is adopted at national level but implemented both nationally and regionally.

Other levels of government

There are three other levels or tiers of government within Belgium that are important and worthy of mention. The Communities (Flemish, French and German) are historic organizations based on Belgium's three underpinning cultures. Notwithstanding this historical significance, the Communities still hold significant responsibility, some of which parallels the power of the Regions.

The Communities for the most part, however, cut across other administrative boundaries, so the Community Councils and the Community executives do exercise their power alongside and not in deference to the Regions. Indeed, the laws of 1980 and subsequent years transfer power not only to the Regions, but in some cases to the Communities. A further complication is added by the geography of the boundaries of the regions/communities which differ in the German Community (Table 9.1).

Table 9.1 Government structure in Belgium: State; region and community

State	Flemish community	Flemish region	French community	Walloon region	German community
Two houses of government	Assembly	Assembly	Assembly	Assembly	Assembly
Ministerial executive	Civil service	Civil service	Civil service	Civil service	Civil service

The two remaining tiers of Government are the Communes and Provinces. There are nine provinces: Anvers, Brabant, Hainaut, Liege, Limbourg, Luxembourg, Namur, Eastern Flanders and Western Flanders. There is a constitutional understanding that the Provinces and the Communes should regulate everything that is of local concern. This is the clearest definition of their roles. In practice, this tends to follow the opposite role from the Regions. Namely, the Provinces and the Communes will assume a measure of responsibility over an issue if matters are not explicitly regulated at national level. Thus, where there is not a body of regularity or other legislation, if the Province or Commune can step in to administer an issue, it will do so.

Each Province and Commune (of which there are some 600) have elected Councils. The Provinces have also taken the step of creating a permanent Provincial Delegation which acts as a non-statutory decision-making body seeking to co-ordinate the actions of the various Provinces.

Decentralization to Provinces and Communes stems not only from National Government, but also Regional Government. To this end, for example, the Regional Council of Wollonia gave the Provinces within that Region the power to agree to (or otherwise) planning applications for changes in land use. The Regional Context for these decisions is maintained because of same decree in 1989 that relinquished some of this power, also made it a prerequisite that Provincial land-use plans needed to be agreed at Regional Council level and that, at the final analysis, the

Provincial decisions can be overturned by Regional Councils under certain circumstances.

ENVIRONMENTAL RESPONSIBILITIES

Given the foregoing analysis, it is perhaps fortunate that the elements of environmental management being discussed here fall almost exclusively within the jurisdiction of the Regional Councils. The original law governing nature conservation was enacted in 1973, and in 1980 the responsibility for its implementation was transferred to the Regions. For this reason it is proposed that the discussion here is focused upon this Regional activity. Were this discussion to try to identify lines of responsibility for all areas of environmental regulations, a different route would probably be needed for each area of legislation. Notwithstanding this attempt at simplification, there are inevitably Regional variations and some duplication between the various tiers of government.

Regional structures

Each Regional Council (Brussels, Walloon and Flanders Regions) has within its administration a Nature Conservation Service (Services de conservation de la Nature). These services are responsible for the purchasing and the management of land to be run as state-owned nature reserves. In designating the nature reserves, the Regional Council liaises with the Minister at National level, and co-operates with the National Council for Nature Conservation (Council Superieur de la Conservation de la Nature).

The Regional Nature Conservation Service consists of representatives from the relevant regional departments, the exact make-up of which varies between the regions. These include those with responsibilities for regional planning, rural affairs, nature conservation (which includes forests and hunting, for example) and, in some cases, water policy.

The Regional Nature conservation structure is complemented by Management Committees, which are constituted of academics, ecologists and scientists. However, their role is only advisory and not executive (Commission Consultative du Parc Naturel, 1977).

The Regional Councils control around 40% of Nature Reserve area in Belgium (Table 9.2), although it has been noted that the designation of Nature Reserves and of other land categories is rapidly becoming a private sector undertaking, driven at least in part in the income to be generated by tourism and environmentally based recreation (Jadot, 1992).

While the Regional Councils represent the most active tier of government in designating and managing nature conservation, it must be noted that notwithstanding Belgium's relatively small size, only one fully designated National Nature Park exists (see below for land designations), which tends to suggest that their level of activity is low.

Table 9.2 Nature Reserves in Belgium, 1987

Reserves	Flanders			Wallonia			Belgium		
	(no.)	Area (hectares)	Area (% of total)	(no.)	Area (hectares)	Area (% of total)	(no.)	Area (hectares)	Area (% of total)
State owned	17	2 930	35.2	21	4 726	44.86	38	7 656	40.6
Private	27	1 037		–	–		–	–	
Voluntary	137	4 357	64.8	122	5 810	55.14	286	11 204	59.4
Total	181	8 324	0.62	143	10 536	0.63	324	18 860	0.63
Forest reserves	1	16.5	–	3	151	–	4	167.5	–

Other structures

The national government still represents the country at international level, and as such there is a central agency responsible for environmental and, more specifically, nature conservation issues. The National Council for Nature Conservation is chaired by a national minister. As is suggested above, however, despite the fact that consultation does occur, inconsistency is evident, which is not surprising given the many layers of Regional and Community government.

At the subregional level, the Provinces and Communes do have some increasing responsibility for nature conservation. This is being slowly released by the Regional Councils and Community Councils. However, much of this responsibility comes as a consequence of other areas of authority being handed over, particularly urban and rural planning. Furthermore, this process is a particularly recent development (for example, in Wollonia, the relevant decree was in April 1989) so the issues that the Provincial and Commune committees have addressed before they included nature conservation have lain elsewhere.

LAND DESIGNATIONS

The law which specifically allows for the creation of natural-history land designations dates from 1973. In turn this was amended in 1980 when the organizational structure was regionalized. The law of 1973 names three types of land designation: nature reserves, forest reserves and nature parks. These are discussed below.

Nature Reserves

Nature reserves are designated to protect the flora and fauna in a partic-ular habitat. The average size of a nature reserve in Belgium is around 60 hectares, although state-owned ones are, on average, six times larger than privately owned ones (Jadot, 1992). There are no less than four types of nature reserves in Belgium. Reserves can be state owned, or privately owned. State owned reserves are designated by the regional council, in consultation with the relevant national council. The land is either owned, leased or otherwise held by the regional authority. On average they are around 201 hectares in size (Table 9.2). Privately owned nature reserves (or authorized reserves) are only acknowledged in the Flanders and Wollonia Regions. Private landowners designate reserves and agree not to undertake certain actions, such as hunting, land management or inter-ference with the natural systems. For this, varying levels of subsidy and support are paid.

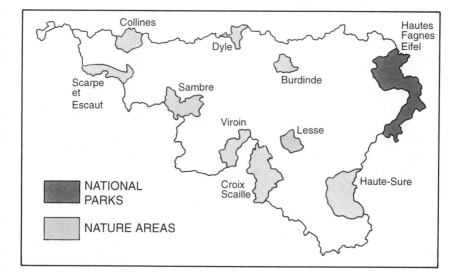

Figure 9.1 National Parks in Belgium.

The state-owned and authorized nature reserves can in turn, take two forms. A fully protected reserve tends to have little or no management, and natural processes are allowed to continue with minimal interference. Alternatively, a specialized nature reserve is conserved through active man-agement procedures. These include the reintroduction of species, habitat restoration or positive conservation.

The work of the Regional Council in managing its reserves is supported by advisory committees. The private reserves tend to be managed by private associations; some 88% of reserves are thus managed. These associations are usually small, locally based organizations.

The rate of establishment of nature reserves is considerably more rapid in the private sector than it is in the public sector (Table 9.3). Some of this reflects the lack of commitment of Regional Councils for nature conservation associated land designations in general.

Table 9.3 Nature Reserve designation in Belgium 1970–87

Reserves	1970		1977		1987	
	no.	area (hectares)	no.	area (hectares)	no.	area (hectares)
State owned	8	5 809	20	6 923	38	7 656
Private	46	5 970	89	6 812	286	11 204
Total	54	11 839	109	13 735	324	18 860

Forest Reserves

Areas of public or privately owned forest can be designated as forest reserves. Again, designation is by the Regional Council, in consultation with the Minister at national level. While the designation of forest reserves is primarily aimed at protecting indigenous species, particularly trees, the designation also allows for limited provision of picnic and recreational facilities. (These are not allowed in nature reserves.)

While most building or other developments are severely restricted, recreational provision is permitted, but only in the context of an agreed management plan. It is the recreational opportunities that designation as a forest reserve brings that often guide nominations rather than the ecological integrity of a particular site.

Nature Parks

The laws, regulations and governing policies for nature parks are extremely complex. This is not only because the procedure itself is complex but, as in other conservation issues there is marked regional variation in system and priorities.

A nature park is designated to 'conserve the character, diversity and scientific interest of the environment, the indigenous flora and fauna, the purity of the air and water, and guarantee the conservation of the quality of the land and soil' (Loi sur la conservation de la nature of 12 July 1973).

The law defines several types of nature park. As above, in the case of nature reserves, one of the basis for distinguishing different types of site is ownership of the site (private or public), but a more important distinction is in the designation of 'regional' or 'national'. A national nature park is designated by the Regional Council. A nature park designated by any other authority (national, regional or provincial), designated a regional nature park.

In 1991, there was only one national Nature Park in Hautes Fagnes Eifel, in the east of the country (Figure 9.1). This park is 67 000 hectares in size, covering 12 municipalities, and is administered on behalf of the region by the Province of Gege. From the date of designation (1984), however, little movement has been made in Belgium to speed up the rate of designation of Nature Parks and, despite a decree in 1985 that was aimed at assisting this process, the two regions of Flanders and Wallonia have proposed 16 new parks, but none have been designated. Furthermore, the decree links the designation of a park area with rural socio-economic development: 'A nature park should be a rural area of major biological and geographical interest, governed in accordance with this decree, by provisions designated to protect the environment in harmony with the aspirations of local people, and with the social and economic factors inherent in the territory in question' (Decret Conseil Regional Walloon, 1985). Thus, the production of a fully agreed management plan is necessary before a park can be designated.

Of the proposed Nature Parks, most are in the range of 10–20 000 hectares. Their designations, when and if it happens, will clearly influence the current proportion of designated land in Belgium, which currently runs at around 2.4% (Table 9.4).

Table 9.4 Areas of designated protected areas in Belgium

'000 km²			
1980	1985	1990	1990 (% of total area)
0.0	0.1	0.7	2.4

Management of designated areas

The foregoing analysis suggest that the state and regional authorities have been relatively slow to take up the opportunities for conservation designation in Belgium. In part this has been due to the fact that the political agenda has been concerned, in large part, with the regionalization process. As a result, the complexities of the organizational structure has made the passing of some legislation difficult. This, coupled with the relatively recent arrival of Belgium into the process of nature conservation (for example, the relevant definitive law was only passed in 1973) means that progress has been relatively slow.

Consequently, the role of the non-governmental organizations has increased and developed (Falk, 1992). A parallel growth has also been experienced in the interest of tourism and recreational concerns in the land designation process. Their interest has been seen as potentially conflicting with the nature conservation interest, but some support for their involvement has been given because of the links that the Government makes between conservation and local socio-economic regeneration (Albarre and Piraux, 1983).

OTHER ISSUES

The management of the natural environment within Belgium not only falls within several tiers of government and private/non-governmental organizations, but also within several departments and agencies within these tiers. For this reason it is necessary to examine briefly some of these other areas of responsibility which have an impact upon nature conservation.

Water management

From an old law, dating back to 1790, the management of water supply in Belgium is the responsibility of the municipalities (Communes) of which there are over 600. This is perhaps the opposite of countries such as France and Spain, where water management is undertaken at regional or even supra-regional level.

Of the 600 or so municipalities, some have joined with others to form intermunicipal agencies or consortiums. Others have handed this responsibility to the national water distribution agency (Societé National des Distributions d'eau, SNDE). In turn, the SNDE has allocated this responsibility to Regional Agencies which were established around 1986/87. Thus, in each of the three regions, there is a mixture of agencies which manages the resource including the regional water distribution agency, the intermunicipal consortiums and up to 100 individual municipalities.

Water is drawn from the rich aquifers within Belgium, and availability has been estimated at over 850 million cubic metres per year (Van den Berg, 1992). The impact of water management upon natural history resources is well documented (National Wetlands Technical Council, 1978) and the impact of such a wide variety of agencies will inevitably be difficult to monitor or regulate, despite the fact that codes of practice and voluntary agreements are in place.

Rural policy

The Regional framework within Belgium is a useful case study for many of the issues facing Europe as a whole. Two regions (Wallonia and Flanders) face predominantly rural problems, one region (Brussels) faces the problem associated with large urban development. As a consequence, the regions of Wollonia and Flanders are trying to integrate their own overall rural policy and this will inevitably have a great influence on nature conservation, not least because the majority of the relevant land designations are within these same regions. It has been stated (Organisation for Economic Co-operation and Development, 1988) that 'In Flanders and Wallonia, a truly integrated rural policy has now emerged.' The reasons for this are probably clear from the foregoing analysis, with a complex organisational structure, large-scale reorganization and historic responsibilities all playing a part. The needs of nature conservation are inevitably linked into this form of integrated planning, and local problems get resolved through local action. However, the creation of a cohesive regional planning system, not only for land-based issues but for other socio-economic considerations, will be helped by the emphasis being placed upon the Regional Development Plans.

These plans are to be the main planning document for all of the Regions, including Brussels. Clearly, the priorities of the Regional Development Plans will vary from region to region, but will none the less provide a cohesive framework around which decisions can be made.

Signing of international conventions

Of the six international conventions mentioned in Chapter 6, Belgium has signed three. It had not committed itself (by 1994) to the Paris (1972), Bonn (1979) or Bern (1979) conventions dealing with cultural/natural heritage; migratory wild animals; and wildlife and natural habitats respectively.

Implementation of EC Directives

Belgium faces its internal organizational problems before that international policy can be adopted at national level, and regionally based implementation inevitably takes a longer period of time. Conversely, in order to adopt international legislation, the national government requires a mandate from the increasingly powerful regional authorities. As a result, the implementation of EC Directives has been somewhat piecemeal. However, as the major changes to internal organizational structures have been resolved, the problems associated with this and the resultant lack of clarity should be easier to resolve. The time would therefore appear right for Belgium, to fully embrace the nature conservation and broader environmental framework of the European Community and follow this through with implementation at the appropriate tier of organization.

SUMMARY

It is evident that, despite its relatively small size, Belgium's internal organizational structure for dealing with nature conservation is as complex as anywhere in Europe. This is not particularly unique to nature conservation, but is symptomatic of the internal tensions arising out of the cultural, political and administrative arrangements. The balance of power between the cultural regions and the political regions is interesting enough, but when coupled with the pan-European issue of centre/regions debate it is not surprising that inaction seems to set in from time to time.

Much of the responsibility for designations lies with the regional governments, the priorities of which have been on the political development of the region. It may partly be a result of this that the national coverage of protected areas is still relatively low in Belgium. Clearly a further determinant of this low coverage is the density of population in Belgium which is one of the highest in Europe.

The types of land designations adopted by Belgium are similar to those found elsewhere in Europe, with the exception that there are no National Parks – a designation which tends to cover larger tracts of land. The underpinning legislation is still relatively recent in Belgium (1973) so there is a large amount of development of protected areas that can take place. The critical factor in this would appear to be whether or not the Belgian government can bring about constitutional arrangements that will allow easy and smooth passage of the relevant acts and laws through what is currently a complex national/regional system.

REFERENCES

Albarre, G. and Piraux, M. (1983) *L'hebergement touristique en region rurale.* Foundation Rurale de Wallonie.

Centre d'études juridiques des problemes regionaux (1991) *Les competences regionales et comminqautaires.* Université de Namur, Namur.

Commission Consultative du Parc Naturel (1977) *Parc Naturel Germano-Belge: Plan de developpement et de protection du paysage.* Dortmund.

Decret Conseil Regional Wallon (1985) *Decret relatif aux Parcs Naturels.* 16 July.

Falk, N. (1992) *Voluntary Work and the Environment.* European Foundation for the Improvement of Working and Living Conditions. Shankhill, Dublin.

Jadot, B. (1992) *Parks and Natures Reserves in Belgium* (pp. 350–353). DocTer, Milan.

National Wetlands Technical Council (1978) *Scientists Report*. Washington DC.

Organisation for Economic Co-operation and Development (1988) New Trends in Rural Policy Making. OECD, Paris.

Organisation for Economic Co-operation and Development (1991) *Indicateurs d'environnement*. OECD, Paris.

Van den Berg, C. (1991) *Water Supply* (pp. 606–608). DocTer, Milan.

Van den Berg, C. (1992) *Water Management*. DocTer, Milan.

<table>
<tr><td>10</td><td>

Denmark

</td></tr>
</table>

Denmark is one of the most northerly countries within the European Community. It has an area of 42 000 km², and a population of around five million. The density of population is therefore around the European average. Denmark sees itself at the forefront of the European environmental movement along with the Netherlands. A combination of 'Atlantic' and 'Central European' biogeographical zones more or less splits the country in half on a north/south axis. There is very little land over 300 m, and much of the land is below 100 m. The western coastline of Denmark has a high density of valuable coastal wetlands due to the low-lying nature of the coast.

The percentage of agricultural land is around the EC average at 79%, with the amount of protected land slightly over the European average at 9.8%.

POLITICAL STRUCTURE

There are several tiers of government within Denmark that are relevant to the environment. These have remained relatively constant over the life of the European Community, unlike Belgium or Spain for example, where recent moves towards the creation of an increased power for autonomous regions has created a major upheaval in local and national politics. This having been said, the 'tradition' in Denmark has been for local/municipal level decision making and therefore some recent trends towards the centralization of some power and authority has caused some confusion in some areas of responsibility. One such area is, not surprisingly, environmental protection, with the Ministry of the Environment in its present form having been created in 1973.

The next section deals with the environmental responsibilities, of the various tiers of government; this section deals with the broader governmental structure.

National government

The national government of Denmark, which is still constitutionally a monarchy, is elected by universal suffrage. There are currently 21 ministries in the government, each one being led by an elected representative, but serviced by an independent administration. Each ministry is, in turn, subdivided into a series of departments, directorates and agencies which are also headed by elected representatives.

The role of central government is perceived as providing a framework and criteria within which local tiers of government can assemble and create their own plans. Thus, on land-use or town-planning issues, the relevant ministry (usually the Ministry of the Environment) will issue directives upon which local councils must base their planning policies. Such a system is comparable to that found in Britain or the Netherlands, for example. This system allows the national government to create a comparable legislative climate across the country (National Environmental Protection Agency, 1990).

Regional and county government

Within Denmark, the concept of Regional and County government are identical. There are 14 such authorities, the councils of which are again elected by universal suffrage and administered by non-political professional staff. The main responsibility of the county administration is land use and physical planning, and as such most of their actions take place within the framework provided largely by the Ministry of the Environment at national level. This remit is executed through the creation of Regional Plans, the basis for which is legally framed in the Urban and Rural Zones Act of 1969, and subsequently amended in 1985 and 1987.

The only exception to this process, largely because it has only recently arrived on the scene as a region in its own right, is the area around Copenhagen. Here, the role of the Regional Council is wider than that of the other Regions/Counties, and incorporates powers usually held by the lower tier of the municipalities. This includes issues such as transport, housing and pollution control.

The Regional Plans which are produced by all the Regions/Counties, including the Metropolitan Region of Copenhagen, have to be approved by the Ministry of the Environment at National level. The first tranche of these approvals were made in 1981, and the second around 1991.

Municipal and local government

There are 277 local or municipal councils, elections for which are held every four years, as indeed is the case for Regional/County elections. The main function of the local government is to manage land-use issues, physical planning and associated issues. However, there are other powers which the local or municipal authorities hold, including several environmental responsibilities. These range from disposal of chemicals and oil waste to nature conservation and the ecological management of some aspects of farming.

The important feature about local government in Denmark is that this particular level of authority follows the directions and policy of the central government and its relevant departments. In this way national policies and initiatives are carried through to local delivery. There are few areas of friction between the various layers of Government, particularly on the environmental issues, largely because the whole of Danish government is greatly committed to environmental protection (National Environmental Protection Agency, 1986).

ENVIRONMENTAL RESPONSIBILITIES

The Danish system of administration was reformed in 1970 since when the responsibility for environmental management has become, if anything, more complicated. However, the environmental singularity of purpose at various levels of government manages to overcome this confusion to a certain extent. During the reforms two processes were at work: first, the responsibility of local and regional government was being consolidated; on the other hand, the central government was attempting to concentrate some environmental power so that emerging international and national policies could be implemented more effectively.

National environmental agencies

The Ministry of the Environment, which is headed by an elected Minister, is ultimately responsible for environmental issues within Denmark. The reality is that this responsibility is delegated to not only regional representatives, but also through the several agencies that act on the minister's instructions. The Minister (and hence the Ministry at a national level) only get involved once there is a problem or a contention within decisions made by these agencies. In this case, a national Environmental Appeal Board steps into resolve the conflicts.

The ministry drew its present responsibility from the 1973 Environmental Protection Act within which the former ministry, which was

responsible initially for environmental protection, was also given the additional responsibility for land-use planning. The relationship between the
central government Ministry and its many agencies is shown in Figure 10.1.
The following discussion analyses the agencies which have a direct responsibility for nature conservation.

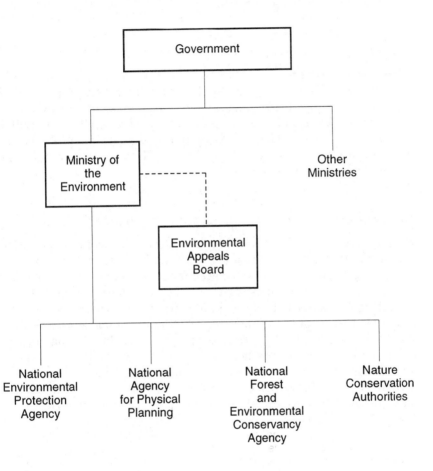

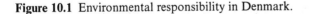

Figure 10.1 Environmental responsibility in Denmark.

National Environmental Protection Agency (NEPA)

The NEPA is responsible for administration for environmental policy at the
National Level. Within the process of national environmental planning

policy, NEPA creates a series of five-year plans. The 1985–90 plan identified three critical areas for the Agency. These were: preservation of human life; protection of natural resources; and the conservation of flora and fauna. These were followed up in the 1990–95 plan. In many cases, the NEPA acts as an environmental regulation body, and adjudicates in controversial decisions made by Regional government.

National Agency for Physical Planning (NAPL)

NAPL is responsible for urban and rural land-use planning and derives its authority from the Urban and Rural Zone Act of 1969. The Agency's responsibility is to provide guidance on land-use planning issues and, if necessary, to resolve problems that arise, regionally or locally, as a result of the guidance being implemented. As a result of its guidance, NAPL expects all local government agencies to prepare land-use plans which include nature conservation designations.

National Forest and Environmental Conservancy Agency

The Forest Act of 1935 was, in many respects, the first piece of land-use legislation in Denmark. Building upon the 'traditional' forestry responsibilities, the Agency also examines the need for stricter conservation measures within its 30 Forestry Districts. With the 1987 amendment to the 1935 Act, the NFECA absorbed the powers of a previously separate agency, the National Agency for the Protection of Nature, Monuments and Sites. With this merger came the bulk of the responsibility for nature conservation; the executive and land-holding power of the Forestry Agency was combined with the conservation ethos of the nature conservation agency (Baldock D., Bower G., and Clark J.). These nature conservation ideals in turn date back to 1917 with the Nature Conservation Act of that year.

Nature Conservation Authorities

Under the same legislation which created the present Ministry for the Environment, the 26 local Nature Conservation Authorities were created. The role of the Nature Conservation Authorities is central to the creation of land-use areas for the protection of nature conservation. The authorities consist of three individuals (nominated by central and local government) who determine applications made under the Conservation of Nature Act. Under this act, as amended in 1978, 'conservation orders' can be applied for on any land by any one of several agencies, including some non-governmental organization. The Nature Conservation Authority decides upon management prescriptions and any necessary levels of compensation.

Environmental Appeal Board (EAB)

Where decisions by the above agencies and authorities are contested, the EAB is the final environmental judicial authority, and answers directly to the Ministry (Figure 10.1).

These four agencies/authorities and the Appeal Board are those which are most directly concerned at a national level with nature conservation and its management. This system is both mirrored and complemented at the Regional and local level.

Regional and local environmental policy

The main responsibility of the Regional/County authorities is for physical planning, particularly the management of water resources, the control or direction of development and the control of pollution or contamination. For our purposes here, the most important of these is the control and directions of physical land use. Included in this responsibility is the proposed designation of specialized nature conservation areas. The National Agency for Physical Planning places upon the Regional Authorities the responsibility for preparing a Regional or County Plan. Through these plans, national directives are enacted.

At the Municipal level, the implementation of the Regional plans is at its most obvious. Construction of infrastructure, the allocation of land for development and, most significantly here, the protection of nature are all areas for which Municipal authorities have some responsibility.

Relationships between levels

It must be said that Denmark has a long history of environmental protection, and included within this has been a commitment to the conservation of natural history. Indeed, the main piece of far-reaching environmental legislation in Denmark, the Environmental Protection Act, was introduced before Denmark joined the EC; 1973 and 1974 respectively. Furthermore, there are several instances where EC regulations have been less stringent than those imposed internally within Denmark. As a result, there is little friction between the National Government, and the directives and guidance it draws-up, and the actual implementation of the legislation. This is usually the case whether the legislation in entirely internal or driven by EC Directives. As a result of Danish environmental awareness, EC policy has been greatly influenced by Danish policy since it became a Member State of the Community.

LAND DESIGNATIONS

Denmark is unusual within Europe in that is does not place great emphasis upon large National Parks, or their equivalent. Instead, the country relies more upon a network of smaller sites, often designated to protect specific habitat types. Similarly, the dominant land uses are agriculture which accounts for 60% of land, and forestry, which covers 19% (Table 10.1). Within Denmark, there is a long history of legislation aimed at not only protecting forestry sites (1805 Conservation of Forests Act, for example) but also the integration of these dominant land uses into the practices of nature conservation. Thus, the need for large protective land designations has not materialized. Notwithstanding this, however, there is still a relatively high proportion of designated land within Denmark (Table 10.2).

Table 10.1 Land use in Denmark

	%
Agriculture	60
Forestry	19
Urban	11
Water/Rivers	5
Other	5
Protected land	9.8

Table 10.2 Area of designated protected areas in Denmark

'000 km²			
1980	1985	1990	1990 (% of total area)
0.1	1.3	4.2	9.8

The basis for the land designation process in Denmark is the Conservation of Nature Act. This was originally passed in 1917, but has been significantly amended since. The Act allows for two types of designation: individual conservation orders and general conservation orders. The former deals with the conservation of very specific habitats, ranging from a group of isolated trees or a pond to a larger mixed habitat. There are several thousand such areas, which carry very stringent regulations.

The general conservation orders cover larger areas, but less stringently, and allow some development or agricultural cultivation to take place within the area providing that the overall integrity of the area is maintained.

There are several strands of policy which help to determine the designation of land in Denmark. Koestler (1991) identifies two; namely habitat type and EC Directives.

Habitat types

There are several specific types of habitats that have been progressively mentioned in the amendments to the 1917 Conservation of Nature Act. These include: watercourses; bogs; privately owned aquatic habitats; heaths, salt marshes; and salt meadows. As is mentioned above, forestry is mentioned specifically in its own Acts. Similarly, the marine environment, which is very important to Denmark both economically and environmentally, is protected in other ways as we shall see below.

By mentioning the six habitat types in the amendments to the conservation of Nature Act, the relevant Nature Conservation Authorities can become actively involved in the protection of that particular habitat type. Furthermore, the Act also lays down detailed constraints to development or cultivation in designated habitat areas. Thus, for example, on salt marshes (Strandsump) areas, the Act requires that the Nature Conservation Authority gives permission for 'cultivation, plantation or any other changes'.

In the Conservation of Nature Act, therefore, the Danish Conservation Authorities have very precise mechanisms for dealing with threats to habitat types, and the power to protect both specific habitats and more general 'natural environments'.

EC Directives

The Danish government is very conscientious about implementing EC Directives and international convention, particularly those relating to aquatic habitats. Thus, the Nature Conservation Authorities have designated some 26 Ramsar Sites (see Chapter 6) and 111 Community Bird Protection Areas, designated to comply with the 1979 EC Directive on the conservation of wild birds. These sites (some of which are more or less identical with each other) cover around 9500 km^2 comprising 2500 km^2 of land and 7000 km^2 of sea or estuarine habitats. Some of these sites (about 20% of the total area) are also covered by the internal protection provided by the Conservation of Nature Act.

The process of land designation is proceeding relatively quickly in Denmark, as opposed to the situation in other Member States such as Spain or the United Kingdom, where the process has slowed down since initial activity following key legislation.

There is a final land designation within Denmark which is worthy of mention: Scientific and Wildlife Reserves. These are sites similar to those protected under an international framework, as discussed above, but which are not designated as international sites. By far the majority of these sites (some 90 in total, with an overall area of 1.1 million hectares) cover aquatic, and particularly marine environments; around 75%. The control of activity on these Scientific and Wildlife Reserves is restricted to traffic, hunting and development.

OTHER ISSUES

It can be gathered from the foregoing discussion that the Danish Government has endeavoured to integrate nature conservation into the activities of the mainstream economy. As a result it is inevitable that other areas of activity, such as agriculture, forestry and water management, are very important elements of the overall picture. Consequently, the following analysis can only scratch the surface of the progress that has been made in integrating the needs of nature conservation into all facets of the economy. Suffice it to say that Denmark is one of the leading supporters of environmental legislation in the Community. Indeed it was partly because of the fear that Community legislation would constrain Denmark's desire for stronger environmental protection that the Danish people initially rejected the Maastricht proposals for stronger European Union.

Agriculture

As elsewhere, the overriding trend in Denmark is for smaller farms to be amalgamated into larger enterprises, and at the same time, production to increase markedly (Danish Farmers Organisation, 1989). Thus, in 1950 there were 200 000 farm enterprises, now there are 82 000. Similarly, every farmer now feeds 160 people as opposed to 27 in 1950.

One consequence of this push for productivity has 'only been possible through methods that strain the environment' (Lizitzyn, 1992). Recently, therefore, the balance has been redressed with a series of laws which ensure that farming methods, and more particularly the chemicals used in farming are approved not only by the agricultural authorities, but also the National Environmental Protection Agency. This process is made slightly easier by the fact that almost all Danish farmers are members of at least one producing and/or distributive co-operative. Thus, access to and assistance with the necessary decision-making processes can be shortened to some extent.

The moves towards greater integration between agriculture and ecology have been maintained in Denmark. A report by the Ministry for the Environment (1987) indicates the preference for lower levels of agricultural productivity, but with larger areas managed under ecologically sustainable agricultural methods. In this debate, the Danes are leading the Community.

Water management and marine environments

The extraction of water in Denmark is cross-boundary so unlike most environmental issues, the administration of water management is undertaken by the County Authorities to the greatest extent. The concern of the water supply agencies is for water quality and continued supply. Most water is extracted from ground water sources and it is generally clean (because of the underlying geology) and relatively plentiful. For those reasons, the continuation of supply and water quality do not usually cause problems for the authorities. Water is thus a very inexpensive resource (Dalgaard-Kundsen, 1992).

Due to the fact that most water is extracted from underground sources, the water authorities do not have very much impact upon the land-based nature conservation. Of far greater importance is the marine environment. The importance not only stems from the geography of Denmark (which is a series of islands), but also from the economic importance of the marine environment. Following the pattern set elsewhere within Danish legislation, the 1980 Act of the Protection of Marine Environment, not only seeks to protect the economic resource of the ocean, but also the natural history interest. This Act is supported and elaborated by several other supplementary Acts and, indeed, earlier Acts.

Where conflicts arise between the economic, water quality and nature conservation interest these are resolved by Forestry and Nature Agency. In order to assist this process, the Agency has mapped over 65% of the Danish seabed. This survey not only covers the natural history, but also the human heritage (shipwrecks and early settlements which have been covered by marine succession) and geology.

Signing of conventions

Denmark has signed the Ramsar, Paris, Washington, London, Berne, Bonn and Rio conventions.

Implementation of EC Directives

The foregoing discussion suggests that the Danish commitment to safeguarding the environment, which necessarily includes nature conservation, is even more stringent and deep rooted than that of the Community and several individual Member States. This has, of itself, caused some friction between the Danes, who wish to move forward with greater protection, and the Community. This friction manifested itself in the rejection of the Maastricht Treaty for European Union in the first referendum in Denmark in 1992. Only after a lot of work by politicians and European executives did the Danish people accept the Treaty in a second referendum.

Directives are implemented either through amendments to existing Acts or legislation, or through circulars/instruction reframing current practice. In most cases there is a relevant piece of legislation which can act as a convenient basis for any necessary amendments.

SUMMARY

A unique feature about nature conservation in Denmark is that the designation of land is not seen as the most important feature of a conservation policy. This having been said, 9.8% of the land is thus designated; over the European average. The Danish government pays equal attention to the nature conservation input into other processes, such as agriculture and water management.

This broader view of nature conservation is exemplified by the types of land designation used in Denmark and the conservation orders, which in the case of 'general conservation orders' are in themselves broadly based and non-specific. Again, this lack of reliance upon specific nature conservation designations sets Denmark apart from its European neighbours. Although the Danish government does have the power to focus conservation orders on precise areas or habitats, this is only part of the broader approach.

The legislative background to nature conservation is relatively long-standing in Denmark, with the original Conservation of Nature Act being passed in 1917, a time when many other European countries were not concerned with nature conservation, at least at the legislative level.

REFERENCES

Baldock, D. et al. (1988) The Organisation of Nature Conservation in Selected EC Countries. IEEP, London.
Dalgaard-Kundsen, O. (1992) Water Management in Denmark. DocTer, Milan.
Danish Farmers Organisation (1989) Facts on Danish Farming. Copenhagen.
Koestler, V. (1992) Parks and Nature Reserves in Denmark. DocTer, Milan.
Lizitzyn, E. (1992) Agriculture and the Environment in Denmark. University of Copenhagen, Copenhagen.

Ministry for the Environment (1987) *Ecological Alternatives in Danish Agriculture*. Kbenhavn.

National Environmental Protection Agency (1986) *Programme of Action for 1985–1990*. Copenhagen.

National Environmental Protection Agency (1990) *Programme of Action for 1990–1995*. Copenhagen.

11	# Finland

Finland joined the EC in 1995, along with its Scandinavian neighbours Sweden and Austria. While being one of the largest countries in the EC (at 305000 km², it is comparable in size to Germany or Italy), Finland is the least densely populated country with only 16 people per km². This point is reflected in the fact that the area has 85% land use coverage of agriculture and forestry, most of which is put over to forestry. This high level of managed rural land-use also reflects the fact that Finland is relatively low lying compared to Sweden, thereby allowing access to most of the country for forestry and agriculture.

The biogeographical zones are 'Central European' and in places 'Arctic', a climate and environment which gives support to one of the EC's indigenous nomadic populations: The Lapps.

Given the low population density, it is perhaps understandable that there is not a perceived need to safeguard the environment through land designations. At 2.4%, Finland is well below the European average.

Correspondingly, the low population density (and consequential reliance upon agriculture and forestry as sources of economic foundation) means that Finland has a low GDP; at 140 in 1992 it was 1% below the EC average.

POLITICAL STRUCTURE

The Finnish Government and Parliament are elected and appointed in the way common to all European Member States, by universal suffrage to two houses of government. The government is appointed by the party with the greatest majority or in some instances through a coalition government. With some of its Nordic neighbours the Finnish government had previously put the issue of membership of the EC to its population in a referendum prior to membership on 1 January 1995. While the Danish people voted to join on that occasion, the Norwegian, Swedish and Finnish people did not. In 1994, Finland and Sweden voted to join, but Norway once again voted to stay out.

The Finnish Government brought a relatively unique perspective to the debate, because of the unstable political conditions of the former Soviet Union in 1993/94 and subsequently as a result, not only did the national government stress the economic rationale for membership, but it also emphasized the potential military assistance that would stem from closer ties with Europe (*Sunday Times*, 1995).

The National Government is structured along common lines: an elected representative is appointed to head a Ministry or Department, the executive of which is managed and staffed by an independent civil service. These Ministries are again common to most European countries: Defence, Industry, Agriculture and Environment, for example.

Local government

At the local level, Finland is divided into Provinces and Counties (similar to Sweden) and at a lower level, Municipalities. The provinces or counties have their own electoral base and have local government systems very similar to those at the national level. For the implementation of national policy, there-fore, local authorities either have delegated responsibility from central government, or their own statutory power that they administer directly. This is also a common pattern to most European countries, as too is the potentiality for confusion and duplication of activity and responsibility in some areas of work. This is increased by the instances where central government implements its responsibility direct through offices in the counties without involving the county administrations.

There is not, however, a great deal of competition between Central and Local government (Törnquist, 1991) as there is between many European regions and their respective national governments. The confusion and potential duplication is relatively minimal.

ENVIRONMENTAL RESPONSIBILITIES

In common with its neighbour, Sweden, Finland has a high degree of cen-tral authority for environmental issues. This is largely a consequence of the relatively sparsely populated nature of much of the country which makes the resourcing of detailed planning, management and monitoring difficult. However, Finland does have a tradition of delegating some of the imple-mentation and management of central environmental strategies to the provinces and counties. It is at this level that much of the expertise in environmental issues is to be found (European Community Committee of the American Chamber of Commerce, 1994). Furthermore, the Finnish government also has a tradition of managing its affairs through agencies that are directly responsible to the Ministries. In this context, there are several environmental agencies that are important parts of the overall picture.

National government

The most important Ministry in the Finnish government with responsibility for the Environment is, not unsurprisingly, the Ministry for the Environment. The Ministry was formed in its current structure in 1983 when two individual Ministries were brought together. This division within the Ministry for the Environment still remains with both parts (Environment and Housing), being led by a junior minister who are responsible to the overall Minister for the Environment.

Many of the functions of the Finnish government, including the Ministry for the Environment, are managed through agencies and institutes that have a relatively large degree of autonomy. For this reason, the work of these agencies (detailed in the next section) is of most relevance here.

Local government

The Provincial and County administrations take on much of the management and implementation role of the national government. This takes two forms: Agency agreements, where the National Government provides the local government with a clear direction for work; and the delegated route, where the central administration defines the broad guidelines for the standards to be met and the local agencies are responsible for meeting these standards. In effect, because of the strong links between the two levels of government, the difference between these two methods is not as marked as it might otherwise be.

The 'directional' responsibility is particularly relevant in land-use issues, where designation and policies about land-based conservation are determined centrally, but the management and implementation of sites and National Parks is undertaken by local agencies, particularly local government departments.

Other agencies

The Finnish Government relies upon a number of agencies to implement strands of its environmental policies. The two most important for nature conservation are the National Board of Water and Environment; and the National Forestry Board.

The National Board of Water and Environment is directly responsible to the Ministry of the Environment, and manages the inland water bodies and rivers of Finland. This is not only a responsibility of water supply, but also water quality and the protection of associated aquatic habitats. The National Board has a network of district offices, which stands outside the local and national governmental structure. As a consequence, the management of water in Finland is elevated to an important position. This is largely because the value and extent of the inland lake system in Finland is of such a high quality that its protection is of utmost importance (Karlson, 1993).

Of equal national significance are the forests of Finland: the country is often referred to as the 'land of lakes and forests', and much of the 85% agriculture and forestry cover in Finland is accounted for by forests. The National Forestry Board is responsible for the management of the state-owned forests. As part of this role, it is also responsible for the integration of nature conservation into the overall management process. This responsibility has been framed in Finnish Law since the 1920s, so the relationship between forests and wildlife has long been recognized in Finland. Recently, the National Forestry Board was renamed the Finnish Forest and Park Service, and now also manages the majority of the country's National Parks and Nature Reserves.

A similar body is the Finnish Forest Research Institute, which undertakes the bulk of the investigation into the effects of acid rain. Clearly they also have other research programmes, but most of their work is focused upon this issue. It is within this framework that the Finnish Forest Research Institute manages several National Parks and Nature Reserves.

LAND DESIGNATIONS

Unlike many countries in Europe, the Finnish government has been accelerating its designation of land over recent years, as Table 11.1 suggests. A large part of the progress has been in the designation of National Parks, with a lot of activity in the early to mid-1980s. The second land designation worthy of particular note, other than National Parks, is that of nature reserves. Both are discussed below.

Table 11.1 Land designation in Finland

'000 km²				
1970	1980	1985	1989	1990 (% of total area)
4.8	4.8	8.0	8.1	2.6

National Parks

There are 30 National Parks in Finland; by far and away the largest number of any Member State of the European Community. Table 11.2 shows the size and dates of designation for these parks, from which it can be seen that the early 1980s, particularly 1982, saw a large increase in designations. Indeed even those National Parks designated prior to 1982 were mostly extended in the 1980s. The reason for this increased activity was the report published by the National Parks Committee (Ministry of the Environment, 1976). On the basis of this report 21 new National Parks were created.

Table 11.2 National parks in Finland

Name	Area (km²)	Date of designation	Main habitats
Eastern Gulf of Finland	5	1982	Islands and coasts
Helvettinjarvi	301	1982	Coniferous forests
Hiidenportti	441	1982	Peatland and heath
Isojarvi	19	1982	Forests and lakes
Kauhaneva – Petijankangas	33	1992	Peatland
Koli	25	1991	Coniferous forest
Kolovesi	23	1990	Lake and islands
Lauhanvuori	36	1982	Boulder field and forests
Lemmenjoki	2855	1956	Natural forest
Liesjarvi	7	1956	Lakes and forest
Linnasaari	36	1956	Lakes and islands
Nuuksio	17	1994	Upland forests and lakes
Oulanka	270	1956	River valleys and gorges
Pallas – Ounastunturi	500	1938	Mountains and forests
Patvinsvo	100	1982	Peatland
Perameri	157	1991	Coast and islands
Petkeljarvi	6	1956	Lake and eskers
Puurinjarvi – Isosuo	23	1993	Raised bog
Pyha – Hakki	12	1956	Ancient forest
Pyhatunturi	43	1938	Peatland and forests
Paijanne	10	1993	Lakeland
Riisituntun	77	1982	Mountains and forest
Rokua	4	1956	Esker and heath
Salamajarvi	60	1982	Peatland and forest
Seitseminen	42	1989	Lakes and forest
South Western Archipeligo	220	1983	Islands and coast
Tammisaar: Archipeligo	39	1989	Islands and coast
Tiilika	34	1982	Lakes and eskers
Torransuo	26	1990	Peatland
Urho – Kekkonen	2500	1983	Mountains, forests and lakes

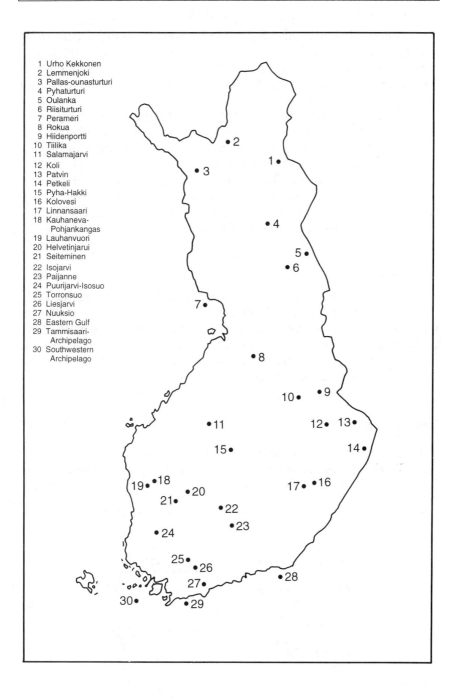

1 Urho Kekkonen
2 Lemmenjoki
3 Pallas-ounasturturi
4 Pyhaturturi
5 Oulanka
6 Riisiturturi
7 Perameri
8 Rokua
9 Hiidenportti
10 Tiilika
11 Salamajarvi
12 Koli
13 Patvin
14 Petkeli
15 Pyha-Hakki
16 Kolovesi
17 Linnansaari
18 Kauhaneva-
   Pohjankangas
19 Lauhanvuori
20 Helvetinjarui
21 Seiteminen
22 Isojarvi
23 Paijanne
24 Puurijarvi-Isosuo
25 Torronsuo
26 Liesjarvi
27 Nuuksio
28 Eastern Gulf
29 Tammisaari-
   Archipelago
30 Southwestern
   Archipelago

Figure 11.1 National parks in Finland.

A feature of the Finnish National Parks is that there are some very small designations; areas that in other countries would qualify as habitats of specific reserves rather than National Parks. This in part explains the large number of parks, and explains why the overall percentage of designated land in Finland is around the European average, despite the large number of National Parks.

The final point worth picking out of Table 11.2 is the importance of the three habitat/landscape types of forest, lakes and peatland, thus emphasizing the alternative name for Finland – the land of lakes and forests (Finnish Forest and Park Service, 1995).

The main rationale for designation is for habitat and environmental protection which is, as we have seen, often at a very localized level in some parks. Educational, recreational and research use is permitted, but there are strict controls on the development of land.

Nature Reserves

Nature reserves are, on average, of a similar size to the National Parks: 19 reserves with a total area of 1500 km^2. However, they do only cover one main habitat type and public access of any kind is severely restricted, if not prohibited altogether. Most of the nature reserves are managed by the Finnish Forest Research Institute, who themselves are restricted in how much activity they can undertake in the reserves.

Other designations

There are several other designations in Finland, which are summarized in Table 11.3. Of particular note is the 'Friendship Park' which is a network of five sites on the Russo-Finnish border, designated to aid co-operation and research.

Table 11.3 Designations in Finland, 1994

Type	Number	Area (km^2)
National Parks	30	7 183
Nature Reserves	19	1 500
Protected Peatlands	173	4 140
Herb-rich forests	53	12
Old-growth forests	92	92
Friendship Park	1	223
Others	38	514
Total	406	13 664

There are over 1000 areas of designated land in private ownership, accounting for around 700 km². It is therefore evident that, as is common elsewhere, much of the designated land is in public ownership.

OTHER ISSUES

The environmental land-use agenda of Finland tends to be dominated by the issue of acid rainfall which affects both Finnish forests and bodies of water. As is evident from Table 11.2, many of the country's National Parks are designated because of the locally significant woodland or lake/river environments. The national importance that is attached to monitoring and managing the quality of rainfall and watercourses cannot be overstretched. Consequently, the management of water is itself an important issue in Finland.

A further important issue is the sparsely populated nature of much of the country. A result of this characteristic is that the rural areas are, in common with other areas of Europe, having severe problems of rural depopulation due to broad economic decline. The importance of integrated rural development is therefore critical for much of the country.

Water management

The management of water collection, distribution and quality is the responsibility of the water agencies that are, in turn, directly responsible to government through the Ministry of the Environment. Like the other agencies mentioned above (forestry and peatland) the water agency has a strong research programme within its operations and several of the larger Finnish lakes are managed for research purposes as well as water management and nature conservation.

Because of this close link between water management and research, the water agencies are themselves very conscious of their responsibility for nature conservation and in many of the National Parks with large areas of water, the water agency operates alongside the Forestry and Parks Service. Furthermore, of the 19 Nature Reserves, 12 are mostly aquatic in nature, and the 173 Protected Peatlands represent a very large natural resource that is overseen by the water agencies.

Integrated rural development

Finland has the lowest population density in the European Community. Much of the concern that arose in 1994 as Finland was deciding whether or not to join the European Community was focused upon these rural areas. If, as was argued in some instances, fishing quotas are reduced and timber production is controlled the traditional rural economy of Finland could be devastated. In the end, this argument did not win, but the problem of declining economic prospects for rural Finland remains a real issue. The Finnish government has not, however, taken a similar route to the Mediterranean countries in trying to alleviate rural inequalities. Rather than create large-scale tourism or infrastructure projects, the Finnish government has 'sought to create localised solutions based on traditional industries where there has always been a tradition of co-operation' (Organisation for Economic Co-operation and Development, 1994). This has created community-owned timber and fishing businesses, and has also introduced the tourist industry, but only to a limited extent.

The Finnish government has also recognized the importance of the natural environment in its plans for integrated rural development through its involvement with several of the key agencies, including the Forestry and Parks Service, the water agencies and the fisheries authorities.

Signing of conventions

Finland is a signatory to all of the conventions mentioned in Chapter 6 and remains a vociferous supporter of international co-operation.

Implementation of EC Directives

With its entry into the European Community, Finland was given only a short run in period during which the national legislation was to be aligned with the European legislation. While this process has not been delayed unduly, it has, none the less, had some inevitable administrative and organizational problems. Notwithstanding these, the overall programme is running to schedule and the assimilation process should be completed by the end of 1998.

SUMMARY

Finland is a now very active member of the European Community and nowhere is this more evident than in the environmental field. Given its susceptibility to internationally caused poor air quality, and its reliance upon clean water and fishing grounds this is to be expected. In many respects, Finland is already leading the rest of Europe in environmental standards.

This enthusiasm is also evident within the sphere of nature conservation, with many Finnish National Parks having been designated since 1990, a trend which is not common across Europe, where most countries are slowing down their designation of National Parks.

REFERENCES

Finnish Forest and Park Service (1995) *Finland's National Parks*. Finnish Forest and Park Service, Helsinki.

Karlson, D. (1993) *The Waterbodies and Rivers of Finland* (translation). Land Use Department, Ministry of the Environment, Helsinki.

Ministry of the Environment (1976) *Report of the National Parks Committee*. Helsinki.

Organisation of Economic Co-operation and Development (1994) *Integrated Rural Development*. OECD, Paris.

Sunday Times (1995) *Europe's new partners*. December.

Törnquist, G. (1991) *The Governance of Finland* (translation). University of Helsinki, Helsinki.

12 | France

France is one of the largest countries in the European Community with an area of 549 km². The proportion of agricultural land is 83% and, as a result, France contains approximately one-third of all the agricultural land in the Community and, in 1990, over 1.5 million people continued to derive their livelihood directly from working on the land. In economic and political terms the agricultural community continues 'to exhort an influence even greater than their numbers suggest' (Hermans, 1994).

Geographically and climatically, France has remarkable diversity unparalleled anywhere within the European Community with 'Atlantic', 'Central European', 'Alpine' and 'Mediterranean' biogeographical zones. The diversity is reflected in the agriculture of the country, with intensive, large prosperous farms of the north being counterbalanced with smaller family-managed mixed holdings in the southern regions such as Provence and Languedoc-Roussillon. This agricultural balance is reflected in the general economy with the Northern and Eastern parts of the country being at the hub of conventional Community economic activity, and the Southern regions being much less developed, and more reliant upon agriculture as a basic industry.

POLITICAL STRUCTURE

France has several layers of government in common with most European countries. This brings with it all the opportunities and problems found elsewhere.

National government is based along lines found throughout the Community; a nationally elected government being responsible for a series of Ministries wherein elected Ministers operate with full-time officers and staff. The actual remit of various Ministries changes with time, as issues and external political pressures change, but for our purposes the two most important are the Ministry of the Environment and the Ministry of Agriculture, both of which have a direct impact upon the protection of the environment. At National level, the Ministry of the Environment is headed by a 'Ministre de lèque' – a relatively junior minister, while the Ministry of Agriculture is headed by a suitably powerful minister. This clearly reflects their respective levels of importance at national level. Indeed, prior to a ministerial reorganization in 1972, the responsibilities for nature conservation, now with the Ministry of the Environment, lay with the Ministry of Agriculture.

Plate 9 Regional parks in France protect not only the environment, but also people's opportunities for recreation. On tourist routes, these pressures can be intense.

At Regional level, 22 regions operate through a similar elected representative/full-time officer structure. Most of the work of the Regional government is in the area of planning, transportation and economic regeneration. At this level, the efforts of the political and professional staff are aimed at 'conforming to the aspirations of a specific population' (Bourne, 1990). The process of regionalization is still progressing in France having been given legal impetus through legislation in 1982 and 1983. Responsibilities and powers are therefore continually being developed and consolidated. This in turn helps to account for the changes witnessed at National level to ministerial responsibilities, particularly in the Ministry of the Environment as we shall see later.

The next level of government in France is the *département*, of which there are 96. *Départements* are responsible mostly for the detailed work and management which is necessary in the day-to-day running of communities. This includes such issues as road and traffic management, town planning, housing development, land drainage and land management. *Départements* are managed by a Prefect.

At the neighbourhood level France operates local town councils and communes at the supply and purchasing level of agricultural production. For our purposes, however, these levels of social and economic organization are not directly relevant. Of greater importance are the six *Agences Financières* de Bassin which control the financial management of water, including water supply, waste management, pollution control and some larger irrigation schemes. These Regional watershed Authorities clearly have a limited remit, based on the control and supply of water, but they do play a role within wildlife and landscape management, and, to a limited extent, influence other regional and *département* decisions on local issues. Their power and responsibilities are derived directly from central government through the Ministry of the Environment (Ullman *et al.*, 1983).

These several tiers of local and national government clearly provide both opportunities and problems, in much the same way that these exist wherever tiers of authority exist. All levels of government are democratically elected and therefore scope exists for political co-operation or confrontation. At the management level, similar degrees of co-operation or confrontation can exist over where lines of responsibility or policy priorities lie. This situation is not unique to France, but it is fair to say that given the strength of the regional movement – a movement also found elsewhere in Europe, but absent in some countries – and the attendant power which the Regional Authorities have, the opportunities and problems are potentially greater. Thus, at all levels of government, initiatives are taking place independently from other levels of government; this is the case with nature and landscape conservation, although progress is relatively slow. 'Except in a few areas the State has not surrendered many of its powers to local governments, and for the department of the Minister in charge of the

Environment, decentralisation does not alter much' (Lambrechts, 1987). This is despite the fact that the 1983 legislation was, among other things, specifically aimed at 'sharing responsibility between the State and the territorial units which vie with the State for the protection of the environment and improvement of the quality of life'.

ENVIRONMENTAL RESPONSIBILITIES

The preceding discussion identifies the vertical structure of French Government, from the State to the Commune. Other than the different political layers, there are several Ministries which have responsibility for various aspects of environmental protection. Reference has already been made to the Ministry of the Environment and the Ministry of Agriculture. Other ministries which have limited influences upon the environmental protection process are the Ministry of Industry and the Ministry of Culture. If this arrangement of interlinking responsibilities is combined with the various layers of political representation, we can gain an impression of the complexity of environmental management in France. It is this complexity which once prompted General de Gaulle to say something to the effect of 'How on earth can you govern a country which makes over 300 different sorts of cheese?'. Briefly, the environmental responsibilities of the various Ministries are as follows.

Ministry of the Environment

The Ministry of the Environment has been subjected to a relatively large amount of change both before it split from the Ministry of Agriculture in 1972, and after this date, when it became a Ministry in its own right. Since 1972, the Ministry of the Environment first expanded and more recently contracted in size and influence within the central administration. In 1982, the formerly large Ministry was reduced to cover two policy areas – nature conservation and pollution – in conjunction with other ministries, such as Planning and Agriculture. Following this, in 1986, the services were placed under a wide ministerial framework, with a relatively junior minister heading the Ministry of the Environment: a *Ministre délègue*. (Ministerie de l'Environnement, 1984, 1991)

The responsibilities and organization structure are shown in Figure 12.1. Most of the affairs directly concerned with the conservation of natural environments (no distinction is drawn between nature conservation and landscape conservation) are directed through the Directorate for Nature Protection (*Direction pour la Protection de la Nature*). This Directorate is, however, headed by an agriculturist, which is based on an agreement between the Ministries of the Environment and Agriculture. This in turn reflects the fact that prior to 1972 the responsibility for nature conservation lay with the Ministry of Agriculture. The Directorate is responsible for managing National Parks and National Nature Reserves, and coastal conservation. The Directorate also represents France at the international level, both at global conventions and at the European Community; again however, the relatively junior status of the Ministry of the Environment dictates that international agreements are ratified by the *Quai d'Orsay* (the foreign office).

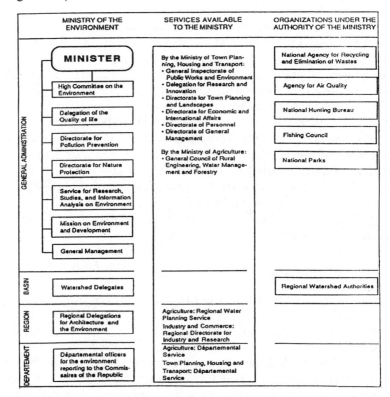

Figure 12.1 Organization chart of the Ministry of the Environment.

Management of land is either directly, or less commonly, through regional departments. The Ministry's regional responsibilities usually lie in other areas of concern.

There are several responsibilities of the Ministry of the Environment which are of particular concern here. The High Committee of the Environment (*Haute Comité de l'Environnement*) is a multiorganizational group of around 55 members, which is chaired by the Minister. The

Committee includes members of voluntary groups, academic institutes, non-government organizations, trade unions and so on. While the agenda of this group is not exclusively concerned with nature conservation, it does represent a relatively high level of discussion between the various groups, many of which are directly or indirectly involved with conservation issues.

The second responsibility of the Ministry of the Environment is the Delegation of the Quality of Life (*Délègation à la Qualité de la Vie*) which is given chaired by the Minister. The Delegation is attended by 24 ministers, who are duty bound to attend, and a further 20 can be called into attend the meetings as required. The topics of discussion will cover a wide spectrum, including conservation, but issues such as pollution control, water management and forestry and agriculture are also addressed.

Between them, the Committee and the Delegation provide a valuable national forum for the discussion and possible resolution of environmental issues including conservation. Direct outcomes of this dialogue include the growing importance of the voluntary conservation movement in France and the agreements made between the Ministry of the Environment, the Ministry of Agriculture and the National Forestry Office; both of these are discussed later in the chapter.

A further major responsibility of the Ministry, which is of direct relevance is that of the National Hunting Office (*Office National de la Chasse*) which in theory is directly responsible to the Minister. In truth, however, the National Hunting Office represents a very strong lobby of both individuals and various national and regional federations and organizations of hunters. A national service of field officers operate to control illegal hunting, which is managed by the National Hunting Office. The national laws are in turn altered locally within each *département*, where the local President of the Hunting Federation manages the service, but the local Prefect can amend administrative details, such as the periods during which hunting is permitted. In practice therefore, the hunting lobby, as co-ordinated through the National Hunting Office, is a major determinant of government policy both as an independent agency and through its contact with the Ministry. For example, the Directive on the Conservation of Wild Birds (Commission of the European Communities, 1979) was opposed strongly by the National Hunting Office, who felt that is would interfere with their hunting, and many concessions were gained to allow localized interpretations of the Directive.

The final direct responsibility held by the Ministry of the Environment is that of controlling the six Watershed Delegations. (*Agence Financière de Bassin*). These authorities are responsible for all the water management within their areas. This includes major drainage and flood control works, pollution control and irrigation. Some of the responsibility for these operations are devolved, particularly down to the *département* level. At this level, it is the requirement of the local landowners, particularly the farmers which is paramount. The thrust for the large amount of land drainage which France has witnessed since 1980 is due both to the pressure from farmers and from the influential 'Sabin report' (Conseil Economique et Social, 1979) a major basis of which is that these works are necessary to aid agricultural intensification.

The complexities of water management in France at both a ministerial level and at the political/geographical level dictate that co-ordination is vital (as indeed it is throughout the conservation field). This is achieved through the *Délègation à la Qualité de la Vie.*

At the Regional and *Département* level, the Minister of the Environment has various levels of representation. In the Regions, the Minister has his own agents in the Regional Delegations for Architecture and the Environment, although their principal responsibilities at Regional level are for urban development, pollution control, environmental impact assessment and monitoring the application of legislation. Conservation *per se* still tends to be dealt with from the central organizations.

At the level of the *Département*, the Minister of the Environment does not have direct representation, so its interests are administered by the representatives of other Ministries, notably those of Town Planning, Housing and Transport and Agriculture. This split from direct ministerial responsibility in the *Départements* is very important, because many of the major issues are resolved at this local level – water management, hunting, forestry management and rural development to name just a few. At a local level therefore, the interests of conservation are not directly represented (Prieur, 1984b).

Other ministries

It is evident from the foregoing discussion that the role of the Ministry of the Environment is only one part of the overall web of responsibilities for conservation. For our purposes, three further Ministries are important.

Ministry of Agriculture

La Ministère de l'Agriculture is responsible for an enormous range of activities. Most obviously, it represents the interests of the agricultural producers, but also has a much wider brief of help in the process of rural development, resolving regional disparities and managing the nation's forests, through the National Forest Office. Most of the national and community inspired attempts at agricultural restructuring, farm income support and economic regeneration of rural areas are channelled through the Ministry of Agriculture. At the smaller level, the Ministry's representatives in the *Département* administer the central policy.

There are two underlying concerns for the agricultural policy makers in France (Delorme, 1987): maintaining the French position as the world's second largest exporter of food products and also resolving the structural problems associated with farm size, incomes and tenure. These are the two processes identified as being central to Community policy. Indeed, it is possible to plot the development of Community policy and its relationship to French national policy in a number of areas, but nowhere is the comparison clearer than in agricultural policy. The impact of Community and French national agricultural policy on the environment is discussed later in this chapter, but for the meantime it is enough simply to note that the influence is inevitably great, as it is elsewhere in Europe.

Ministry of Industry, Post and Telecommunications

La Ministère de l'Industrie, des Postes et Téléphone et du Tourisme has the important responsibility for controlling and implementing tourist development, specifically in rural areas, and coastal and mountain areas. As it is these areas that are often of the most valuable for conservation, this role is clearly crucial.

Ministry of Culture and the Arts

The Ministry of Culture and Communication is responsible for managing historical monuments of national significance. While many of these are built structures, some are prehistoric and therefore of intrinsic importance to the landscape.

Summary

It is clear that the management of the environment is a complex issue in France (as it is elsewhere) with various ministries and different levels of Government assuming different roles. To some extent, this is resolved through the Delegation of the Quality of Life at ministerial level. However, in practical terms, much of the responsibility for conservation operate at Regional, Watershed or *département* level. As a result, confusion and duality can enter the system. Furthermore, the Ministry of the Environment retains central control over some issues (such as managing National Parks), while other issues are devolved (control of hunting for example) and other are managed completely independently from the Ministry. The control and co-ordination of this overall process is therefore critical, which makes the central role of the Ministry of the Environment of great importance.

LAND DESIGNATIONS

The land designations in France which are designed to protect the natural environment reflect the political and natural make-up of the country. Of greatest importance here are the designations of Forests, National Parks, Nature Reserves, and Regional Natural Parks.

Forests

Around 25% of France is wooded – a relatively high proportion – which reflects the long history of forestry management. This dates back to 1669, with the Ordinances de Colbert. This in turn led to the Forestry Code which was first drawn up in 1827 and amended in 1951, 1964 and 1979.

Table 12.1 Forests in France, 1990; a) size and b) ownership structures

a	Ownership	Regulated	Non-regulated	Total '000 hectares
	State	1 508	–	1 508
	Departement	13	–	13
	Communes	2 351	142	2 493
	Public Agencies	40	–	40
	Private	11	8 895	8 906
	Total			12 960

b	Size (hectares)	No. of owners
	< 10	1 445 000
	10–50	63 000
	50–100	11 000
	100–200	700
	200–500	2 600
	500+	700

Since 1984, the National Forests have been managed by the Ministry of Agriculture. A specific Secretary of State for Forests administers the Office of National Forests (ONF). The overriding brief of the ONF is to develop national reserves of timber and, through its officials at *Département* level,

to organize networks of production and marketing. Figure 12.2 shows why
this is necessary; by far the greatest proportion of forestry owners manage
woodland of less than 10 hectares

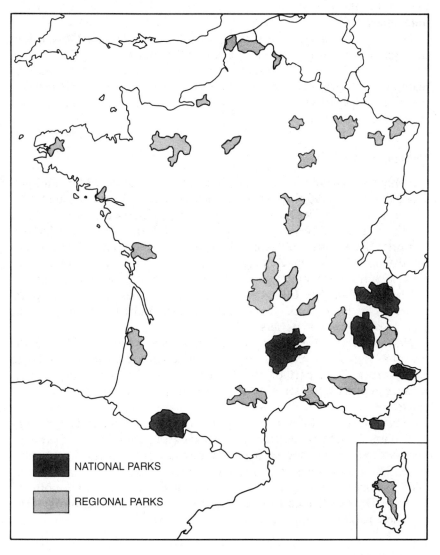

Figure 12.2 National Parks in France.

The importance of the forests for nature conservation stems from their size
and land coverage rather than any specific policy inherent in their management. This importance is further enhanced in state-owned forests which are

'regulated'. This means that certain land uses and activities, particularly hunting, are regulated in some way. Conversely, the importance of private woodland is reflected in the data in Figure 12.2, which shows that by far the largest proportion of woodland is privately owned and unregulated.

Forestry Action Areas are designated by the National Government through the Code Rural (a generic term for the concept of multi landuse in rural France). These areas are designated to take account of the need to maintain biological equilibrium. The local Prefect monitors adherence to the regulations. In 1991, 21 such areas were designated, which covered around 225 000 Hectares.

National Parks

Les Parcs Nationaux in France are designated to protect wildlife and natural habitats. In 1990 there were six such National Parks, covering 0.52% of the country. The National Parks are managed by the States authorities, having been established by national decree following a public inquiry. National Parks are split into 3 zones: the Peripheral Zone (*Zone Péripherque*) the Central Zone (*Zone Central*) and the Full Reserve (*Zone Intègrale*). It is interesting to compare this system with the United Nations' MAB programme (see Chapter 6) which also identifies these three ascending zones of importance. In the Central Zone and the Full Reserve the State has considerable powers.

National Parks were first defined in France as late as 1960 in the National Parks Act of that year. The underlying aim of the Act is to 'safeguard a finite part of the National Territory from human interference, in order to preserve its original beauty and conserve its biological assets'.

Given the size of France, the opportunity to create large and at the same time 'natural' National Parks has been taken (see Figure 12.3 for their location). Recreation is allowed in the Peripheral Zone, but not in the inner zones. This restriction is often lax, however, with major development taking place in some peripheral zones to accommodate tourism. Furthermore, the National Forestry Commission and the military can pursue its own policies anywhere within a National Park.

Nature Reserves

These too are designated by the State, through the Department of the Environment, and more specifically by the Directorate of Nature Conservation. A target of 100 such reserves was set in 1972, and by 1990 over 80 had been designated. The reserves were all originally managed and owned by the state but, more recently, many have been established on private land. This brings problems of management. In 1990 the ratio of public to private reserves was approximately 2.5:1.

Nature reserves are much smaller than National Parks with an average of 1000 Hectares for public reserves and only 85 hectares for private reserves. (National Parks average at about 57 000 hectares). This has led some commentators to suggest that the spread of habitats protected by the reserves is not comprehensive (Orme, 1989).

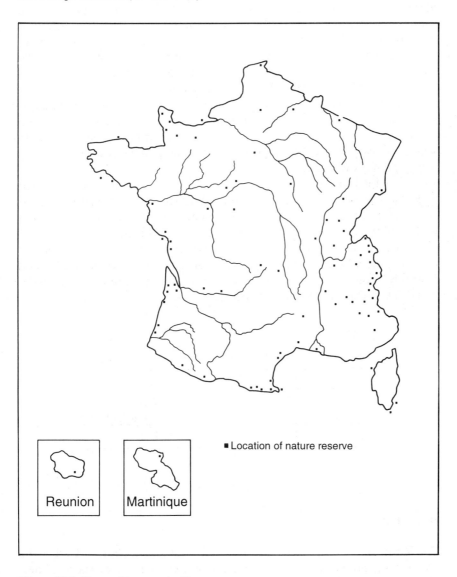

Reunion   Martinique   ■ Location of nature reserve

Figure 12.3 Nature Reserves in France.

Regional Natural Parks

As we saw previously, the strength of French regions began its recent climb in 1972. Three years after this, the power to designate and manage Regional Natural Parks was conferred upon the Regions. These regional land designations are targeted at protecting cultural and landscape qualities, as well as natural history. This sets them apart from the National Parks in their objectives. Furthermore, the Regional Natural Parks are managed by a committee drawn together with representation from the Regions, *Départements*, Municipalities and others. Funding is met by the local communities, with some state subsidies where appropriate – and this usually means for nature conservation. However, the role of tourism and recreation provision in Regional Natural Parks is increasing.

As a rule, Regional Natural Parks are nearly three times as large as National Parks (145 000 hectares as opposed to 55 000 hectares). As a consequence, control is less rigorous and towns, villages and communities as well as industry flourish within their boundaries; much of the land also lies within private ownership.

One of the local benefits of such a designation is that built development within a delegated area must face a special tax; the *Tax Départemental pour les Espaces Vertes* (TDEV). Thus, by designating land as a Regional Natural Park, additional resources for its management can be raised.

Management is through a small executive group, but these groups do not have the same direct regularity powers that apply for National Parks, and must rely upon administrative and other structures that are already in place, as well as establishing local agreements.

Table 12.2 Area of designated protected areas in France

	'000 km²		
1980	*1985*	*1990*	*1990 (% of total area)*
12.8	16.5	47.8	8.7

Other designations

The Directorate for the Protection of Nature has a direct link with all of the above designations, albeit in an increasingly remote form. Other local designations do exist such as: Voluntary reserves (created entirely at a landowner's initiative); areas of biotope protection (which are designated at the level of the *département*); and publicly owned biological reserves (many of which are in national forests arising out of an interdepartmental agreement of 1981). In all, approximately 200 of these additional sites exist, covering over 15 000 hectares.

Summary

The system of land designation and the means of financing the management of these designations has evolved in France as a result of many factors. As a consequence, the central Department of the Environment has a decreasingly significant role, while the role of the Regions is increasing. For example; National Nature Reserves and Regional Natural Parks are all managed regionally, with no central office directly involved in their management. While this accords with the spirit of the 1972 regionalization policy, it does mean that there is a gap in the direct link between local and national policy. How much this policy is based upon a philosophical commitment to decentralisation and how much to budgetary considerations is difficult to say (Baldock *et al.*, 1988).

There is no doubt, however, that since the early 1960s the French Government at all levels has become increasingly aware of the responsibilities for nature conservation, and has acted upon these responsibilities.

OTHER ISSUES

Despite its size, even within France land that has as its prime function nature conservation is rare. As a result, other land-use considerations are relevant and important. Of these four are particularly worthy of discussion: agricultural change, hunting, water management and tourism/leisure.

Agricultural change

As in all European countries, the agriculture industry in France has seen rapid changes. Despite this, as we have seen, cultivated agricultural land in France still accounts for 60% of the total area of country and about one-third of the total cultivated land within the community. The pattern witnessed since the beginning of the European Community is similar to elsewhere; intensification, amalgamations, population loss and, from the 1970s onwards, a slow compromise between the erstwhile conflicting objectives of farming and nature conservation.

The change that was heralded by the reform of the Common Agricultural Policy, which in itself was largely a result of French agricultural thinking, has exposed French farmers to yet more changes. Much of French agriculture in the less favoured regions is subsidized through the Common Agricultural Policy. As a result, these areas, which are also valuable for nature conservation will witness some of the greatest change. This inevitably takes time to develop patterns, but it has been estimated that some six million hectares of land will be taken out of cultivated agricultural production in only a ten-year period from 1988–98 (Delorme, 1987). The benefits of this for nature conservation remain uncertain (Devaud, 1991) despite the coming together of agricultural and environmental interests.

Hunting

Closely tied into the rural and agricultural way of life is hunting which is a widely practised activity across much of France; *La Chasse* is an integral part of rural life and dominates not only land-use debates but also much of the political and legislative debate. The National Hunting Office (ONC) is a national agency responsible, at a national level, to the Minister of the Environment. However, at a local level, the ONC officers are also obliged to note and follow decisions made at *départemental* level by the Prefect. Thus, if a Prefect determines that locally, some particular species of bird can be hunted, or an open season extended, the ONC officer must follow this, even if this goes against EC Directives (Baldock, 1988). As it is the same prefects which can also make local orders for the protection of some species or habitats, the potential for conflict is clear.

The hunting lobby is very strong in France, and the ONC has been criticized, particularly by nature conservationists, of only pursuing the interest of hunters and failing to control various aspects of hunting policy, such as 'traditional' methods of capture or trapping or the long-standing hunting of species that are now protected.

It is still the right of every French citizen to hunt, within the constraints of land ownership and locally administered codes. The national framework is held within the Code Rural but as we have seen, the implementation of this at local level is dependent as much on prefectoral decision as it is upon national policies (Prieur, 1984).

Water management

In France, the management of the water cycle is undertaken by a series of agencies that cross many ministerial and regional boundaries. At the national level, the ministry with the greatest degree of authority is the Ministry of the Environment. However, as the responsibilities of this Ministry are undertaken through other agencies at the departmental level, this continuity is broken. The agencies which administer water supply within each water basin (*Agences Financières de Basin*) legally link national and departmental obligations.

One of the most significant impacts of the management of the water cycle is that on important wetlands. The debate about the needs of agriculture and the provision of water and, conversely, drainage, was part of the wider debate about agricultural improvements (Conseil Economique et Social, 1979). It was estimated in 1982 for example that of 25 major wetland sites important for wildfowl, 12 were already being drained, and eight were vulnerable or open to impending encroachment (Chantrel, 1982). Perhaps ironically, this report was prepared by the National Hunting Office.

The overriding priority of the water basin committees is to provide clean drinking water to the population, to provide agriculture industry with its needs, be it drainage or irrigation, and to provide industry with its needs. In 1987, the basin committees developed their fifth Programme of Policies, which continued these existing priorities. As elsewhere between agencies in France, the needs of nature conservation are being accommodated within these policies, albeit slowly (Blanchard, 1991).

Tourism and leisure

Most National Parks in France are in mountainous areas. Not only is this a poor reflection of the range of habitat types across the country, but it also leaves the network of National Parks open to pressure from development of tourism facilities, particularly from ski-lifts for winter recreation. As has been evident elsewhere, the pressure for recreational development is widespread, and indeed was for several years a conflict that was present even within the EC regeneration programmes. In France, this pressure is particularly intense because of the distribution of the National Parks.

The potential conflict between tourism and the environment is more widespread than just in the National Park network (Michaud, 1983). It has been suggested that the very areas that are most susceptible to damage due to pressure – coasts, mountains, river valleys and rural areas – are also the most delicate. Two statistics produced by *Le Cente Permanent d' Initiation à l'Environnement* will exemplify this point. Some 70% of France's 8500 campsites are on the coast, and for the 10 years between 1980 and 1990, levels of visits to the mountains during winter increased by 10% per annum; in 1988 alone 7 billion Francs were invested in ski-lifts.

The French tourists as well as the French Government have increasingly become aware of the potential conflict and have taken some steps to relieve the problem. Indeed, the development of Regional Nature Parks can be considered such a step. This is because these Parks are created not only to protect the landscape, but also to try to accommodate the demands of recreation. Growing liaison between National Park authorities and Regional Park authorities will spread the good practices of both (Orme, 1989).

Signing of international conventions

Of the eight international conventions mentioned in Chapter 6, France has signed all of them. However, for two (the Bonn and the Berne conventions) France had not, in 1993, begun the process of enforcement.

Implementation of EC Directives

There is no internal, Parliamentary discussion of EC Directives within the French political system. Hence, ratification can be speedy, but implementation or enforcement can be relatively slow as with the Bonn and Berne conventions. The central government department drafts the relevant legislation and its enactment is then passed to the relevant level or organization. As the political structure is so complex, and given that some government departments do not have direct representation at Regional or *Département* level, the necessary continuity is hard to maintain.

A further complication it that the Prefect within each *Département* has often conflicting responsibilities and powers, as with hunting and species protection for example. All this being said, however, the French government has a good record on ratification and adoption of EC Directives, and has some similar problems to all EC countries in ensuring implementation on the ground.

SUMMARY

The French system of land designation can, in many ways, be considered as an important basis of comparison across Europe. France is one of the founding members of the European Community and has thus been in an important position to influence policy at a European level including nature conservation policy. Furthermore, the area of land covered by land designations is almost exactly the European average. Finally, the types of land designation, and the political shift in responsibility for designations are also comparable to many European countries. The initial emphasis on National Parks has recently given way to an emphasis on Regional Parks. Clearly, the political shift in the focus of power is not the only criteria which determines designation, but it is influential. In many ways, therefore, France exemplifies many of the trends found in Europe.

A further feature of the French conservation scene is the influence of the farming industry (83% of the land is agricultural or forestry) and, by extension, the hunting movement. This manifests itself at both the level of individual species and at the level of overall designation where hunting falls into conflict with 'permitted uses' of conservation areas.

Notwithstanding these conflicts, the French national and regional governments have designated protective land use on some of the most delicate and valuable coastal, alpine and forest habitats in Europe and remain central (politically and geographically) to the success of any European networks for conservation sites.

REFERENCES

Blanschard, M. (1991) Water supply in France, in *European Environmental Yearbook*. DocTer, Milan.

Bourne, I. (1990) Landscape Architects in France. *Landscape Design*, **186**.

Chantrel, C. (1982) *Element d'étude pour un bilan économique de la transformation des zones humides par l'agriculture*. Office National de la Chasse, Paris.

Commission of the European Communities (1979) *Directive of the Conservation of Wild Birds*. OJ L103 25.4.79. Brussels.

Conseil Economique et Social (1979) *Water and the Needs of Agriculture*. Ministerie de l'Environnement, Paris.

Delorme, H. (1987) An outline of French views on land conversion programmes, in *Removing Land from Agriculture*. CPRE/IEEP, London.

Despax, M. (1980) *Droit de l'Environnement*. Litec, Paris.

Deveraud, J. (1991) Agriculture and the environment, in *European Environmental Yearbook*. DocTer, Milan.

Federation des Parcs Naturels de France (1986) *Les Parcs Naturels Regionaux*. FPNF, Paris.

Hermans, B. (1994) *Wetlands Drainage in Europe*. IEEP, London.

Lambrechts, C. (1987) Organisational structure in France, in *European Environmental Yearbook*. DocTer, Milan.

Michaud, J.L. (1983) *Le tourisme face à la environnement*. Presses Universitaires de France, Paris.

Ministerie de l'Environnement (1984) *L'état de l'environnment*, Paris.

Ministerie de l'Environnement (1991) *L'état de l'environnment*, Paris.

Prieur, M. (1984a) *Forests et Environnment*, Limogues.

Prieur, M. (1984b) La politique regionale de l'environnement en France, in *Revue Juridique de l'Environnment*, (Vol. 2) Université de Sorbonne, Paris.

Ullman, G. and Achard E. (1983) *Guide practique des Procedures judiciaries et adminstratives*. Grenoble Universit Press.

Germany

13

The following analysis concentrates upon the former Federal Republic of Germany (West Germany) for a number of very practical reasons. First, the information that allows any meaningful comparison with other Member States only exists for the former West Germany. Second, the concerns of the 'new' Unified Germany, following the break-up of the former Eastern Bloc in the early 1990s, has been with economic and social stability. As a result, environmental legislation, particularly that relating to nature conservation, has not progressed very rapidly. Any moves in former East Germany are therefore aimed at bringing that area up to existing standards. Finally, the actual systems themselves are in such a state of change that any assessment would be futile. This will remain the case for many years to come. Ironically, it was the reunification of Germany, among other very significant events in the 1990s that marked the start of the period of uncertainty within the European Community and hence a lessening of the impetus to full environmental competence for the European Commission.

The Federal Republic of Germany, along with its Western neighbour, France, is not only one of the largest of the countries within the European Community at 399 km² since reunification, but is also widely recognized as one of the principal powers within the Community and, following recent moves for the re-unification of the Federal Republic and the German Democratic Republic, the economic strength of this Member State looks set to increase (Organisation for Economic Co-operation and Development, 1994), with a GDP of 19.7, well above the European average.

Despite its large size, Germany is far more ecologically homogenous than its large neighbour France. It is almost entirely of 'Central European' bio-geography and, with the exception of some bands of land predominantly in the south, land is under 300 m. Furthermore a belt of land in the extreme south is over 2000 m, where the Alpine belt begins to rise towards Switzerland and northern Italy.

POLITICAL STRUCTURE

The German Constitution identifies three levels of governmental administration. The central government is headed by two elected houses, which are in turn headed by the Chancellor. The three levels of government that are most commonly identified are: Federal; State or Lander; and local.

The Federal administration has, since 1992, been extended to incorporate the former East Germany, while the federal structure consisting of state and local administrations has similarly been extended. The major difficulty in this process of extensions is the development of local and state mechanisms in the eastern regions. The changeover from a centralized political system to one where the states, municipalities and other areas have a high degree of autonomy is clearly going to be difficult.

National government

The Federal Republic, as defined here, originally consisted of 11 States (or Lander). The Federal Authority, or Bund, has the principal responsibility for developing and enacting legislation which, by and large passes to the states and other levels of local government for implementation. For this, and other historic reasons, the Federal government has its autonomy enshrined within the Federal constitution, as well as the State and other local government agencies.

Within the Bund, the administrative responsibilities were reorganized as recently as 1986, when ministerial areas of responsibility were reallocated. The mechanisms for managing ministerial portfolios did not change; there continues to be an elected minister which heads each ministry. In turn, the ministries are subdivided into divisions. Within these, the administration is undertaken by professional civil servants and officers. As is explained below, the environmental responsibilities saw some of the most significant changes following the reorganization in 1986.

State government

The States, or Lander, are comparable to the regions found in other European countries. However, the fact that these states were, until relatively recently, self-governing kingdoms, means that the historic strength of the States is great. For this reason, most authority within the country lies with the state.

The 11 states making up the German Federal Republic which joined the European Community were: Bayern; Baden-Württemberg; Saarland; Rheinland-Pfalz; Hessen; Nordhein-Westfalen; Niedersachsen; Bremen; Hamburg; Berlin; and Schleswig-Holstein. With the reunification of Germany, 10 additional states have begun the process of integration into the Federal Republic.

The organization of the Lander varies considerably, with some retaining large 'traditional' ministries such as Agriculture or Industry, while others have followed the Federal lead, and reorganized into newer, multifunctional ministries. As the governments of the Lander are elected independently of the Federal government, the state administration does not necessarily reflect the Federal priorities, regardless of the internal structures.

However, notwithstanding this autonomy, the State governments can also, from time to time, act as the agent of the Federal government and implement Federal policy. Thus, the State can act independently or in co-ordination with the central authority. Needless to say, there is a great degree of variations within this overall picture between the states.

Local government

There are four distinct levels of local government in Germany, namely Counties (Bezirke), Physical Planning Regions (Regionen), District (Kreise) and Municipalities or Communes (Gemeinden). Local government is given a relatively high degree of autonomy by the German Constitution or Basic Law. By far the most significant of these local levels of government are the communes and the districts. As was noted above, the lower levels of local government derive their authority in a number of ways; by implementing State or Federal legislation on an agency basis for example, or by managing areas for which they have sole and direct responsibility.

The Basic Law identifies three distinct methods for the implementation of legislation which governs the relationship between the municipalities, the districts, the States and the Federal government. These are:

- legislative jurisdiction to be administered only by the Federal government;
- legislative jurisdiction to be implemented concurrently by the states and the Federal government;
- legislation which is administered in detail by the states, but for which a framework is provided by the Federal government.

The relationship between the States and the lower levels of local government are equally well defined. Thus, it is conceivable that some forms of legislation could pass directly through from Federal to municipal government, while others would need to pass through three separate legislative processes, with each successive part of the process becoming increasingly detailed.

The two remaining levels of local government (Planning regions and Counties) do not, for the most part, have executive powers and tend to concentrate upon providing a physical plan within which local decisions can be made. As these plans achieve legal status, usually at State level, the role of the Planning regions is increasingly to monitor local decisions against the planned framework. Increasingly, these plans cover not only land-use issues but also broader environmental issues that are affected by land use, such as pollution. The function and importance of these plans is, therefore, growing (Koblhammer, 1987).

ENVIRONMENTAL RESPONSIBILITIES

It is stated above that there are three formally defined routes through which the responsibility for legislative implementation may progress: Federal; concurrent; and 'State based'. It is into the latter two categories that environmental legislation falls predominantly. Notwithstanding this localization of the responsibility for environmental implementation, the Federal government maintains its responsibility for providing a national framework. Therefore, it is with Federal environmental organizations that this analysis begins.

Federal structure

Figure 13.1 shows the structure of the Federal Ministry for Environment, Nature Protection and Reactor Safety. This Ministry was formed only relatively recently, in 1986. Until this time, environmental responsibility was spread between two ministries: the Interior; and Food, Agriculture and Forestry. With the creation of the new Ministry, very specific powers were transferred to the new organization, including: environmental planning and co-ordination (except spatial planning); water resources policy; nature conservation; landscape planning (David, 1992). Furthermore, the Ministry represents the country at international conferences, and consequently helps to develop the relevant frameworks.

The Ministry (usually referred to as BMU) only spends some 1% of its budget on nature conservation and landscape protection. This is, however, a misleading figure (Baldock, 1988). The issues of nature conservation and landscape are not usually separated within German legislation, and both are implemented by State or Local Authorities, or indeed all public and government agencies. The 1976 Nature Conservation and Landscape Management Act (Federal Government, 1976) lays a responsibility upon all public bodies to 'support the aims of nature and landscape conservation within the limits of their own competence'.

In order to co-ordinate cross-ministerial activity on environmental issues, a Cabinet Committee was also created in 1986. Furthermore, an advisory group of experts was also drawn together (*Umweltrat*).

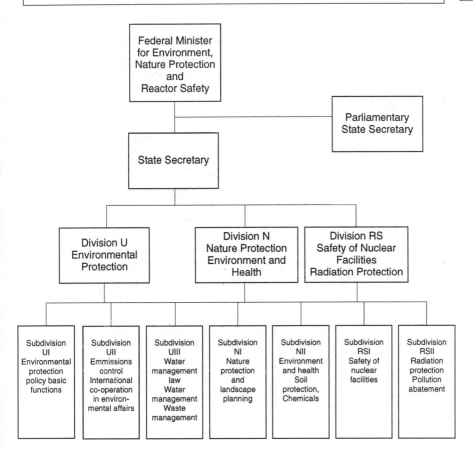

Figure 13.1 Federal Ministry for Environment, Nature Protection and Reactor Safety.

The contact between the Federal and State governments (Bund and Lander) is through the Conference of Ministers. For environmental matters, the most important are the Environment and Agriculture meeting. The role of these meetings and standing committees is to ensure, as far as possible, that there is a logical progression in policy making and implementation through these layers of government.

State responsibilities and structures

The framework, both Federal and international, within which the individual German states operate is identical. As a result, and also partly as a result of the Conference of Ministers discussed above, the Acts that are introduced by the various State Governments are, to a large extent also similar if not identical. However, the organizational structures are far from identical. The clearest result of this is that the environmental issues which are covered by a single ministry of Federal level can be covered by several ministries at State level. Similarly, the 'tradition' of earlier administration for encompassing environmental issues within other ministries (notably agriculture and/or forestry) still prevails in several states.

In Baden-Wurttemberg for example, a Ministry for the Environment was created as recently as 1987. While in Schleswig-Holstein none has as yet been created. Instead, the environment is covered by a division of the Ministry of Food, Agriculture and Forestry, although it is often debated within the State whether or not an Environmental Ministry would be of benefit to Schleswig-Holstein (Baldock, 1988).

Another model can be found in Bayern, where the Environment is part of the Ministry of State Development and Environmental Issues. This reflects the importance of the State-led physical planning process, as discussed above. Perhaps the most wide-ranging State ministry is found in Nordrhein-Westfalen where it covers environment, physical planning and agriculture.

With only a few exceptions, in most States the national ministries do not have local or regional basis; for the executive function they rely upon the various levels of local government. Thus, while the States carry a large proportion of the constitutional authority for legislation, the implementation is quite often carried out at a more local level.

Other agencies

The Federal Government established a research agency to inform the decision making of the BMU when it was formed in 1986. Thus, the Federal Research Institute for Nature Conservation and Landscape Ecology (BFANL) undertakes research into most of the functions covered by the corresponding Division within the BMU. These include: species protection and control of the 'red list' of endangered species; nature conservation; game research; landscape management; environmental impact assessments; and habitat loss and protection.

LAND DESIGNATIONS

The Federal Nature Conservation Law of 1976 set the framework for the system of land designations in Germany. In addition to this, numerous State laws influence the land designations, as too do the Regional Planning Programmes. The process of managing the various land designations is undertaken by the State Authorities rather than the Federal government.

This is in common with most environmental issues in Germany (University of Bonn, 1993).

The Nature Conservation Law identifies four types of land designation which provide the basis for nature conservation in Germany. Collectively, they cover some 11% of land in the country (Table 13.1). The individual designations are discussed below.

Table 13.1 Area of designated protected areas in Germany

	'000 km²		
1980	1985	1990	1990 (% of total area)
2.9	5.3	29.6 [49.5]	11.0 [13.9]

National Parks

The National Parks are relatively large, with the smallest being 13 000 hectares, and the largest 285 000 hectares (Table 13.2). The overriding criteria for a National Park is that it must 'be sited in a region that has suffered little or no human influence, thus ensuring as a priority the protection of the indigenous fauna and flora and retaining the greatest possible variety of species' (Article 14 of the Federal Law). Only as far as is compatible with this primary objective can recreation or access be permitted in National Parks.

Table 13.2 National Parks in the Federal Republic of Germany (Natur und Landschaft, 1987, **62**, 4)

Name of National Park	Year of institution	Address	Area (hectares)
Bayerischer Wald	1986	8352 Freyunger Str. 2 Grafenau	13 000
Berchtesgarden	1976	8243 Ramsau, Berchtesgaden	21 000
Niedersächsisches			240 000
Wattenmeer	1985		
Schleswig-Holsteinisches			
Wattenmeer	1985		285 000

As is explained above, there is no clear distinction made in legislation between nature conservation and landscape protection. As a consequence, National Parks in Germany seek to protect both of these elements of the natural heritage.

The initiative for designating National Parks come from either the Federal, or more usually, the State government.

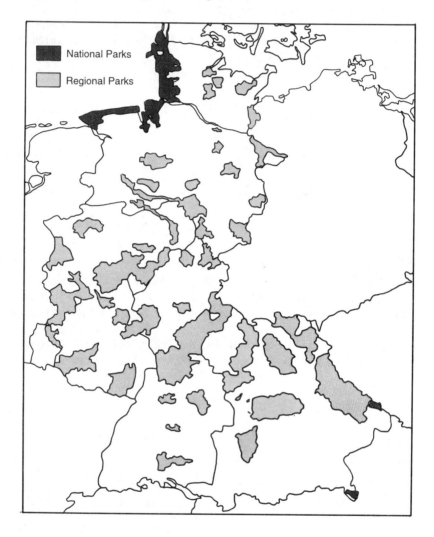

Figure 13.2 National Parks in Germany.

Nature Parks

The requirements for a Nature Park, as defined in Article 16 of the Federal Law are that the area should be sufficiently large (they range from 4000 hectares to 200 000 hectares) worthy of protection and just as critically, suitable for recreational use and some tourism development. To this end, Nature Parks must be planned and managed, by the State Authorities, to accommodate access and recreation.

There are over 65 Nature Parks in Germany, and they account for the bulk of the designated areas in the country. Some, such as Luneburger Heide (Luneburger Heath) were designated as special sites as long ago as 1920, and were absorbed into the new structure with the advent of the Nature Conservation Law of 1976.

The Nature Parks contain many smaller, more specific types of land designation, and are not continuous tracts of unspoiled or inaccessible land. Therefore, they can be compared to British National Parks or French and Belgian Regional Nature Parks in their form and objectives.

Nature Protection Areas

Article 13 of the Nature Conservation Law of 1976 defines a Nature Protection Area as an area of land that requires special measures to protect: living communities; certain species; scientific/natural/historical interests; uniqueness and/or beauty. This protection includes the banning of all activities which might destroy or damage the integrity of the area that is being protected.

However, as with Nature Parks, public access may be permitted if this access is compatible with the protection of the area.

Table 13.3 Nature protection areas in Germany

Size (hectares	1976		1986		1976–86
	No.	%	No.	%	%
0– 0.9	29	2.6	35	1.5	−1.1
1– 4.9	212	19.1	321	13.5	−5.6
5– 9.9	168	15.1	381	6.0	0.9
10– 19.9	187	16.8	443	18.6	1.8
20– 49.9	214	19.2	523	22.0	2.7
50– 99.9	118	10.6	278	11.7	1.1
100– 199.9	78	7.0	178	7.7	0.7
200– 499.9	48	4.3	125	5.3	0.9
500– 999.9	26	2.3	57	2.4	0.1
1000–4999.9	21	1.9	27	1.1	0.8
> 5000	11	1.0	6	0.3	0.7
Total	1112	100.0	2380	100.0	–

By and large, the Nature Protection Areas are relatively small, and concentrate upon protecting specific features such as ponds, clumps of trees or well-defined habitats. Table 13.3 shows that over 50% of Nature Protection Areas were 50 hectares or less in size in 1986. This compares with the smallest Nature Park in the same year of 15 000 hectares. Clearly, therefore Nature Protection Areas are smallish nature reserves, and can be located within the boundaries of the larger parks, thus offering two-tier protection for the most valuable sites within a generally valuable environment.

Landscape Protection Zones

Having said that the German Federal Law on Nature Conservation does not draw a clear distinction between nature conservation and landscape conservation, the designation of Landscape Protection Zones covers specific landscape features, such as trees, geological or heritage features. This is a designation, therefore, focusing on landscape issues, rather than nature/landscape.

As with Nature Protection Areas, Landscape Protection Zones are relatively small, and concentrate upon protecting very precise features of the landscape.

Summary

Finke (1991) suggests that 'it can be assumed that the designation of national parks and nature reserves has largely been completed'. As a result, the foregoing analysis for the former West Germany could be seen as being comprehensive. The next phase of the process, therefore, would be to extend this coverage into the Eastern part of the country.

The theme of slowing down of land designation is one which repeats itself across Europe, with the initial rushes of activity now slowing down. Another recurring theme is that of pressure on valuable habitats and environment from leisure or recreational activities. Finke (1991) argues that 'the greatest danger for conservation areas today is presented by the wide range of leisure activities'. This is increasingly one of the greatest demands upon natural environment across Europe and indeed the world.

The main responsibility for designation lies with the States, which operate within the framework provided by the Federal Laws. Smaller land designations are often the joint responsibility of the State and the Counties/Municipalities.

OTHER ISSUES

The variety of landscapes and habitats within Germany range from the Alpine summits to the lowland pastures of Schleswig-Holstein. As a result, the variety of other issues that determine the efficiency of nature conservation measures is equally as great. Agriculture, water management, and leisure planning all have an impact upon nature conservation to a varying degree.

The following analysis looks at these three areas of policy development within Germany and briefly assesses their impact.

Agriculture

The rationalization of the Common Agricultural Policy has been felt as hard in Germany as anywhere. This is partly because the original Mansholt Plan was created to a large extent with German input. The amalgamation of farms and the consequential loss of the number of people earning their living from farming led to an intensification of agricultural practices, and social problems in rural areas in the 1980s (Schopen, 1987).

As a means of resolving these pressures, and of resolving the scandal of the intervening prices reaching unacceptable levels, the German government undertook four measures: promoting alternative crops; promoting new crops; restriction of quota levels; and removing land from agriculture (so-called set-aside). Thus, the pressures for intensification, as cited above, have given way to the need for the removal of land from agricultural production.

Connected to this is the move towards incorporating ecological policies in agricultural processes. While it is accepted that this process has a long way to go, it is felt that there have been some positive moves in this direction, (Schopen, 1987). One tradition of this is the amount of subsidy offered to farmers to safeguard landscape and ecological features (Table 13.4).

Table 13.4 Average compensation payments in the Republic of Germany, 1986

Programme aims	Dm per hectare per annum
Preservation of water meadows and marshlands	490
Preservation of arid grassland areas	440
Protectionof meadow breeding birds and fowl	375
Preservation and maintenance of orchards	375
Preservation and care of hedges, woods and thickets	3500
Protection of flora and fauna perimeters around ploughland and meadows	1610
Restrictions on ploughing green meadowland, restoring ploughed land to green meadowland	250

However, notwithstanding these trends, 'damage caused to the environment, resulting from modern agricultural practice continues to increase' (Gotter and Wenk, 1988).

Water management

The Water Resources Acts of 1957, amended in 1986, lays down the guidelines for the management of water quality and supply. This work is administered by the 21 Federal States and, as a result, there is relatively little institutional confusion between water management and other nature conservation functions. However, the issues of water quality and the possible conflicts between water extraction and conservation still remain (Mooler, 1987). For example, over 14 000 water extraction plants clearly have an impact upon wetland habitat quality. Where this happens in designated areas, the pressure for water supply usually takes precedence. Similarly, it has been estimated that 11% of Germany's surface area is required for catchment of good quality water. More often than not this restricts the volume of agricultural production that can take place within the catchment area, and can restrict the land available for nature conservation.

The main areas of conflict remain the balance of water quality, and the impact that drainage has on delicate wetland habitats.

Recreation and tourism

There is no overall legislative framework for recreation and tourism in Germany, and as a result the provision of recreational development usually rests with local authorities, with any broader initiatives being formed as an amalgamation of these initiatives.

The creation of the Nature Parks was, in part, a response to the demands for recreation and leisure opportunities in the natural environment. These parks are usually identified within Regional Plans as being the focus for leisure activity. However, it is rare that centres of urban population contribute to the management of these rural areas.

The concentration of some leisure activity in very delicate areas has led to the usual problems of habitat and environmental damage. This has been particularly noticeable in the Alps and on the Baltic Coast. In order to try to combat this, and to prevent similar situations arising elsewhere, Regional Ministries draw up tourism plans which seek to regulate the flow of recreational and tourism traffic. However, these plans run into difficulties because of the administrative arrangement between States, Lander and the Regions.

Signing of conventions

By 1989, Germany had signed all of the conventions discussed in Chapter 6.

Implementation of EC Directives

The formal adoption and implementation of EC Directives is determined by several criteria. Thus, the efficiency of the process varies. These criteria include issues ranging from the process of interpreting the Directives to the more widespread problems associated with the implementation of laws through a multistructured system, and those associated with the conflict between EC law and Federal or State laws.

On this latter issue, a good case in point is provided by the Nature Protection Law. At State level in Germany, species of animals and plants are protected from harmful interference except 'for reasons of farming and forestry exploitation'. By comparison, the EC Directive 79/439 (Birds and their Habitats; see Chapter 5) determines that this clause is inconsistent with protection of rarer species. Thus, in 1987, for example, the European Court deemed that this 'farming clause' was illegal. At a lower level of administrative jurisdiction, the Lander gives permission for hunting, which again is often in contravention of EC Directives. This latter point is complicated by the fact that several layers of legislation need to be amended before the Lander can adjust their own laws.

It must be stressed that in the former of these cases, the German Federal and State Governments do not contest the conflicts and are amending their own National Legislation. None the less, the process remains a relatively slow one. Therefore, in cases where the inconsistency is contested, longer delays are inevitable. This is the case in the latter example, where the Lander wish to continue to allow hunting of certain members of the crow family (*Corvidae*) in contravention to the EC Directive.

SUMMARY

The overriding priority for all of German socio-political activity since 1990/91 has been the process of reunification. Against this backdrop, all other issues have taken second place. Furthermore, the single most important facet of reunification has been the economic restructuring that has been necessary. Within this immense challenge (and it is worth keeping the enormity of the impact of reunification in mind) the process of nature conservation clearly faltered.

Part of this was directly as a result of the need to bring the former East Germany into line with West German practice. In reality, this meant that environmental designations (and indeed all environmental legislation) had to be reframed to bring all of the reunified Germany onto the same level. Subsequently, the effort has been in putting administrative and operational systems in place. This in itself has been an enormous task, and one which will take several more years to complete.

For this reason, it is somewhat false to try to compare the systems and processes in the two parts of the formerly divided Germany.

Ultimately, the framework will contain the land designation components discussed in this chapter, but it is also evident that the wider environmental concerns will begin to be equally important. This is because two other elements have increased in significance – one a consequence of reunification and one a result of changes at a European level. The first issue is that of pollution which was significantly worse in 'East' German industry than in the 'West'. Consequently, the environmental work of the German Government has begun to focus more on this aspect. The second change is that of the Common Agricultural Policy (CAP), which was influenced heavily by Germany through the Mansholt Plan. Now, CAP is about to be influenced by the changes taking place in political opinion about the CAP. This in turn will influence the existing pattern of farming in Western Germany and will also modernize the Eastern European agriculture industry.

REFERENCES

David C.-H. (1992) The organisational structure of German Government, in *European Environmental Yearbook*, DocTer, Milan.

Federal Government (1976) *Bundesnaturshut – gesetz*. Bonn.

Finke, L. (1991) *Parks and Nature reserves in Germany* (translation). University of Dortmund, Dortmund.

Gotter, F. and Wenk, H (1988) Produktion von Landshaft. *Agra-Europe*, **28**(17). Sanderbeilage.

Koblhammer, W. (1987) *Umweltgutachten*. Stuttgart.

Mooler, M.W. (1987) *Wasserversorgung in der Bundesrepublik Deutchsland*. Bundesminister des Innen, Bonn.

Schopen, W. (1987) Removing land from agriculture in Germany, in *Farming and the Environment*. IEEP, London.

University of Bonn (1993) *Natur und Landschaft*, **68**(4). Bonn.

Greece

14

Greece is a relatively recent entrant to the European Community, having signed the Treaty of Rome in 1981. It is also one of the newest democracies within the EC, having adopted its new constitution in 1975. These facts, coupled with Greece's location on the south-eastern corner of Europe, suggest that Greece's role within the European community is emerging at the same time as its internal democratic system. In these respects, there are parallels with Spain (see Chapter 20).

The country itself is similar to its fellow Mediterranean Member States. Its biogeographical status is almost exclusively Mediterranean with its corresponding relatively low rainfall and high average temperatures. Greece's population density is one of the lowest in the EC, notwithstanding the very low densities of the two most recent Scandinavian countries. Perhaps surprisingly, the agricultural land only covers 54% of the country; however, this is explained by the fact that a large proportion of the land is classified as rough forest or scrubland, which is not defined as either agricultural or forestry land use.

Greece's entry to the EC was based upon its need to regenerate its mainstream economy; with a GDP of $7800 per capita in 1992, Greece was then the poorest country in the Community. Perhaps this partly explains why only 0.8% of the country is protected by conservation designations because it has been evident that Greece's priorities have remained in economic development over the recent past.

POLITICAL STRUCTURES

Greece has traditionally had a centralized administration, focused on the decision making within the capital. Even with the new constitution of 1975, this history was maintained. Thus, the government of the regions and prefectives is through appointed representatives of the central government ministries. For this reason, the most significant governmental structure is clearly at the National level, with the government of the Regions (*Peripheries*), prefectives (*Nomoi*) and municipalities all localized agents of the central government.

Plate 10 The many islands in Greece provide many valuable habitats, but also opportunities for tourism.

National government

Government elections are by universal suffrage, with two levels of elected representations being present. The President of the Republic and the Chamber of Deputies are responsible for legislative functions, and the Prime Minister is responsible for the executive and implementation roles.

This executive arm of the Government is serviced by a professional and paid Civil Service with the work being departmentalized into a number of ministries. These ministries are each headed by an elected minister. This model is common throughout most of the European Community. There are some 13 ministries within the Greek government, which again are common across Europe: Ministry of Transport, Ministry of Agriculture, and Ministry of Foreign Affairs, for example. Others, however, reflect Greece's

Table 14.1 Ministries and their environmental responsibilities in Greece

Ministry	Responsibilities
Ministry of the Environment, Physical Planning and Public Works	Co-ordination of various public and private agencies for monitoring and for Environmental Protection projects. Transboundary pollution. National parks. Protection of the atmosphere. Quality controls for recreational waters. Monitoring of chemical and biological (e.g. coliform) environmental quality variables. Control of industrial emissions and effluents discharged to the atmosphere, into sewage networks or natural waters. The Ministry 'shadows' the independent Organizations for Water Supply and Sewerage of the area of Athens and Thessaloniki. The Ministry is also responsible for the physical and city planning issues.
Ministry of Merchant Marine	Protection of Marine Environment from oil spills, vessel waste and dumping into the sea. Inspection and control of coastal industries, tourism etc. Installations. Imposition of fines.
Ministry of Health, Welfare and Social Security	Evaluation of all bacteriological results of sea water analyses, further bacteriological determination in sea water, shellfish etc. (at the Central Public Health Laboratory, the Athens School of Hygiene), classification of the beaches according to the quality of their waters. Management, cleansing and improvement of sewerage and waste disposal systems.
Ministry of Agriculture	Protection of forests, National parks, fishing resources. Monitoring of rivers, inspection of areas of aquaculture etc. Control of hunting and uses of chemicals in agriculture.
Ministry of Macedonia and Thrace	Study, monitoring, control of air pollution of Thessaloniki, water pollution and sea waters of Thermaikos Gulf and various gulfs and other sites of Northern Greece. Many responsibilities of the Ministry of the Environment and other services have been recently passed to this Ministry.
Ministry of Industry Research and Technology	Co-ordination and financing of scientific research on environmental issues. The Ministry 'shadows' the National Centre of Marine Research.
Ministry of Commerce	It 'shadows' the general chemical laboratory (of the State) that has branches in all Prefectures. Several analyses of environmental variables are carried out there.

Table 14.1 (*cont'd*)

Ministry	Responsibilities
Ministry of Foreign Affairs	Transboundary pollution, international collaboration for the protection of seas, rivers etc. within UNEP, OECD, UNESCO (IOC) etc.
Ministry of Transport	Legislation, monitoring and control of car emissions.
Ministry of Interior	Responsible for the sewerage networks and new treatment plants of municipalities.
Hellenic Bank of Industrial Development	Control and treatment of the industrial effluents within the designated 'industrial sites' organized and operating under its supervision.
Ministry of Tourism	Monitoring and control of effluents from hotels and other tourist installations, planning of tourist development.

history and source of traditional wealth, such as the Ministry of Merchant Marine or The Ministry of Tourism. Table 14.1 identifies some of these ministries, as well as their environmental functions.

It is accepted wisdom that the Greek economy fits one of the models identified in Chapter 3. The central urban centre around Athens suffers the environmental problems faced by many larger conurbations. For example, air pollution levels in Athens were, in the early 1990s, amongst the worst in the world (Siskos, 1991). Conversely, the rural areas of the country suffer the decline associated with many of Europe's remoter rural locations. These include depopulation, unstable economic base and low levels of local expectations. Consequently, in the new constitution of 1975, the focus for much of the new government was economic regeneration in rural areas. As a result, the central government structure was geared towards this objective, with the Ministries of Agriculture, Tourism and Physical Planning being very powerful. This has changed slightly since the early periods of the new structure, but the underlying objectives still remain important. Article 24 of the new constitution, for example, declares that 'The State should take all measures necessary to develop sources of national wealth in the atmosphere, in underground and underwater deposits, to promote regional developments and advance especially the economy of mountainous, insular and border areas'.

Local government

The centralizing of most of the authority of government in Greece is reflected in the nature of local government. Greece has 54 *Nomoi*

(Prefectives, or subregions). The system of administering these *Nomoi is* consistent throughout the country. In each area, all the central government ministries are represented. The head of each of these local ministries and the overall co-ordinating agent, the Prefect, are each appointed by central government for a 1–4 year period. The Prefect and his or her Prefectoral Council have several areas of delegated responsibility and authority, but all decisions are subject to possible central government amendment.

In 1989, the country's prefectives organized themselves into non-constitutional regional assemblies (*Peripheries*). There are 13 regions, each headed by a *Peripheriacis* whose task is to co-ordinate the work of each Prefective within each Region. As indicated, this work is potentially complicated by the fact that the role of the *Peripheriacis* is not contained within the 1975 constitution. As a result, the role only carries the authority that regional Prefects are willing to release to it.

At a more localized level of government, the municipalities or town councils have some powers delegated to them by the Prefectives. These powers are directly linked to the Prefectives through the same system which links the Prefectives and the State. The type of responsibility that is delegated is relatively localized work such as litter collection, the provision of sewage treatment works or small construction schemes.

ENVIRONMENTAL RESPONSIBILITIES

It is noted above that the primary objective of the Greek Government when it was formally constituted in 1975 was that of economic regeneration. This was undertaken on a sectorally based system (Organisation for Economic Co-operation and Development, 1988). Thus, the Ministries of Agriculture, Merchant Marine, Tourism, Industry and so on were established. Consequently, the issues of environmental conservation were separated and split among many ministries. This situation has not changed dramatically (as Table 14.1 suggests) although in 1985 the Ministry of Physical Planning, Housing and the Environment merged with the Ministry of Public Works under the new name of Ministry of the Environment, Physical Planning and Public Works.

This unification indicates several features of the environmental management process in Greece which have been highlighted by Scoullos (1991) and the Organisation for Economic Co-operation and Development (1985). First, the unification did not cover many aspects of the environmental management as Table 14.1 shows. Thus, the process of combining all of the relevant environmental responsibilities (or indeed most of them) was not carried through. This situation is not by any means unique to Greece. The second point is that the dominant feature of the new, large

Ministry is the physical planning and public works. Thus, the constitutional objective of improving the economic capacity of the rural and island areas is the overriding concern of the unified ministry, rather than that of determining environmental standards and protection criteria and regulations.

Finally, the issues of nature conservation and land designations are not part of the 'new' ministry but are still the responsibility of the more traditional ministries, particularly agriculture. This brings with it the potential difficulty in balancing different objectives and priorities within the same organizations. Again, it must be stressed that this is not unique to Greece, but the combination of these factors gives a particular weighting to the work of the Greek government.

At the Regional level, it has already been indicated that the Prefectives reflect the national government even down to the fact the Prefects themselves are appointed centrally. Consequently, the environmental responsibilities of the various ministries are also managed through the Prefects, and their other centrally appointed colleagues on the Prefectural Council.

Table 14.2 National parks in Greece (Scoulos, 1991a)

Name	Year of desig- nation	Location (Prefecture– Periphery)	Address	Area (hectare)
Olympos	1938	Pieria–Macedonia	Directorate of Forests, Katerini/Piera	3 998
Parnassus	1938	Evrytania–Phokis	Directorate of Forests, Amphissa	3 513
Parnis	1961	Attiki	Directorate of Forests, Attiki	3 812
Ainos	1962	Cephalonia	Directorate of Forests, Caphaloma	2 162
Gorge of Samaria	1962	Crete	Directorate of Forests, Hania/Kreta	4 850
Oeta	1966	Lamia–Thessaly	Directorate of Forests, Lamia	7 210
Pindos Range	1966	Grevena–Epirus	Directorate of Forests, Greneva	10 140
Vikos-Aoos	1973	Ioannina–Epirus	Directorate of Forests, Jannina/Epirus	3 300
Lake Prespa	1974	Florina– Macedonia	Directorate of Forests, Florinia	21 200
Sounion	1974	Attikionia	Directorate of Forests, Attiki	3 500

The National and local responsibility for nature conservation, particularly the designation of national parks and other protected areas, rests between the Ministry for the Environment and the Ministry of Agriculture. With only a handful of staff at National level, the Ministry for the Environment is particularly badly equipped to designate sites, without the added responsibility for managing them. Thus, the Ministry of Agriculture, with a significantly larger staff, both at National and local level, tend to administer and manage important sites.

Heritage landscapes

One of the earliest land-based protection laws in Greece was enacted in 1932. The Law for the Protection of Antiquities was, however, only concerned with historic sites and historic landscapes. Nature, as such, was not included in such a process. Thus, the Ministry of Culture is inevitably included in the protection of landscape. For this reason, for example, the first two protected areas within Greece are important for their historic or cultural background as much as for their natural history. Olympus and Parnassus (Table 14.2) were both designated in 1938, and whilst both are now designated as National Parks, both were originally designated by the Ministry of Culture to protect their historic interests.

Within Greece, perhaps more so than in any European country, the linking of heritage and archaeological importance of sites with natural history, is a very important consideration. For this reason, the recently established inter-ministerial boards draw upon a range of expertise, including natural historians and archaeologists.

Interministerial Committees

With the growth of international frameworks for nature conservation and indeed other environmental issues, there grew a pressing need within the Greek government to establish a cross-issue committee to attempt to co-ordinate the environmental work of the state. The International Committee was therefore formed out of the three Ministries of Agriculture, Environment and National Economy. It is interesting at this point to note that the latter ministry was included to the exclusion of the Ministry of Culture, thus breaking with the 'traditional' linking of heritage and natural history.

None the less, the Interministerial Committee does draw upon expertise from a wide range of consultants, academics and its own staff, and does work within international guidelines. The committee for example seeks to draw up multifunctional management plans for some of the more contentious areas including some highly pressured National Parks. The site of the Prespa National Park in the northern most area of Greece is one such case, where the pressure to develop lake side tourism has led to the need for a strong management plan (Scoullos, 1991).

Non-governmental agencies

One of the most influential non-governmental agencies in Greece is the Hellenic Society for the Protection of the Environment and Cultural Heritage (*Elliniki Etairia*). Here we see direct links between the natural and cultural heritage. *Elliniki Etairia* has been particularly forceful and successful in bringing pressure to bear on some sensitive planning decisions associated with vulnerable sites. These include the case of Lake Prespa cited above, and the historically important site of Delphi where an aluminium smelting plant had been proposed in 1987.

LAND DESIGNATIONS

Early legislation in Greece was principally concerned with the historic and culturally important sites of the country. Thus, in the 1932 legislation mentioned above, natural landscape and natural history were not mentioned. It was only in 1971 that the natural environment was legally acknowledged as being appropriate for protection in its own right. As we have already seen, however, early 'historic' sites also tended to protect natural landscape because of the close parallels between artificial features and their location within the natural environment. Following on from the 1971 legislation, and the new constitution of 1975 and subsequent laws, there is now a series of land designations which are used within Greece to protect the natural environment, as distinct from heritage landscapes. The most important of these are: National Parks, Aesthetic Forests and Natural Monuments. Others relate primarily to hunting and restriction to the game season.

National Parks

Greece has ten National Parks. Some of these are parks that have become designated as National Parks following earlier protection for artificial features (Mount Olympus being the best-known example), while others followed later with more specific legislation. Table 14.2 gives details about the National Parks and Figure 14.1 shows their locations.

The designation of National Parks in Greece has been a complicated process, however, and some designations may have been held up as a result. Following on from the designation of historic landscapes after the 1932 legislation, the responsibility for designated land lay with the Ministry of Culture. With legislation in 1971 and 1975, the Ministry of Physical

Planning, Public Works and the Environment became responsible for managing National Parks, but never had the resources to do so. As a practical reality, therefore, the Ministry of Agriculture takes up the management responsibility. As a means of trying to overcome some of this interministerial cross-working, legislation of 1986 sought to transfer some of the responsibilities from the Ministry of Agriculture to the Ministry of Physical Planning, Public Works and the Environment. However, this has not yet happened in full.

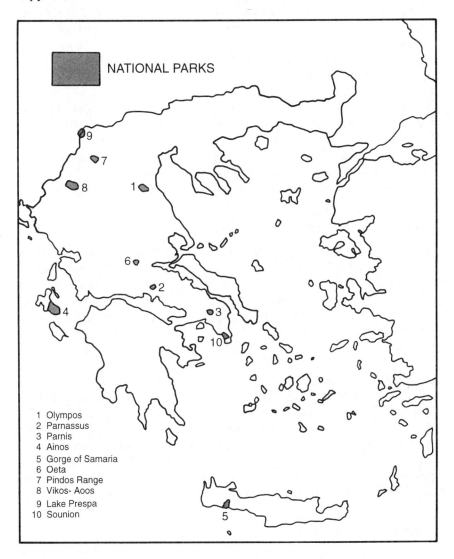

NATIONAL PARKS

1 Olympos
2 Parnassus
3 Parnis
4 Ainos
5 Gorge of Samaria
6 Oeta
7 Pindos Range
8 Vikos- Aoos
9 Lake Prespa
10 Sounion

Figure 14.1 National Parks in Greece.

As a consequence, the responsibility for designating National Parks lies with the Ministry of the Environment, but management lies with the Ministry of Agriculture, usually the Directorate of Forestry. Consequently, the Interministerial Committee spends some of its time on these joint management issues.

National Parks in Greece are designated to protect the natural integrity of the areas so defined, and no reference is made for tourism or recreational pressure. This is, however, a potential problem because, far from deflecting such pressure, no policy framework has been provided in which to deal with such issues. This is particularly relevant given the ever-growing tourist industry, particularly in coastal and island areas, and gives the overriding economic priorities for rural, coastal and island areas. Thus, by initially ignoring the recreation/tourism issue, the situation has, in the longer term, been made worse.

The natural or semi-natural forests of Greece forms the basis of many of the National Parks. Indeed, the importance of forests within the natural history of Greece can be seen from Table 14.2. This also brings with it the single most damaging problem for many National Parks in Greece: forest fires. Annually forest fires destroy up to 120 000 hectares, and some of the most important areas are within National Parks (Cassios, 1980).

Aesthetic Forests and Natural Monuments

Both of these land designations are the responsibility of the Ministry of Physical Planning, Public Works and the Environment. The former designation gives a clear indication to the origin of the whole National Parks movement in Greece. The management of forests and associated landscapes has long been associated with the management of the environment in general. The Aesthetic Forests and the Natural Monuments tend to be smaller than the National Parks, being similar to the specific habitat or biotope designation of other Member States. The overall area of land covered by these two designations is around 10% of that covered by National Parks. Indeed, as is common, the smaller designated areas tend to overlap in some areas with the larger designations. The greatest difficulty facing the Ministry of the Environment is the lack of staff time to prepare management plans for the sites, so designation is the only means available to the authorities to protect the sites from damage. This tends to be a negative responsibility, in that positive management measures cannot be undertaken without a plan so all that can be achieved is restriction of on-site action and activities.

Other designations

There is a large number of other types of land designation in Greece, which fulfil various functions. Some of these overlap with the designated areas mentioned above. For example, the Ramsar and Barcelona conventions have both given rise in Greece to land designations aimed specifically at fulfilling the objectives of those conventions. Some include some of the National Parks (such as the Gorge of Scimaria, or Sounion) or Aesthetic Forests (such as Skiathos Island or Pefkios-Xylokastron). Many of these Ramsar and Barcelona convention sites are a mixture of island and marine environments and are therefore relatively large, up to 100 000 hectares in some cases.

The Greek government has only designated areas that fulfil the objectives of the EC Birds Directive and the more recent Habitats Directive. Within the former category all the National Parks have been included, and some specific sites outside this framework. Similarly, with the Habitats Directive sites, National Parks and Aesthetic Forests feature relatively strongly.

The remaining designations relate specifically to hunting which is an important feature of Greek rural life, as indeed it is in many European countries. The types of designation/control include: Permanent Hunting Reserves; Controlled Hunting Grounds; Temporary Controlled Areas; Game Reserves; and Restricted Areas. It has been estimated that the area of land in Greece covered in some way by regulations to conserve wildlife (but ultimately so that it can be hunted) amounts to 5% of the land area (Organisation for Economic Co-operation and Development, 1981).

Finally, mention is usually made of the Athos Peninsula which is a large area controlled by Greek Orthodox Monks. Their policies of protection have made this area of land a de-facto nature or National Park, the quality of which would match the best of the officially designated areas.

OTHER ISSUES

Table 14.3 identifies the land use of Greece, and it is immediately apparent that forests (in their various forms) account for a large amount of land in

Table 14.3 Land use in Greece, 1992 (Directorate of Forestry, Ministry of Agriculture, 1992)

Type	(Area million hectares)	% of total
Cultivated land	3.96	30.0
Forests: Full	2.51	19.0
Partial	3.24	24.5
Rough	2.49	18.9
Lakes etc.	0.31	2.3
Urban	0.47	3.6
Rocks/barren	0.22	1.7
Total	13.2	100.0

Greece. Accordingly, the issues surrounding their management and upkeep have a great impact upon nature conservation. So too, of course, do the policies associated with agriculture, water management and, as is pointed out above, hunting.

Agriculture

Table 14.3 indicates that some 30% of land in Greece is 'cultivated' for agricultural use. Furthermore, there is a certain proportion of the land classified as forest that is used for rough grazing. The main conflict arising between agriculture and nature conservation stems not from the intensive use of chemical fertilizers or herbicides, but from problems associated with soil erosion (Modinos, 1992).

The reasons for this erosion vary. In the river watersheds and mountainous areas, for example, overgrazing which does not permit natural regeneration of woodland means that the seasonal heavy rains wash away the soil layers. It has been estimated that 3.5 million hectares, are thus affected. In other areas the wind accounts for the erosion.

In more intensively cultivated areas the process of crop rotation and shifting cultivation has also led to impoverished soil. Again, an estimate of land thus affected is put at 800 000 hectares (Modinos, 1992).

The Greek constitution dictates that the priorities for the government include those of increasing the economic well-being of the mountainous and island farming communities. There will therefore be increasing pressure to increase the intensity and geographic spread of the modern agricultural management. Without careful policy and planning, therefore, the problems of soil erosion could increase. Connected to this process, is the problem of salination; because of the increasing demand for larger quantities of water for irrigation, the water is both reused and drawn from greater depths. As a consequence, the quality of the water has decreased, and salts and high quantities of mineral are now found in much irrigation water. This and the previous problems are exacerbated by the fact that the Greek climate is so hot, and thus the regeneration of forests, the restoration of soil and the quantity of available water will always remain potential areas for concern (Ministry of Agriculture, 1992).

Water management

Given the foregoing analysis, it will come as no surprise that agriculture, rather than industry, is the main consumer of water in Greece (Zeris, 1993). The management of water supplies, and indeed all other issues, is controlled by local and municipal corporations funded by the State. The authority and responsibility of these corporations stems from the 1980 Law 'Concerning the establishment and operation of water supply and sewage companies'.

The supply of good quality water is a major concern for many areas of Greece. On the islands, for example, where there is little or no possibility for building reservoirs, water has to be shipped in by tanker, especially during the summer months, when tourists increase the demand.

The agricultural and domestic demands for water mean that aquatic and associated habitats are being compromised by lowered water tables, dried river or stream beds and poorer water quality. This is not to imply that water quality or supply is not regulated – normal EC standards apply, quite naturally. However, the gradual increase in demand clearly has an impact upon the nature conservation interests of the surrounding areas.

The large civil engineering projects needed to create reservoirs or to accomplish the diversion of water courses do bring some benefits for conservation. For example, Ramsar sites in Greece are artificially created, or at least have artificial components within them. Thus, the overall, often detrimental impact of major adjustments to water courses and basins needs to be balanced with the possible gains to be made in the creation of bodies of water and wetlands.

In order to meet EC standards, much of the older water treatment infrastructure is being upgraded within Greece. So the two main priorities in the management of Greek water resources is getting the supply to all users, and in ensuring the high quality of this supply. This is identical to other Member States. However, given the dry climate of Greece, it is a large and costly task. Added to this, the seasonality of much of the demand contributes to the management problems. Inevitably, therefore, the environment can suffer in the wake of large civil engineering projects.

Cultural heritage

Before the Greek government recognized its important Natural Heritage, it had acknowledged the vital significance of its cultural heritage, most noticeably the Greco-Roman legacy. Consequently early legislation was focused upon this facet of the country's importance, rather than the natural environment. This is worthy of note here for several reasons. First, the early conservation legislation in Greece addressed the need to protect cultural sites (the 1932 Law of Antiquities being a good example). The second point of importance is that the structure developed to deal with the management of antiquities was later adopted to manage the natural resources, i.e. a centralized framework. However, and this is a further point of significance, the early importance of the cultural heritage was reflected through a ministerial status. The somewhat later status of the natural heritage has meant, that no such comparable Ministerial status exists (UNESCO, 1989). Indeed, as we have seen, much of the physical management of the natural resource is undertaken through the Ministry of Agriculture, not the Ministry of the Environment.

Signing of conventions

Greece has signed all the conventions mentioned in Chapter 6 of this book with the exception of the Washington convention on trade in endangered species (CITES) and the Paris convention on water pollution.

Implementation of EC Directives

Following Greece's membership of the EC in 1980, a 5–8 year period of adoption and implementation of policies and directives was approved. While this got off to a relatively slow start (Scoullos and Kaberis, 1991) progress was made after this. Attention has been concentrated upon the policies of water quality and, more recently, waste disposal and toxic substances. The Directives associated with nature conservation have received recent attention.

The process of amending existing, often general, legislation to accommodate newer, more detailed and targeted Directives is inevitably a time-consuming process. None the less, this is the mechanism that has been chosen by the Greek government. The picture is further complicated by the involvement of several Ministries in each piece of legislation. This has been somewhat alleviated by the formalized cross-ministerial working, and new awareness of the need for progress.

Adoption of Directives is one issue, but far more important work is done in the implementation of the legislation. In this context, it has been argued (Scoullos and Kaberis, 1991) that Greece has been slower than it should in adopting the relevant legislation. Partly, this has been due to weaknesses at the appropriate technical level; a weakness which is now being addressed.

SUMMARY

There are a number of characteristics which Greece exhibits that are worthy of note as summary. Most significantly, in terms of the management system adopted, is the highly centralized nature of all of the Greek administrative system. Consequently, the management of nature conservation interests is similarly built up from a central core. Perhaps the most unique feature of the Greek organizational structure is that the protection of the natural environment is linked very closely with the protection of the cultural heritage. For example, Mount Olympus is designated as a National Park as much for its historic importance as for its natural history. This mirrors the broader definition of 'heritage' adopted by the United Nations in its designation of World Heritage Areas. However, within Europe it is a unique combination, particularly where the link is made at the organizational level.

The reason for this is easily identified; quite clearly the importance of the Greek cultural heritage was identified much earlier than that of the natural heritage. Consequently, the latter was aligned with the former in Greece, whereas in other countries, this alignment was with landscape or forestry authorities.

Probably as a result of this early concentration upon the cultural heritage, the importance of nature conservation did not develop significantly over this period. Furthermore, the concern of the 1970s and 1980s was almost exclusively economic development in Greece. Thus, the rural areas were developed for tourism and through other traditional economic means. Despite this effort, the GDP of Greece is still the lowest in Europe, but a change has been witnessed in the Greek view on environmental protection. This has resulted in a greater awareness of the damage potentially done to the environment by large-scale development. It has also resulted in more action to alleviate this damage, partly through pressure from European legislation and through new constraints on the grant regimes available from the EC.

REFERENCES

Cassios, C.A. (1980) *National Parks and Nature Reserves in Greece*. Nature and National Parks (Vol. 67). Department of the Environment, London.

Ministry of Agriculture (1992) *Land Use Change in Greece*. Ministry of Agriculture, Athens.

Modinos, M. (1992) Agriculture and the environment, in *European Environmental Yearbook*, DocTer, Milan.

Organisation for Economic Co-operation and Development (1981) *A Review of Environmental Policies in Greece*. OECD, Paris.

Organisation for Economic Co-operation and Development (1985) *Environmental Policy in Greece*. OECD, Paris.

Organisation for Economic Co-operation and Development (1988) *New Trends in Rural Policy Making*. OECD, Paris.

Scoullos, M. and Kaberis, H. (1991) EC policy implementation, in *European Environmental Yearbook*, DocTer, Milan.

Scoullos, M. (1991) Environmental organisational structure, in *European Environmental Yearbook*, DocTer, Milan.

Siskos, A. (1991) *Air Pollution in Athens*. Ministry of the Environment, Athens.

UNESCO (1989) *La Protection du Patrimone Culturel – Manvel des legislation nationales*. Paris.

Zeris, C. (1993) *Hydraulic Research and Planning*. Ministry of Public Works, Athens.

Irish Republic | 15

The Irish Republic was formally established in 1922, which makes it one of the newest States within the European Community. As a former colony of Britain, much of the legislation which precedes this date was based on British law and the country's position as a part of Britain. Consequently, the Irish Republic has had a massive internal agenda of reorganizing its political and administrative structures, as well as more recently accommodating changes necessitated by membership of the EC.

The country itself is dominated in land-use and employment terms by the agriculture industry, with 87% of land in some form of managed agricultural or forestry use. A further 5% is estimated as being non-managed agricultural use, such as rough grazing. Coupled with its low per capita Gross Domestic Product, this makes Ireland one of the poorer states in the EC. It is also one of the least densely populated, with an average of only 51 per km^2, compared to an EC average of 117. For three centuries, Ireland has had a history of emigration, largely to the United States of America and the United Kingdom.

Positioned on the western edge of the EC, the Irish biogeography is exclusively 'Atlantic'. Together with its relatively low-lying topography, this gives Ireland a varied natural history. Furthermore, being an island has also led to some variations not only from the European mainland but also from its neighbour, the UK; the absence of snakes in Ireland being the most famous example.

POLITICAL STRUCTURE

Having gained independence in 1922, the Irish people moved away from some of the organizational structures that had been part of its link with Britain. The resultant political system has therefore got some similar elements to Britain but also many in common with other EC countries.

National government

The Irish National Government has two elected houses, both of which have seats awarded through proportional representation. The two houses, the Dail and the Senate, are respectively the 'lower' and 'upper' houses. The two most important Heads of State are the Prime Minister (who is leader of the majority party in the Dail) and the Irish President, who tends to function in a non-executive role as Head of State.

The executive work of the Irish Parliament is implemented through a Departmental structure, each one of which is headed-up by a Minister of State, with sub-ministers supporting the Minister. The Departmental arrangements within the Irish Republic are similar to those found in many other countries, with Agriculture, Environment, Energy, Marine, Foreign Affairs, Forestry Fisheries and Tourism, and Labour being among the more important.

The administration of the departments is managed through a non-political civil service directly responsible to the Ministers.

Local government

Unlike the National Government, the organization of local government still relies upon the system put into place when Ireland was governed as part of the United Kingdom.

The 1898 Local Government Act divided the country into a number of organizational structures. These are: 27 County Councils, 4 County Borough Corporations, 7 Borough Corporations, 49 Urban District Councils, and 28 Incorporated Towns. By far the most important of these are the County Councils and the County Borough Corporations which cover the four largest cities in Ireland.

The County Councils and County Borough Corporations operate in two different ways. First, under some circumstances the authorities can act as agents for the central government under the direct control of the relevant minister. For the most part these matters are managed by the Department of the Environment, and relate mostly to planning or land-use issues. However, some of these direct mandates come from other Departments, notably Agriculture, Health and Welfare.

The other component of the County Councils and County Borough Councils work is that which is directly controlled by the locally elected representatives. The split in powers is defined by statute, and is also administratively split, with the County Manager taking a central role.

The powers of the major local authorities cover a number of areas, including housing; transport; water supply; development control and incentives; education; recreation; and environmental protection.

There exists, therefore, a balance between the function of implementing central government policy, and implementing local policies that have been drawn up by locally elected representatives (Scannel 1992).

ENVIRONMENTAL RESPONSIBILITIES

There exists within the Irish Republic, as elsewhere, a split in responsibility for environmental issues. This necessarily includes nature conservation and other land-based environmental issues. This split has two main directions: across and between departments; and vertically between the various levels of government. As intimated, this pattern is represented in other countries but perhaps what makes the situation unique is the fact that, given the relatively recent formation of the nation, the pitfalls of split-functions could have been avoided. The fact that they were not reflects the fact that other issues were at the top of the young nation's agenda. However, the Irish Republic did take the opportunity to use its Presidency of the European Community to focus on the global, European and national environment, and consequently addressed some of these issues (Institute for Environmental Studies, 1992).

National responsibilities

The focus on the environment brought about by the Irish Presidency of the European Community was not the first move towards rationalizing the environmental responsibilities of National Government. In 1986, some parts of the Department of Forestry, Fisheries and Tourism were linked into the Department of Finance to bring together the land-based management of conservation areas. Figure 15.1 shows the situation prior to and after this reorganization. As a consequence of these changes, the two most significant departments are, somewhat ironically, the Department of Finance and the Department of the Environment. The Department of Finance has, more recently, passed some of its responsibility to the Department of the Environment, but the bulk of the management responsibilities still remain with the Treasury.

The role of the Department of the Environment is less clear, at least in the area of land-based conservation. The brief of the Department of the Environment is very broad, and includes most of the issues recognized at European level as being relevant. Thus, waste management, pollution control, Environmental Impact Assessment and monitoring of EC directives lies with the Department. For natural history, however, the Department has little significant input. The most influential section of the Department which had an impact on land management was *An Foras Forbartha* (Planning and Research Section) but this was abolished in 1987, with no cohesive plan for its work to be undertaken after that date. As a result, the research function was broadly absorbed back into the main work of the Department.

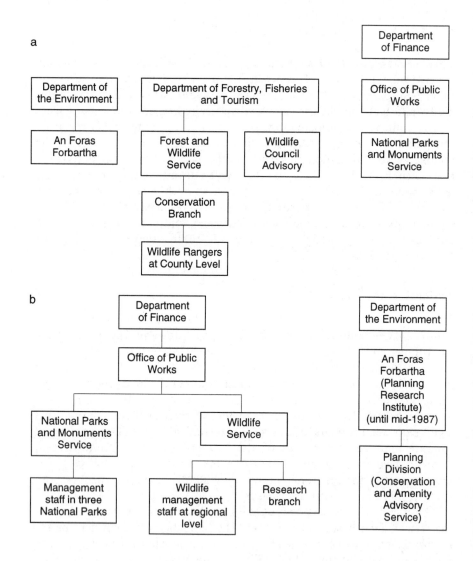

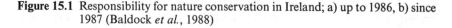

Figure 15.1 Responsibility for nature conservation in Ireland; a) up to 1986, b) since 1987 (Baldock *et al.*, 1988)

Consequently, the main implementation work for environmental conservation depends upon the type of work in question. As Figure 15.1 shows, for nature conservation this is, uniquely, with the Department of Finance. For other issues, it is with the more usual Department of the Environment.

Local government responsibilities

As was indicated earlier, the Local Government authorities in the Irish Republic perform their duties in two ways: as agents of central government, or as their own independently elected organizations. The range of environmental responsibilities is therefore wide, but of varying authority. There are eight general headings which reflect these responsibilities: Housing and Buildings; Road Transportation and Safety; Water Supply and Sanitation; Development, Incentives and Controls; Environmental Protection; Recreation and Amenity; Agriculture, Education, Health and Welfare; General/Miscellaneous Services.

Within each of these areas of responsibility, the precise areas of relationship and the differences between reserved and executive functions are laid down in legislation. Overall, the management is largely under the supervision of the Minister for the Environment (with other ministers being more or less important in the eight areas of responsibility defined above), while it is the actual management which is split. It is this interface which is the subject of the legislation.

One of the more important functions of local authorities in the Irish Republic is to safeguard the public consultation in the system of government. This is particularly relevant for the environmental responsibilities, where individual and non-governmental organizations tend to be particularly active in Ireland (Falk, 1992). The Planning Appeals Board is the channel through which complaints or local input is made to the decision-making process. These decisions can be at a strategic, issue or locally based level, and there is a well-established tradition of voluntary sector input into all levels of public decision. This tradition is most keenly seen at the local government level, with much less at National level: 'Extensive provision is made for public participation in environmental decision-making by local authorities, but not in internal decision-making by government departments' (Scannel, 1992).

Wildlife Service

Of the many agencies within Government in Ireland, the most significant for our purposes is the Wildlife Service.

The Service was formally known as the Forest and Wildlife Service, and has been a somewhat moveable agency, having been within three ministries since 1960. Currently, it is a separate unit from the Forestry Service. The Wildlife Service now resides within the Office of Public Works in the

Department of Finance (Figure 15.1). The Forestry Service has become a state-owned commercial agency (Coillte), established under the 1988 Forestry Act. Responsibility for the Service interestingly lies with the Department of Energy.

The Wildlife Service has several functions. One of its principal functions is to provide the ranger service which is employed at County or local level to enforce the Wildlife Act of 1976. Like all ranger services, the role is moving towards that of education and interpretation, but the location within the organizational structure is still in the Wildlife Service.

Another function of the Wildlife Service is to undertake research of species and habitats. This research has, as part of its overall objective, the identification of sites that are suitable and worthy of nomination for wildlife reserve status. The Service therefore has a vital role in implementing the Habitats Directive of the European Community.

Finally, the Wildlife Service can, if funds allow, purchase land where this is the best means of affording it protection. However, this capital budget is small and, consequently, these powers are of limited value (Baldock *et al.*, 1988).

Other agencies

There is a relatively chequered pattern of government-based advisory and executive environmental agencies within the Irish Republic. Two policy and advisory-based organizations (The Wildlife Advisory Council and *An Foras Forbartha*) were both abolished in 1987 despite having played important co-ordinating roles for central government. *An Foras Forbartha*, for example, drew up the 'Blue Book', a list of nationally important 'Areas of Scientific Interest' and also prepared the environmental overview, 'The State of the Environment' in 1985 (*An Foras Forbortha*, 1985).

One agency that has survived is the National Parks and Monuments Service. The Service not only manages the country's 200 000 or so sites of archaeological importance, but also the National Parks and some smaller areas. This management includes the physical management of the sites and also the environmental education and visitor management that inevitably follows from the designation of a National Park.

The movement between different Departments suffered by the Wildlife Service has not been witnessed by the National Parks and Monuments Service. However, the overall effect of the various adjustments has affected the efficiency of the Irish government to deliver its environmental programmes (Blackwell and Convey, 1983).

LAND DESIGNATIONS

Given the predominantly rural nature of the Irish landscape and natural environment, it may come as a surprise to find that only 0.4% of the land is covered by a protected status for nature conservation (Table 15.1). This is, however, a reflection of the perceived urgency for such designations rather than the quality of Irish habitats. Despite this low level of coverage, the species within the overall habitats are no less vulnerable in Ireland than they are elsewhere in Europe and the rest of the world (Table 15.2).

Table 15.1 Areas of designated protected areas in Ireland

	'000 km²		
1980	1985	1990	1990 (% of total area)
0.1	0.2	0.3	0.4

Table 15.2 Percentage of threatened species in Ireland

Species	% that are threatened
Mammals	16.1
Birds	24.7
Fish	–
Reptiles	–
Amphibians	33.3
Vascular plants	–

National Parks

There are few National Parks in the Irish Republic, as shown in Figure 15.2, and these are concentrated in the sparsely populated west of the country. These vary in size from 400 hectares to 10 000 hectares. The National Parks are all owned by central government and managed by the National Parks

Table 15.3 National Park areas in Ireland

Name	Year of institution	Area (hectares)
Killarney	1932	10 129
Glenveagh	1975	10 000
Connemara Letterfrack	1980	2 180
Burren	1978	400

Service. Inevitably, however, management agreements are made with local landowners so that appropriate land management practices are upheld. The main policy guidelines for the National Parks are that forestry and peat-cutting are phased out and ultimately stopped in perpetuity. There is also a heavy commitment to providing education and access to Irish National Parks so, in this respect, they resemble British National Parks rather than, say, the French or German examples which are more protectionist.

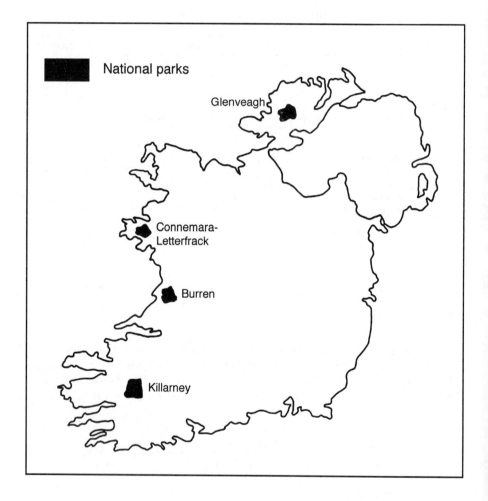

Figure 15.2 National Parks in Ireland.

Nature Reserves

There are around 65 Nature Reserves in the Irish Republic which are managed by the State. Most are on state-owned land also. The power to designate and manage Nature Reserves is given by the 1976 Wildlife Act, since when all delegations have been made. The reserves vary in size from 4 to 2250 hectares, and cover predominantly woodlands, peatlands, and estuaries as the dominant types (44%, 16% and 11% respectively).

The aim of the Nature Reserve designation is to protect named habitats and/or named species found on the reserve. To do this, certain damaging activities are restricted and positive management of the site takes place through the state ranger service. While educational and visitor use is not the primary aim, it is evident that the reserves have a vulnerable role to play in education. As a result, some of the larger or less delicate habitats have had educational programmes developed. This is particularly true for some of the more recently designated reserves, such as Clara Bog, in County Offaly, and Pollardstown Fen, in Kildare, both of which were acquired following prolonged public fund-raising campaigns.

Other designations

As elsewhere in Europe, there is a plethora of land designations which have been used to solve specific issues or have been piloted and are awaiting further policy development or proposals. There are three such land designations in Ireland that are worth considering here.

1. Refuges for Faunas have been designated on private land to protect habitats and to restrict hunting. Some 70 or more of these exist, and cover relatively small areas of land. These are also sometimes referred to as Wildfowl Sanctuaries because most of the sites seek to restrict wildfowling.
2. Environment Park. There is currently only one such site in the Irish Republic, around Slieve Bloom in Central Ireland. The concept of the Environment Park is relatively young, with the Slieve Bloom park having been designated in 1988. In its aims, it is similar to the French Regional Parks, with agreements between local authorities, landowners and tourism interests forming the basis of an environmentally based recreation and educational industry. The arrangements are still relatively informal and are awaiting further impetus to put the venture on a more statutory basis.
3. Heritage Zones are a relatively untested concept, but are a pilot idea designated to protect clusters of natural and artificial heritage sites and monuments. The concept would also go some way to protecting larger

areas of high landscape quality such as the wider area of the Burren Connemara or the Wicklow Mountains. The concept has been tested in the Clonmacnoise Heritage Zone.

Summary

The pattern of designations in the Irish Republic has been somewhat sporadic. For example, one of the pieces of research undertaken by *An Foras Forbartha* was the assembly of the list of Areas of Scientific Interest. Although some of these sites have been designated as Nature Reserves, the list as a whole has largely been forgotten. Similarly, the four National Parks do not look set to expand nor are new ones likely to be designated in the short to medium term. However, there are land designations that have been introduced over the past few years which have endeavoured to address the new agendas of 'green tourism' and broader heritage protection. As part of this agenda, the 1991 'Plan for National Recovery' lays great emphasis on the natural heritage of Ireland and how it is necessary to protect this heritage to safeguard not only the natural environment but also the long-term economic well-being of the country.

OTHER ISSUES

The Irish economy is traditionally dependent upon the agriculture industry and, despite the guidelines for diversification laid down in the Plan for National Recovery, this continues to be the case. Consequently, the most significant issues that impact upon nature conservation in Ireland are the management of agricultural land, and the related management of water in the country.

Agriculture

The Department of Agriculture has full responsibility for farming and food production in Ireland. By and large, the Irish agricultural policy has followed the Common Agricultural Policy, so is now gradually switching from maximizing farm output to farm diversification and improved structures. During this process, from 1975 to 1991, the number of farms fell from 227 900 to around 215 000 (Department of Agriculture, 1992), although over a comparable period (1975–85) land use did not alter significantly (Table 15.4).

The relevance of these changes is that together with some of the increases in livestock figures, they reflect an intensification of agricultural management across most of Ireland. Other factors suggest that the process of change to the environment continues, albeit in different ways. In recent years, for example, private forestry has become more significant, with grants covering 85% of preparation, planting and establishment costs in some areas. Furthermore, the Environmentally Sensitive Areas Scheme had not been adopted in Ireland as late as 1991, although plans were brought forward in 1992.

Table 15.4 Agricultural land-use change in Ireland

	1975 (million hectares)	1980 (million hectares)	1985 (million hectares)
Total area	6.89	6.89	6.89
Utilized area	5.71	5.70	5.71
Crops and pasture	4.69	4.70	4.70
Pasture	3.17	2.93	2.96
Hay and silage	1.07	1.21	1.24
Arable crops	0.46	0.55	0.50

It has been suggested (Hickie, 1991) that 'The main reason that some habitats still remain relatively intact is low intensity farming rather than conservation policies.' However, with the Irish Presidency of the European Council in 1990, the Government took the opportunity to re-establish its commitment to nature conservation and the development of environmental policy (Department of the Environment, 1990).

Water management

The geomorphological and climatic characteristics make the discharge of water 'a major preoccupation in Ireland' (Baldock, 1984). The main mountain ranges lie on the periphery of the country and large expanses of the central area are low-lying bog and fen. The driving force for this water management is the agriculture industry. Wet soils and slow drainage are serious disadvantages to a new and developing agriculture, but provide valuable wildlife habitats.

It has been variously estimated that from 1949 to 1980, some 1.2 million hectares of land (one-fifth of all agricultural land) received grants towards improving drainage. This annual rate of 31 000 hectares was not achieved in France, for example, until as late as 1974/75.

Drainage falls into two categories: main arterial improvements, and field-based improvements. The overall impact of this is unclear because little data exists for the pre-drainage environment. However, the impact is generally considered to be great (European Parliament, 1983; Merne

1990). It ranges from impact upon species of animals and plants, to the wholesale drainage of bogs and fens to the alteration to watercourses and their flow. This programme of drainage was initially supported by the European Community, but now policies within Europe mean that stricter environmental guidelines are now used when offering this grant-aid. As a result, the hoped-for balance between economic well-being, environmental protection and 'green tourism' could be achieved.

Signing of conventions

In 1993, Ireland had signed six of the eight major nature conservation conventions identified in Chapter 6. It had not signed either the Paris or Washington (CITES) conventions.

Implementation of EC Directives

Implementation of EC policy is through three mechanisms in the Irish Republic. The first is through 'Administrative Circulars' through which the Department of the Environment draws the attention of the responsible authority to relevant directives and instructions. The authority concerned is usually the County Council or equivalent. The second route for implementation is more satisfactory than the informal process of circulating information. The Department of the Environment can make legally binding Regulations under Section 3 of the Irish European Communities Act. This route is now the most common in Irish law.

The third and most comprehensive mechanism is to enact a specific piece of legislation to cover the European Directive. This has happened in some areas of environmental law (such as the Air Pollution Act of 1987) but not specifically nature conservation.

The speed of enactment or implementation can therefore, in theory, be very quick, but little information currently exists to test whether the administrative speed is matched in practice (Cabot, 1991). With the abolition of *An Foras Forbartha* and its replacement with a government department-run Environmental Research Unit, the gathering of this field-based information has been somewhat disjointed.

SUMMARY

When Ireland took over the Presidency of the European Commission in 1990, it chose to make the environment the cornerstone of its action programme. This, in many ways, represented a 'coming of age' for environmental policy making within the Irish Republic. After its break from British rule in 1922, the Irish Republic was concerned initially with its own development and its own identity. A lot of effort went into the protection of the cultural identity (particularly the language and the music). The natural environment was never perceived to be under threat.

In the 1980s, however, the need for the protection of the environment became an area of concern. This was focused on a number of significant and individual issues: the loss of the blanket-peat for fuel (particularly at the then recently opened peat fired power stations), and the development of deep-sea oil termini on valuable and attractive coastlines.

In a situation similar to that found in Greece, the Irish have begun to develop a sound basis for environmental protection, but this does not rely to any significant extent upon protectionist designations. With a low population density and a low GDP, the Irish also have the lowest area of protected land. This does not reflect a low value for these habitats or landscapes, but does reflect a 'phase' of environmental policy development which has been omitted due to the characteristics of the development of the Irish nation. The Irish now have the opportunity to move straight towards integrated conservation, having 'missed out' the designation of large areas of land.

REFERENCES

An Foras Forbartha (1985) *The State of the Environment*. DoE, Dublin.

An Foras Forbartha (1986) *Irish Environmental Statistics*. DoE, Dublin.

Baldock, D. (1984) *Wetland drainage in Europe*. International Institute for Environment and Development, London.

Blackwell, J. and Convey, F.J. (eds) (1983) *Promise and Performance: Irish Environmental Policy Analysed*. University of Dublin Press, Dublin.

Cabot, D. (1991) EC policy and implementation, in European Environmental Yearbook, DocTer, Milan.

Department of Agriculture (1992) *Agricultural Statistics*. Dublin.

Department of the Environment (1990) *An Environmental Action Programme*. DoE, Dublin.

European Parliament (1983) *Report on the Protection of Irish Bogs*. Working document 1-1180/82. Strasbourg.

Falk, N. (1992) *Voluntary Work and the Environment*. European Foundation for the Improvement of Living and Working Conditions, Shankhill, Co. Dublin, Ireland.

Hickie, D. (1991) Agriculture and the Environment, in *European Environmental Yearbook*, DocTer, Milan.

Institute for Environmental Studies (1992) *European Environmental Yearbook*. DocTer, Milan.

Merne, O.J. (1990) *Impact of Drainage on Wildlife*. National Board for Science and Technology, Dublin.

Organisation for Economic Co-operation and Development (1994) *Environmental Indicators*. OECD, Paris.

Scannel, Y. (1992) Organisational structure in the Irish Republic, in *European Environmental Yearbook*, DocTer, Milan.

Italy

16

Italy was one of the first Mediterranean countries to join the European Community, and as such has done a lot to shape the Community's policy towards the southern Member States. Within a single country, the variation between the industrialized areas of Europe and the traditional, peasant economies can be seen very clearly. So can the variations in habitat zones with 'central European', 'Alpine' and 'Mediterranean' zones all being present: only France has a comparable variety, but France is over twice as large.

With a population density slightly higher than the EC average, Italy is rapidly trying to improve its agricultural industry, as well as its other industrial base. However, as becomes evident in the following analysis, one of the main problems (if not *the* main problem) that has faced Italy over the latter part of the 20th century has been political uncertainty. There has been in Italy a rapid and continuing succession of coalition or single party government which has meant that continuity of policies has been difficult if not impossible.

POLITICAL STRUCTURES

Italy has undergone significant internal political change over the period since 1992. Triggered largely by allegations of political scandal, the changes have involved all levels of government, culminating in 1994 with a new government elected under new rules. However, the basic political structure of the country remains the same, with a division of power and responsibility between three levels of government: National, Regional and Provincial.

National government

The National Government in Italy has two elected houses of representatives. These are the House of Deputies and the Senate. The elections to appoint Members of Parliament and the Government of the day were up until 1993, by proportional representation. The Italian system was so constituted that the elected government very often found it difficult if not impossible to govern effectively. Consequently, over the decades that Italy has been a member of the European Community there have been upwards of 20 changes of government. This naturally brings with it serious problems of lack of continuity, lack of sustained policy initiative and, it must be said, low morale and esteem for the process of Government. The recent changes in the electoral process at National level have been initiated in order to overcome some of these operational and organizational shortcomings.

The elected representatives, as elsewhere, are served by a full-time executive organization; the Civil Service. Some of the key parts within this Civil Service remain political appointments, and each Ministry is headed by an elected Minister of State. The leading elected representative is the President of the Republic, who heads the government.

The Italian constitution also recognizes the need for an independent judiciary which, as a result of the history of frequent changes in government, has tended to develop its own continuity. The same can be said of the Civil Service which, although in theory is headed by individual Ministers, has also had to develop internal continuity to cope with frequent changes in the elected government (Baldock, D., Bower, G. and Clark, J., 1988). One reflection of this is the power of the government to issue Decree-laws, which are temporary but legally binding directives which must be ratified or revoked by Parliament within a given period.

The relationships between National and Regional governments are relatively confused, not only because of the historic lack of continuity at a national level but also because, under the Italian constitution, some regions have more authority than others.

Regional government

There are 20 regions in Italy (*Regioni*) as shown in Figure 16.1. Each of these has extensive delegated powers under the constitution, although five of these regions have greater powers than the others. These are: Sicily; Sardinia; Trentino-Alte Adige; Friuli-Venezia Giulia; and Val d'Aosta.

The Regional governments are locally elected and all have local responsibility for a wide range of functions, the transfer of which began in the 1960s and 1970s, but originated in the Constitutional Charter of 1948. In

1977, a law was enacted which speeded up this transfer of power, and effectively established the Regions as powerful administrative and political organizations.

1 Valle d'Aosta
2 Piemonte
3 Lombardia
4 Trentino/Altoa
5 Veneto
6 Friuli/V. Giulia
7 Liguria
8 Emelia-Romagna
9 Toscana
10 Marche
11 Umbria
12 Lazio
13 Abruzzo
14 Molise
15 Campania
16 Basilicata
17 Puglia
18 Calabria
19 Sicilia
20 Sardegna

Figure 16.1 Regions in Italy.

The 1977 Act (Presidential Decree 616/77) identified the precise responsibilities that were to be transferred, among which were many environmental issues. A further Law of 1984 (known as the Galasso Decree) identified further powers which were devolved to the Regions, and again there were several environmental issues among them. Notwithstanding these key pieces of legislation, the precise extent of each tier of Governmental responsibility remain relatively unclear. Despite subsequent minor decrees, this situation continues, and is worsened by the inconsistency within Central government (Orme, 1989).

Where issues inevitably overlap or cross Regional boundaries, central government retains some of the responsibility for cross-border co-operation. This is even the case for areas of responsibility which would normally be managed by the Regions. This also adds to some of the confusion, which has led one commentator to remark that 'one consistent aspect of the Italian legislative system is the fragmentation of responsibility' (Onida, 1991).

Provinces and municipalities

The lower levels of Government (around 100 'Provinces' and 8000 *Communi*) function in various ways. They often take responsibility for the day-to-day running and delivery of services for either the Regional or National governments. Alternatively, they are also independently responsible for some aspects of Government. These various levels of authority are inevitably concerned with very localized functions, such as building control, management of waste disposal or repairs to highway infrastructure. The strategic planning work and the major capital works are the responsibility of the Regions, who develop a plan within which the Provinces and Municipalities must operate.

The laws of 1977 and 1984 which built up the authority of Regional government also built up some of the responsibilities of the lower tiers of government, although not to the same extent.

ENVIRONMENTAL RESPONSIBILITIES

The foregoing analysis suggests that the lack of consistency in central and, consequently, Regional government has had a deleterious effect upon all policy areas within the country. Quite clearly, this applies to environmental matters in general and nature conservation in particular. However, more positive development in environmental conservation is the creation of a specialist Department of the Environment (*Ministero dell'Ambiente*) in 1986 with implementations in 1987. Thus at one level, matters have been allowed to develop in an *ad hoc* way, while at another, the government of Italy appears to have addressed some of the problems of inconsistency.

National government

Prior to 1986, the environmental remit of the Italian Central government was spread among several Departments. In 1986, the passing of Law 349 followed three years of work by the Minister of Environment who, up to that point, had been a Minister without a corresponding department. Given the relatively recent formation of the Department, together with the frequent (almost annual) changes to Central government, the Department of the Environment has been slow in organizing its own internal agenda. Indeed, in 1991 Onida (1991), indicated that even five years after its creation, the Department 'had yet to consolidate its structure, and the vigour coming from tradition and experience was lacking'.

The aim of the Department is to 'ensure, within an organic framework, the promotion, conservation and restoration of environmental conditions which safeguard the interests of the community and the quality of life, as well as the identification and development of the nations natural heritage and the protection of natural resources from pollution'. Such a broad remit was drawn from three main contributing departments (Agriculture, Culture and Tourism) with some responsibility remaining with these original departments. Indeed, it is interesting to note that after the formation of the Department of the Environment two drafts of proposed wildlife legislation were prepared; one by the Department of the Environment and one by the Department of Agriculture. Clearly, old habits die hard!

At a central government level, the Department of the Environment has a number of functions. First, it is the competent organization to represent the country at international meetings and fora. Second, the Department co-ordinates environmental activity across several ministries. The Department is also responsible for framing and managing environmental legislation across a wide range of issues reflected in its brief. In order to do this, the Ministry is divided into a number of Directorates, as shown in Figure 16.2, each with a portion of the overall brief.

The final role of the Department of the Environment which is of direct relevance here is that of designating some land-use categories, including National Parks, Sites of International Significance (such as Ramsar sites) and national sites of cross-regional importance.

The Department of the Environment has two advisory committees associated with its work: The Scientific Committee and The National Environmental Council. The latter is a group made up of representatives from the Regions; other local authorities; and representatives from environmental protection organizations in the voluntary sector.

The National Environmental Council also draws members from other governmental departments which have environmental functions within their areas of responsibility. Some of these departments have extended their environmental work since 1987 despite the creation of the Department of the Environment. These other departments include Health, Agriculture and Cultural Heritage. In particular, the Department of Cultural Heritage has acquired broad powers for artificial or cultural components, or where there are a number of individual sites within the landscape that are culturally important.

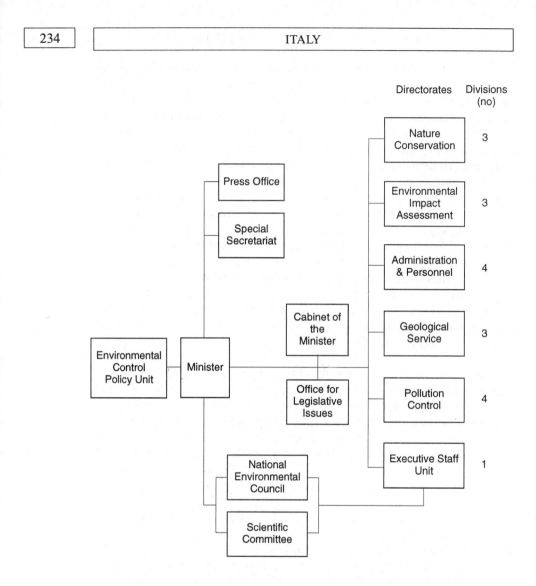

Directorates   Divisions
                (no)

Nature Conservation   3

Environmental Impact Assessment   3

Administration & Personnel   4

Geological Service   3

Pollution Control   4

Executive Staff Unit   1

Press Office

Special Secretariat

Cabinet of the Minister

Office for Legislative Issues

Environmental Control Policy Unit

Minister

National Environmental Council

Scientific Committee

Figure 16.2 Structure of the Italian Department of the Environment.

Of equal, if not greater importance to the Department of Cultural Heritage is the Ministry of Public Works. Initially the 1986 reorganization moved several of the Ministry of Public Works' responsibilities to the newly formed Department. However, from 1989 onwards a series of new laws (particularly Law 183 of May 1989) empowered the Ministry with 'Regulations governing the organisational and functional management in the area of soil protection.' Under the rationale of soil protection and more recently water management, the Ministry can intervene on most planning or

land-use issues, the main responsibility for which rests with another department. The work needed to co-ordinate this and other possible duplication
of work lies with the National Environmental Council (Cirietto, 1983).

The Regions

Since the formative law of 1977, which transferred much of the power from
central government to the Regions, the Regions have been keen to uphold
their environmental and land-use responsibilities. Within each Region, the
Ministries and Departments are structured differently, so there is no single
way in which they respond to environmental needs. Table 16.1 shows the
way in which four of the regions have created Assessorats or Departments
to cover environmental responsibility.

Table 16.1 Environmental administration in four regions of Italy

Region	Administration
Abruzzo	Assessorato for planning, land use and environmental issues; Assessorato for agriculture, forestry and food; Assessorato for education and culture, sports, hunting and fishery.
Liguria	Assessorato for agriculture, forestry, land protection and hydrogeological management; Assessorato for physical planning and economic planning; Assessorato for environment and housing.
Toscana	Assessorato for agriculture and forestry; Assessorato for physical planning and land use; Assessorato for environment and energy.
Veneto	Assessorato for agriculture, forestry, upland economy and EC relations; Assessorato for physical planning, environment protection, mining and extraction; Assessorato for public works and land protection.

As a general principle, the Regions tend to have a large degree of administrative freedom to manage their environmental affairs, but this action is
often controlled to some extent by the National Laws. This principle is,
however, only a very broad guideline, because there are several situations
that contradict this. For example, it was noted earlier that five regions enjoy
greater autonomy than the others. Of these Sicilia and Valle d'Aosta *do*
have the authority to draw up legislation on nature conservation, for
example. In yet another of the more autonomous regions, Trentino-alto
Adige, the authority to draft legislation is transferred to its two
autonomous provinces.

All regions are responsible for land-use planning and control, although again the degree of this varies from Region to Region.

It has been argued that the division of responsibilities between National and Regional government for policy creation and administration respectively causes unnecessary friction. How this should be resolved depends upon which side of the debate is listened to. Onida (1991) sums up the situation by suggesting 'constitutional jurisprudence regards the environment as a "mixed-area" in which State and Regions compete'.

Other levels of government

The Provinces and Municipalities by and large depend upon the Regions for their levels of responsibility. As we have seen, in one region the power to legislate is transferred to the Provinces. However, this is the exception rather than the rule, and most Regional authorities delegate the lower tiers of governments the day-to-day management of some affairs, which includes some environmental responsibilities. This ranges from street cleaning or pollution monitoring to the management of Regional Nature Parks.

LAND DESIGNATIONS

It has been suggested (Palladino, 1987) that there are two major camps in the agencies responsible for nature conservation and landscape conservation in Italy. (The distinction between nature and landscape is not usually made in Italy.) These camps are those who believe in centralized authority, and those who believe in regional responsibility. This is not surprising, given the foregoing analysis, and neither is it surprising, therefore, that the two largest and therefore most important groups of land designations are National Parks and Regional Parks.

National Parks

There are four National Parks in Italy, with a fifth (Calabrian) that has been designated, but no effective on-site management has been created. The legislation that has been used to create the National Parks pre-dates the Second World War, and all but the Calabrian Park were designated in 1935 or earlier.

The reason for this apparent inaction is that the rapid changes in National government and the upheaval caused by the creation of the 'new' Department of the Environment has meant that no cohesive legal structure to designate or properly manage National Parks has ever really had the chance to be formulated. In the four active National Parks, there was some dispute as to who was actually responsible for their management even as late as 1991/92. Figure 16.3 shows the location of the four plus one current National Parks.

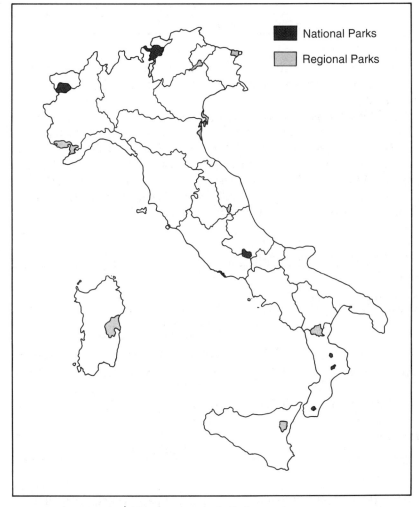

Figure 16.3 National and Regional parks in Italy

Also shown in Figure 16.3 are the proposed next generation of up to eight additional National Parks. Progress on these has been slow, for the reasons outlined above, but some movement is being made, with budgetary allocations being made provisionally in 1993/94. If all of these National Parks are designated, the land area protected in Italy by some designation would rise to around 10% from its current level of around 4.3% (Table 16.2).

Table 16.2 Areas of designated protected areas in Italy

'000 km²			
1980	1985	1990	1990 (% of total area)
4.1	5.2	13.0	4.3

The National Parks that have been designated are spread across Italy, with two in the northern Alpine area, two in central Italy, and one in the southern tip of the mainland.

All of the areas represent mountainous terrain, the importance of which is for both landscapes and nature conservation reasons. They vary in size from 8400 hectares to over 130 000 hectares as Table 16.3 shows. The fauna that are important within the parks include Brown Bear (Circea National Park) and Ibex (Gran Paradiso). Pressure is evident in all of the Parks from visitors and tourists, with over a million people each year visiting some of the most delicate environments in the country.

Table 16.3 National Parks in Italy

Name	Year of institution	Address	Area (hectare)
Parco del Gran Paradiso	1922	Via della Rocca 47, 10123 Torino Via Losanna 5 11100 Aosta	58 000
Parco degli Abruzzi	1923	67032 Pescasseroli	100 000
Parco del Circeo	1934	Via C. Alberto 53, 04016 Sabaudia	8 400
Parco dello Stelvio	1935	Via Monte Braulio 56, 23032 Bormio	134 620
Parco della Calabria	1968	Viale della Repubblica 126, 87100 Cosenza	15 344

After the slow and sporadic progress of the past decades, there are new signs that the National government in Italy will begin to address this problem of visitor pressure and the more important issues of resources, commitment and a policy framework.

Regional Parks

There are over 75 Regional Parks in Italy, which vary in size from less than 100 hectares to over 25 000 hectares. Whereas the National Parks are managed by Central Government staff and rangers, the Regional Parks are managed either by Regional staff or if delegated Provincial or Municipal staff and rangers.

The delegation of authority for planning from National to Regional government in 1986 led to a large number of Regional Parks being established in the late 1980s, although some were designated earlier. The fact that each region is responsible for designation and management means that there is no absolute consistency in policies, but the Regional Parks do have some points in common. Unlike National Parks, where development and economic activity is not allowed, Regional Parks encourage tourist and recreational development, and also the development of agriculture and forestry activities. The reason for these policies is that the Regional Parks tend to be situated close to centres of population, so Regional Parks often act as an environmental recreational resource as much as a means of protecting the natural environment.

Management of the Regional Parks varies according to size, location and policies on the balance between conservation and recreation. Some, such as the large (96 000 hectares) Ticino Park in Lombardy/Piedmont are zoned like National Parks to offer maximum protection for the core area, which amounts to about 1% of the Park area. In this example, some 18% of the designated area is developed.

Other designations

There is a small number of other types of land designations that are worthy of note and, particularly in the case of Italy, it is worth noting the contribution of the non-governmental sector. This is an active sector in Italy, largely because some of the difficulties at government level have left a vacuum, into which the NGOs have stepped.

State Nature Reserves

These are administered by the Department of Agriculture at a State level. There are some 130 such reserves which cover a variety of habitats but for the purposes of management are the responsibility of the Forestry Division. With an overall area of 100 000 hectares the average size is much smaller than that of the National or Regional Parks. Correspondingly, State Nature reserves seek to protect very specific habitats or species, and the designation therefore controls certain potentially damaging activity, and the land ownership passes to the State.

International Park

One of these has been agreed between Italy, France and Switzerland. The National Level agreement seeks to give National Park status to the

Montblanc Massif. The international dimension adds weight to the great importance of this area to all three countries, and indeed to Europe as a whole.

Non-governmental organizations

These are very active in Italy, with both popular and professionally based associations having wide memberships. The general involvement of NGOs is discussed later in this chapter, but it is worth noting here that some of the larger organizations do manage reserves. These include the Italian Association for the Protection of Birds (*Lega Italia Protezione Uccelli*) and the National Federation of Nature (*Federazione Nazional Pro Natura*).

OTHER ISSUES

The foregoing analysis suggests that the political process within Italy is, in itself, a major determinant of the success or otherwise of nature conservation in the country. Clearly this process also determines the parameters within which other departments and agencies operate. Consequently, there are a number of related departments, issues and organizations which have a bearing upon nature conservation in Italy.

Agriculture

Agriculture, and the closely associated land use of forestry, remain very important in Italy. As Table 16.4 reveals, agriculture and forestry account for over 50% of land use, compared to a European average of around 85%. This balance is not mirrored within the whole country because most of the agricultural land is concentrated in the southern regions. This, in turn, brings with it problems of an internally unbalanced economy. This is being exacerbated by the structural changes partly brought about by the changes to the Common Agricultural Policy. The need to reduce surpluses and change agricultural practice to balance the needs of agriculture with those of the environment are having a great impact upon the Italian agriculture.

Table 16.4 Agricultural land use in Italy

Land area ('000 km²)	Arable/crop land ('000 km²)	% of land area	Wooded areas ('000 km²)	% of land area
294	120	41	68	24

The Department of Agriculture plans its work through a series of five-year plans. This co-ordinates not only the State's work but also that of the regions. The issues that the industry face are not only those of structural change, but also of the increasing responsibility for better environmental performance. The plan attempts to address this by identifying the issues of importance, such as the use of chemicals and fertilizers, and of the impact of agriculture on the water courses and soil. It has been estimated (Albrizio, 1991) that only 15% of the agriculture budget goes towards environmental protection, against 44% to support farm prices. This situation, it must be said, is not unique but merely a reflection on the broad difficulty of balancing the needs of agriculture and those of the environment.

Hunting

In common with France and Spain, Italy has a very strong tradition of organized hunting, enjoyed by thousands of agricultural workers. In some countries, hunting (other than fishing) tends to be an elite sport, but not so in Italy. Two issues are therefore important. First, the political lobby associated with hunting is very strong and consequently, the laws that control hunting are relatively weak. This means that some species that are protected elsewhere in Europe are not in Italy. The second issue is that the hunters are also trying to roll-back even this restricted legislation to allow, say, more hunting in National Parks. It is the Regional or even Provincial authorities that issue hunting licences and as a result, the potential conflict that exists between the various tiers are exploited by too many licences being issued for designated areas (Orme, 1989).

Water management

Under a decree dating back to 1932, all spring, river and lake waters in Italy are public, and placed under the authority of the Ministry of Public Works. Groundwater, however, is not public, which causes confusion over the management of the resource and the pollution that affects it.

The Regions administer most of the planning functions associated with public water, while the Provinces monitor extraction and water-usage licences. The Municipalities, some 8000 or more, deal with day-to-day water management and home or industry installation.

In total, Italy has an adequate supply of water. However, there are some inequalities in the geographical distribution. The issues facing the authorities are therefore dominated by three main issues: (1) extraction (through wells; by the management of rivers and lakes in the northern mountains; and the extraction of water from lowland rivers, such as the Po Valley); (2) distribution (predominantly from the North to the dry, relatively arid south); and (3) pollution control. All of these issues are made more difficult by the fragmentation of the management system as described above, and the subsequent poorly maintained distribution infrastructure (European Commission, 1978).

Non-governmental agencies

Italy has a vibrant and active non-governmental or voluntary sector some of which, such as the Lega Italia Protezione Uccelli (Italian Association for the Protection of Birds) dates back over 100 years. The largest is a broad-ranging organization called Italia Nostra (Our Italy) which originated in the professional classes of Italy. Initially, the aim of Italia Nostra was to protect the cultural heritage (predominantly Roman) of the country. However, this brief widened to accommodate the natural environment. Founded in 1955, Italia Nostra has over 30 000 members with many local branches (Orme, 1989).

There are several strong national branches of international organizations such as World Wide Fund for Nature and Friends of the Earth, and a number of increasingly influential and land-owning NGOs. Two of these – Fondo l'Ambiente Italiano and Federazione Nazional pro Natura – raise funds specifically for protecting the environment and owning and thereby protecting the natural environment.

At a more local level, small groups (many of which are members of the Federazione mentioned above) participate in direct action or lobbying to protect smaller local sites. Falk (1992) suggests that the activity of the voluntary or NGO sector in Italy compensates to a smaller degree for the confusion witnessed in National and Regional government.

Signing of conventions

Italy has signed all of the Treaties mentioned in Chapter 6, but it has been stressed that given the fragmentation of Government in general and the management of the environment in particular, the implementation of these Treaties is not as advanced as elsewhere (Grassi, 1983).

Implementation of EC Directives

The State Government accepted in 1987 that there were many EC Directives that were not being implemented in Italy. Consequently, a decree was passed giving the State government power to implement over 100 EC Directives, some of which were inevitably environmental. Notwithstanding this bold step, the problems associated with inconsistency remains between the State, its various departments and the Regions . This is because as we have seen, the State government draws up guidelines and policies but Regions deliver the implementation and management.

Not all the Directives fall into the gap between National and Regional government, and in some instances, such as noise pollution or waste management, progress is much quicker. However, in most instances 'to be implemented, Directives require greater collaboration between Central Government and the Regions' (Capria, 1991).

SUMMARY

There are several characteristics of the Italian system of managing the environment that are worthy of note. However, the single most influential characteristic is not specific to nature conservation. The feature that has been most obvious within Italian policies has been the almost constant turnover of governments. The almost annual round of elections that are designed to create a majority government have succeeded, in many spheres of activity, simply to freeze any progress. This has been the case with nature conservation, so for example despite being one of the earliest proponents of the need for protected landscapes, the area of the country thus designated is half the European average.

It must be said, that this confusion at a national political level continues. In 1995, many of the nation's senior politicians were facing charges of corruption – a product surely of the lack of clear direction and consistency of control (*The Times*, 1995).

As a consequence of this lack of consistent direction from a national government, two other characteristics of nature conservation have developed in Italy: the relative strength of the regions, and the importance of the voluntary or non-governmental sector in conservation.

Arguably, the balance of power between the regions and the central government is as much a cause as an effect of inconsistent government at the national level. However, what is clear is that the lack of central management of government has allowed the regions to develop (as contrasted to Spain for example where a formerly strong central government is controlling the release of authority to the regions). This is manifested in nature conservation by the growth in importance, say, in regional parks.

The other characteristic noted above is that of the importance of the voluntary sector. Either at the local town or neighbourhood level, or at a regional/national level, non-governmental agencies are as active as anywhere else in Europe. Much of this activity arose out of the Italian interest and concern for the cultural history of the country (comparable with Greece in this way) but has developed into a wider concern for natural landscape and cultural history.

REFERENCES

Albrizio, E. (1992) *Agriculture and the Environment in Italy.* DocTer, Milan.

Baldock, D. *et al.* (1988) *The Organisation of Nature Conservation in Selected European Countries.* Institute of European Environmental Policy, London.

Capria, A. (1991) EC policy and implementation, in *European Environmental Yearbook.* DocTer, Milan.

Cirietto, P. (1983) *Ordinamentu di Governo e Comitat: Interministerial.* University of Naples, Faculty of Law.

European Commission (1978) *Studio di Sintes: Sulle risorse in acque sotterranee dell Italia.* European Commission, Brussels.

Falk, N. (1992) *Voluntary Work and the Environment.* European Foundation for the Improvement of Working and Living Conditions. Shankhill, Dublin.

Grassi, S. (1983) Parlamento, Governo e Regioni ed attuazione delle directive communtarie, in *Regionu,* **652**.

Onida, V. (1991) Organisational structure, in *European Environmental Yearbook.* DocTer, Milan.

Orme, E. (1989) *Nature Conservation and the Role of the Land Manager.* College of Estate Management, Reading.

Palladino, S. (1987) *Parks and Nature Reserves.* Ministero dell Ambiente, Rimini.

The Times (1995) Italian Politics on Trial, 19 August.

Luxembourg

17

Luxembourg is the smallest country in the European Community and as such has different issues and priorities which face it. The country is dominated at many levels by Luxembourg City, the focus for most socio-economic activity in the country. Being only 3 km² in size, with a population of 390 000, the population density is around average, but over 60% of these live in Luxembourg city, leaving over 85% of the land as agricultural or forestry. Furthermore, over 20% of the land is protected in some way by conservation designations; the highest formal designation level in Europe. The biogeography of the country is exclusively 'Central European', like that of its much larger neighbour Germany and, in parts, Belgium and France.

The smallest country in the European Community also has the record of having the highest level of Gross Domestic Products in the EC. At $21 000 per capita it is over $6000 more than the average, and over twice as much as the poorest country, Greece.

POLITICAL STRUCTURES

Luxembourg is unique within the European Community as it is the only Grand Duchy in the EC. This position, rather like the Monarchy in the UK, does not however regulate or in anyway control the day-to-day management of political affairs within the country, except that, formally, the decrees and laws are issued by the Grand Duke. This law or Ducal decree is translated into an implementation decree by the government or relevant minister through a ministerial decree.

The size of Luxembourg more or less dictates that the process of government is almost entirely undertaken at a National level. Consequently, the difficulties of communication and policy formulation found between various layers of government in other countries are not in evidence. None the less, there are political layers of government within Luxembourg other than the National one.

National government

The formal process of governmental policy and law making is influenced by the constitution of the country as a Grand Duchy. This predominantly manifests itself through the legislative and law-making process. The government system is, however, comparable to those found in other European Member States. A government, elected by universal suffrage (Chamber of Deputies), is organized into ministries or departments, the heads of which are elected representatives, but the executive work of which is undertaken by a paid and full-time Civil Service.

One of the significant features of Luxembourg's governmental system is how it reflects the location and size of the country. The country is much more dependent upon the surrounding countries than a larger country would be. Consequently, its economy, geography and, in part, political systems reflect this. For example, the tourist industry is very important because Luxembourg is a destination for many visitors from Germany and France on its eastern and southern borders respectively. The industry therefore has its own department reflecting the importance of the service sector in general and tourism in particular. Similarly, transnational issues such as pollution have a much longer history of legislation in Luxembourg than they do in other Member States (Aluseau, 1987).

Water quality, for example, has been protected by Ducal decree since 1669, and currently involves five ministries: Environment; Health; Public Works; Agriculture and Viniculture; and Labour and Social Security.

The ministerial structures, as can be gathered from this, are again similar to those found elsewhere, with Environment, Finance, Health and others being main components of the overall structure.

Other levels of government

The size of the Grand Duchy is in part a reflection of its history. Both of these factors contribute to the homogeneity of the country, at least in terms of its political structure, if not its environmental and geographical structure. As a consequence, regional (or the equivalent of county or department politics) do not exist to any great extent. There are government administrations through some of the larger communes, of which there are 14. The legislation for these starts as a National Decree which gives the local agencies the authority to issue communal regulations which in turn bring individual communities into line with central government policy.

For our purposes here, however, there are no specific or unique powers that local government holds in Luxembourg that are of direct relevance.

ENVIRONMENTAL RESPONSIBILITIES

Given the lack of potential areas of confusion or conflict between various levels or tiers of government, the management of environmental responsibility could, in theory at least, be simplified from that in other countries where, for example, the National/Regional debate is more intense. This is

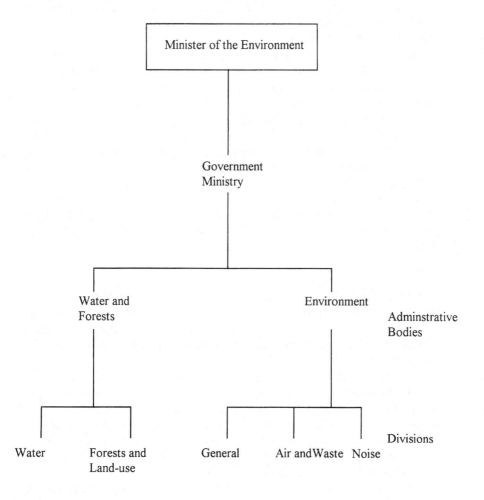

Figure 17.1 Organizational structure of the Ministry of the Environment in Luxembourg.

true in part, but the partial division of responsibility for environmental issues does remain at a National level. However, even here the scale of the activities within Luxembourg makes the process easier.

The most influential department is the Ministry of the Environment which, since 1984, has managed the greatest proportion of the environmental portfolio. The Ministry is subdivided into two main administrative bodies (Water and Forests; Environment). These are further subdivided into five divisions, as shown in Figure 17.1. The role of the administrative bodies is much the same as most Civil Service organizations and includes the drafting of legislation, the monitoring of the environment, offering advice to a range of agencies, and having some executive powers to manage environmental issues. This process is funded through the Environmental Protection Fund.

The other Ministries that are involved in elements of environmental protection include Agriculture and Viniculture; Health; and Public Works. In order to co-ordinate the activity of these ministries, the Minister for the Environment chairs the National Environmental Protection Committee. Founded at the same time as the Ministry, this organization draws together not only the relevant ministries but also private companies, 'city' and town officials from the country's communities, non-governmental agencies, and other representatives from economic and social areas of responsibility. The main and official function of the Committee is to inform Ministers and to co-ordinate interministerial action. The group also acts as a channel for communications, an umbrella organization for different levels of activity and continually updates Luxembourg's Code (Raume-Degreve, 1992).

Other agencies

Due to the overriding control that central government has on environmental processes in Luxembourg, the involvement of other agencies (either public, voluntary or private) is very much dictated and managed by central government. All other activities are undertaken, in some way, on behalf of the central agencies.

Environmental implementation is led, by and large, by the preparation of environmental strategies. These are created by the various communities within Luxembourg. It has been suggested that base-line data for these plans were inconsistent and of poor coverage in the early 1980s (Chambre de Deputes, 1985). As a consequence, mostly private sector agencies and individuals were employed by the Government to update and improve the environmental base data. It is upon the basis of these data that 'green policies' as they are referred to are drawn up. The implementation of the policies within these plans are the responsibility of a number of agencies, including the State, the Communities and Private Sector.

LAND DESIGNATIONS

The majority of land designations arise out of the planning process described above. Locally important 'green zones' are identified alongside other planning and land-use considerations. At a National level, the larger land designations are drawn up by the Forestry Division of the Department of the Environment. As some 30% (87 500 hectares) of Luxembourg is under either natural or commercial forests, the link between conservation and forestry is inevitable (Administration de l'Environnement, 1988).

National protected areas

The Protected Areas, as designated at National level, are established to protect natural environments, and specific flora and fauna. Table 17.1 identifies the seven designated sites and their areas. From the division between core area and buffer zone, it is evident that the Protected Areas are managed on similar lines to the French Nature Parks. In Luxembourg, all development in the core area is prohibited, as too is hunting. Some milder forms of development are permitted in the buffer zone, but hunting is still banned.

Table 17.1 Protected areas in Luxembourg

Name	Core area (hectares)	Buffer zone (hectares)
Roserbann	25	333
Mierscherdall	28	139
Aarnnescht	40	27
Beufrerdurgermuer	1	20
Telpescholzlei	2	63
Sonnbierg	15	–
Fensterdall	2	9

The whole of the Protected Area, including the buffer zone is managed by the Forests and Water Administration, specifically through the Forestry and Land Use division.

The legislative competence for designating Protected Areas comes from the 1982 Law on the Preservation of the Countryside. This same law also allowed for the designation of National Parks. However, National Parks in Luxembourg are much less important than Protected Areas. The two National Parks in the country are not protected or managed by the State, and are almost entirely in private agricultural ownership. Whereas most of the Protected Areas are focused upon the forests of Luxembourg, the National Parks are more concerned with reconciling economic activity (such as agriculture and tourism) rather than protecting wildlife *per se*. In these joint objectives they loosely mirror National Parks in the United Kingdom, although the latter have much tighter planning and management controls to them.

Other areas

There are two further types of designation in Luxembourg which are worthy of note here.

The so-called 'green zones' as defined in the planning documents prepared at Commune level are managed by the Forestry Division, in co-operation with the Ministry of State which is ultimately responsible for land-use planning. These green zones seek, at a local level, to not only protect the natural environment, but also reconcile some of the potential conflicts of pressure on the land resource. The main mechanism for accomplishing this is by the careful definition of urban or community perimeters.

The second type of designation is really a 'reverse designation' area where wildlife is not protected but which by definition means that in other areas wildlife is protected. In common with many European Countries, there is a strong tradition of hunting among the working, predominantly agricultural community. The hunt in Luxembourg is however, restricted to some 600, relatively small areas across the country. These sites are all under 100 hectares in area, and many are much smaller than this. Consequently, for some 2000 km² of the country, hunting is not permitted. The main difficulty in managing this potentially forward-looking policy on hunting is that, in 1990, there were only two national inspectors for the whole of the country.

OTHER ISSUES

The issues which have a bearing on the management of nature conservation in Luxembourg are influenced by the size of the country. Agriculture, water management and the broader issues of economic development (through 'green tourism' for example) all have as a common factor the size of the country. Integration of many objectives in relatively small areas of land are common place. Thus, in the management of these issues, this integration is evident, in policy if not in practice.

Water management

The national management of supply of water is undertaken by the General Commission of Water Protection. This Commission handles the planning and financing of the water supply programme. Localized supply is managed by Commune-based consortia which are formed under the overall co-ordination of the Luxembourg Water Services Association.

Over two-thirds of the country's water is drawn from aquifers in the southern half of the country (Gutland). In the northern part (Oesling) the topography means that artificial lakes and reservoirs have been constructed.

The main issues facing Luxembourg are those of consistency of supply and quality. The geomorphology, as described above, means that constant management of the volume of reserves is necessary, particularly in the reservoirs to the north. Being a small country, Luxembourg cannot call upon reserves of water from various regions as, for example, could the UK or France. The issue of quality is similarly important. In the north, the multi-use of the main reservoir system poses problems for the control of water quality, particularly in the Esch/Sure lake. In the south of the country, the quality of groundwater is a function of the quality of the soil through which the water passes. As a result, the water is affected particularly by the amount of fertilizer or other chemicals that are used in the forestry or agriculture industries. In this context, the Grand Duchy has issued several Ducal regulations over the past decade to regulate and control outflows into the water system (Ministère de l'Environnement, various years).

Agriculture and forestry

A large part of Luxembourg's economy is based upon primary production, notably forestry and agriculture, and these industries are represented at ministerial level by their different ministries. This could potentially cause conflict, as it does elsewhere, but it is apparent that Luxembourg has accepted that, because of its size, the total integration of most land/water-based activities needs to be an objective rather than segregation. Thus, it is the policy of the Ministry of Agriculture to regulate and actively monitor the impact of agricultural production on the water supply and, at a broader level, the overall environment (Everling, 1975). Similarly, in the forestry industry the concern is equally as evident. The management of water and forests falls within the same division at the Department of the Environment; as around half of the country's water supply lies under land covered by forests, the link is clear (Administration de l'Environnement, 1988).

Signing of conventions

Luxembourg has signed all of the relevant international conventions with the exception of Ramsar. This has not been signed because, in the eyes of the Luxembourg Government, there are no significantly important sites within the country.

Implementation of EC Directives

Due to the small size of the country and because of the corresponding centralized nature of much of the policy formulation and implementation, Luxembourg's ability to implement directives is potentially much easier than in other Member States. It has also been made evident that the country has identified the need for integration of its many land-based pressures. Consequently, Luxembourg has a relatively good track record of introducing and, indeed, implementing EC policy and directives (STATEC, 1988).

While all areas of environmental protection are of concern to a country of Luxembourg's size, it is safe to say that more concern is expressed over issues that have an impact upon Luxembourg from outside its own boundaries. Thus, issues such as air pollution, water pollution, waste management and toxic substance management are more important than, say, establishing a programme of land designations. However, that does not mean to say that progress is not made on all fronts. Indeed, in its own words 'Luxembourg deserves a good conduct medal' (Kromarek, 1992).

SUMMARY

Despite its small size (or indeed, because of it) Luxembourg has, on its own analysis a good record of upholding the spirit of EC environmental policy. This record is maintained in its designations of land for nature conservation. The area thus designated is over twice the European average, and is the highest in Europe. Similarly, Luxembourg has the highest proportion of forestry and agricultural land in Europe (85%). The reason for this is relatively straightforward: the city of Luxembourg is the only centre of population of any size in the small country – the rest is allocated for rural and/or conservation land uses. Notwithstanding this, Luxembourg's Gross Domestic Product is the highest in Europe, reflecting the country's strong position as a finance and 'invisible earnings' centre for Europe and, indeed, the world.

The link between rural land use and protected/designated land is shown in the fact that most of the Protected Areas are forests in state or private ownership. The further emphasis on the need for 'green zones' around centres of population reflects the country's concern for safeguarding against the spread of urban areas into the forests and agricultural areas.

These processes of designation and protection are made all the easier by the fact that the small size of the country enables direct control without intervening layers of regional or other local government structures.

REFERENCES

Administration de l'Environnement (1988) *Invetaire de la foret Luxembourgoise.* Luxembourg la Ville.

Aluseau, R. (1987) *L'eau potable au Grand-Duche de Luxembourg.* Department of the Environment, Luxembourg la Ville.

Chambre de Deputes (1985) *L'etat de l'environnement naturel humaine au Grand Duche de Luxembourg.* No. 2933 Session Ordinaire. Luxembourg la Ville.

Everling, R. (1975) *La responsibilité civile du polluer en drait Luxembourgoise.* Presses Universitaires.

Kromarek, D. (1992) EC policy and implementation, in *European Environmental Yearbook*, DocTer, Milan.

Ministère de l'Environnement (various years) *Rapport d'Activité.* Luxembourg la Ville.

Raume-Degreve, R. (1992) Organisational Structure, in *European Environmental Yearbook*, DocTer, Milan.

STATEC (1988) *Le Grand Duche en Chiffres.* Luxembourg la Ville.

The Netherlands is one of the smallest European countries, situated in the north west of mainland Europe. It has a temperate/atlantic climate covering 34 000 km². Its most unique feature is its low-lying topography, with very little land over 300 m, and a significant proportion being beneath sea level. Consequently, a large part of the nature conservation importance of the Netherlands stems from its wetlands, particularly the coastal wetlands.

A further significant feature of the Netherlands is the fact that it has the largest population density in the EC, and therefore has always seen major pressure on its agriculture industry, which at 68% covers less land than in most of Europe; only Belgium is comparable. None the less, there is still a slightly higher than average percentage of land protected through conservation designations (9.5% compared to 8.4%). This reflects the Dutch commitment to environmental protection which, as the following discussion reveals, is one of the strongest if not the strongest in the EC.

POLITICAL STRUCTURES

The Netherlands, in common with Spain and the United Kingdom, is a monarchy which means that the monarch is, in constitutional terms, the head of State and all acts of government are done in the name of the monarch. How much this 'theoretical' situation is reflected in the day-to-day management of affairs varies; the monarch has a much more clearly defined role in government than in, say, the United Kingdom. The Dutch model defines 'The Crown' (i.e. the State) as the monarch and the ministers together. In this way, neither the monarch nor the ministers can make any legislative or constitutionally binding decision without the agreement of the other. The highest advisory body to the Crown is the Council of the State, presided over by the monarch. Other advisory councils exist with the constitution, and of particular relevance to the environment are the Council for Nature and the Council for Physical Planning.

In the day-to-day affairs of the country, however, it is the Government that undertakes most of the work and leads most of the legislative initiatives. Consequently, it is with this part of the process that we are concerned here.

National government

The Parliament (*Staten-Generaal*) consists, as elsewhere in Europe, of two houses: the First and Second Chambers. The Second Chamber is by far the most important and is made up of around 150 elected representatives. The Second Chamber acts as a controlling body, and consists of 75 indirectly or non-elected representatives. The government, which is constituted by the monarch and his/her ministers, is answerable to the Parliament, and vice versa. For a bill to become law, it must be approved by both the government and the two Chambers, with both the Second Chamber and the government having the authority to promote and initiate legislation. The ministers, who are part of the government but not constitutionally part of Parliament, have responsibility for various portfolios. These include: Agriculture and Fisheries; Economic Affairs; Welfare, Public Health and Cultural Affairs; Social Affairs and Employment; and Housing, Physical Planning and the Environment. The last reorganization of this structure was in 1982.

Each of these ministries has both an executive and policy-making role and a regulatory role through various inspectorates. The inspectorates' role is in itself two-sided, with the regulation of private sector companies being one strand of its work, and the monitoring of regional and provincial government being another component of its work, thus 'bridging the gap between central and decentralised government' (Aalders, 1992).

Regional and local government

The Netherlands is divided into 12 Provinces or Regions. The role of central government is largely to develop and formulate overall policy, and the role of Provincial government is mostly to execute this national policy, supported by the finances supplied by National government. The Provinces have their own collection of agents and agencies which constitutes Provincial Government. These are: the Commissioner for the Monarch (which represents a direct link with the government); Deputees-General (which are locally elected representatives); and the States-Provincial (which is the overall governing organization, representing the two former elements of government).

The regions have control over the broad physical planning process, but this only occurs within the overall framework provided by the National government. Within this process of physical planning, Provincial government takes the responsibility for most decisions concerning transport, infrastructure, building, waste management but all of them, with three exceptions, have handed their responsibility for water management on to water authorities.

The 700 or so Dutch Municipalities represent the most localized form of government and consist of a Mayor; a Council of Mayor and Alderman; and a Municipal Council. The powers and responsibilities of the Municipalities are not great, and their authority covers local implementation of national and regional plans, mostly on issues associated with the protection of local rights (covered by the Public Nuisance Act of 1952) or with the delivery of local services (such as domestic waste disposal or street cleaning and the management of local public areas). Perhaps the most significant function of the Municipalities is in the regulation and monitoring of building and housing activity to ensure that it conforms with the Provincial Physical Plan.

It must be said, however, that the Regional and local government system within the Netherlands does not represent a strong movement as it does, say, in its neighbour Belgium, and the responsibilities reflect as much the implementation of national policy as they do the development of local initiatives. This is largely a consequence of the size of the country and the lack of an historic and cultural regionalization of great strength.

ENVIRONMENTAL RESPONSIBILITIES

There is a long history of nature conservation and general environmental concern in the Netherlands. This is in part a result of the topography of the country which has resulted in a clear and widespread awareness of the relationship between the environment and the well-being of the people. Pressure on land availability, the need for continual reclamation and drainage of land and the consequent need for pure water to safeguard the quality of the reclaimed land have all concentrated the national interest for several centuries. One of the earliest pieces of legislation that can be considered as 'modern' relates to land reclamation and dates back to 1810. Closely allied to this concern with the need to reclaim land from the sea has been the need to protect agricultural interests and to safeguard water quality. Not surprisingly, therefore, the Ministries of Agriculture and Water Management have many of the broader environmental responsibilities within their authority.

National government

Since the government reorganization of ministerial responsibility of 1982, the two principal agencies concerned with environmental protection within government are the Ministry of Housing, Physical Planning and the Environment, and the Ministry of Agriculture and Fisheries, although as mentioned above, the Ministry of Water Management also has some significant responsibility.

The role of the Ministry of Housing, Planning and Environment has the overall co-ordinating role for the environment, although it lost control of some specific areas of responsibility such as nature conservation in 1982 with the reorganization. Figure 18.1 shows the divisions of the Ministry at the level of Directorate-General. This central role gives the Ministry an important function not only at the national level, where it co-ordinates the work of all the ministries with an environmental interest, but also at the international level; the Minister of Housing, Physical Planning and Environment represents the Netherlands at the Council of Ministers for example, and also at international conventions. Both the Physical Planning Directorate and the Environmental Health Directorate have direct inputs into environmental management in the country. Clearly, in the former's case this is through the land-use designation process. In the latter it is through the regulation of environmental performance and through the research and advisory work of the Ministry's many sub-committees and bodies.

The Ministry of Agriculture and Fisheries has two large subdivisions or Directorates-General. The Directorate-General for Rural Areas and Quality Control has a large brief, which includes agricultural land management, research, nature conservation, open-air recreation, forestry and farm diversification. Whereas in some countries the fact that the responsibility for nature conservation is within the Ministry of Agriculture can be seen as representing a secondary role for nature conservation, in the Netherlands it is more a sign of the real progress towards integrating agriculture and nature conservation (Orme, 1989). Purely in terms of the role of managing the natural environment, the Directorate of Nature Environment and Fauna Management within the large Directorate-General encompasses most of the issues. The individual sections within the Directorate cover: landscape and nature conservation; open spaces; fauna and species management; hunting; and fauna research. It has been argued that not only does this close and active relationship between agriculture and nature conservation reflect a commitment on the part of the

Dutch authorities, but is has also helped to force the pace of changes in Europe, particularly to the Common Agricultural Policy (Central Council for Environmental Health, 1992). In a combination of roles where both areas of responsibility have strong support (agricultural production and environmental protection) a healthy relationship appears to have been created.

Other sections within the Ministry of Agriculture and Fisheries include the State Forestry Service, which has responsibility for the nation's 141 000 hectares of State Forest (Table 18.1).

Table 18.1 Area of land use in the Netherlands

Land area ('000 km²)	Arable/crop land ('000 km²)	% of land area	Wooded areas ('000 km²)	% of land area
34	9	27	3	9

Other national agencies

All Ministries within the Netherlands have a number of associated organizations which are independent of but report to and advise the Minister and his/her staff. Their independence is usually safeguarded through the involvement of non-governmental organizations, academics and other external agencies. Both the Ministry of Agriculture and Fisheries, and the Ministry of Housing, Physical Planning and Environment have a large number of these associated bodies to advise them. Those that support the Ministry of Agriculture include: The Forestry Information Council; Nature Protection Council; Advisory Council on the Threatened and Exotic Species Act; Provisional Committees on National Parks; Hunting Council; and State Institute for Research. These bodies and others draw upon a wide area of expertise and seek to link the views of often conflicting interest groups in order to come to a commonly accepted solution to environmental problems. For example, the Hunting Council contains conservationists, hunting organizations and agricultural representatives among others.

Similarly the Ministry of Housing, Physical Planning and the Environment has a range of advisory and associated bodies including: the Technical Committee for Soil Protection; Environment and Nature Research Council; and the Committee on Environmental Impact Assessment.

Voluntary organizations

The Netherlands has a tradition of voluntary sector or non-governmental organizational involvement in the environment that is deep-rooted and now firmly embedded in the official nature conservation processes. The work of the voluntary agencies is twofold. First some, such as the Dutch Society for the Preservation of Birds and the Association for the Conservation of Natural Monuments, own and manage conservation sites, thereby protecting them. The second and equally important role of the voluntary sector is in the support and advice that they give to the government agencies. Into this category come the organizations which make up the Nature and Environment Foundation. The government encourages and supports this involvement of the voluntary sector at both levels, a situation which has similarities with other European countries but is better organized here than anywhere else in Europe.

The voluntary organizations are well supported in the Netherlands. The three mentioned above for example have around 45 000, 250 000 and 1 000 000 members respectively. In land-holding terms, the organizations are similarly important, with the Dutch Society for the Preservation of Birds holding some 20 000 hectares, and the Nature and Environment Foundation member organization holding 3000 sites covering 50 000 hectares (Orme, 1989).

At the other end of the scale, smaller or more specific groups also attract support. The National Society for the Protection of the Wadden Sea focuses upon one area of wetland, yet still attracts 30–35 000 members. The Ecological Cycle Foundation in Arnhem on the other hand survives largely without a formal membership, but still manages to employ over 25 people (Falk, 1992).

The voluntary sector in the Netherlands is therefore a significant National and Regional/local force in the broad spectrum of environmental conservation. As we have seen here, this is similarly true in the specific area of nature conservation.

Regional agencies

The main role of regional and local organizations is the implementation of policies established at the national level. This involves the enforcement of land-use plans or the fine detail but with the local need at the forefront of the planning process. Similarly, it might involve the management of protected areas or the regulation and monitoring of environmental performances. By far the most active role is in physical planning which drives much of the development process in the Netherlands. For example, even at the level of the municipality, the authorities have agencies which buy and hold land for development or renewal. The reason for this is the overall rapid changes in land use and, inevitably the scarcity of land and the nature of much of the land which is reclaimed and/or below sea level. The objective of the physical planning process has been defined as 'At National and Provincial level, policies are directed at controlling the location of urban growth, decreasing the growth of mobility, conserving areas with natural and landscape value – an important element of all of these is the "compact city" policy' (Brussaard, 1987).

LAND DESIGNATIONS

It is evident that the Netherlands is both a small and a densely populated country, with a strong agriculture industry. The population per square kilometre is around 350 for example compared to, say, 225 in the UK and 192 in Italy. For these reasons, land is at a premium and areas of natural landscape and of a high ecological value are relatively scarce, and where they are found they are small. Thus, in a country that is justifiably proud of its environmental record, the percentage cover of land protected through land designation is large at nearly 9.5% (Table 18.2). None the less, there are a number of designations, including nature reserves and National Parks, and the physical planning laws allow for less stringent forms of protection. This is the case in most European countries and is therefore not discussed specifically here.

Table 18.2 Areas of designated protected areas in the Netherlands

'000 km²			
1980	1985	1990	1990 (% of total area)
1.1	1.6	3.6	9.5

National Parks

There are eight National Parks in the Netherlands. It the general policy that National Parks should be over 1000 hectares in size and seek not only to protect natural habitats and landscape that cover the designated areas but also seek to support limited and educationally based recreation. In having this dual objective of conservation and recreation, they are similar to the UK National Parks. Dutch National Parks, however, are State owned and have little or no other land use within their boundaries.

Table 18.3 lists the Dutch National Parks, from which the low-lying and wetland characteristics of the country can be gathered, with marsh, dunes and heath being prevalent within the designations. The Parks are managed by staff employed directly by the Ministry of Agriculture and Fisheries. The legal background for the establishment of the National Parks is the Nature Conservation Act of 1967. The Act similarly underpins the other types of designation and the broader protection of the countries flora and fauna.

Table 18.3 National Parks in the Netherlands

Name	Year of designation	Type	Address	Area (hectares)
Hoge Veluwe	1935	Woodland and heath	Apeldoornseweg, 250 Hoenderloo	5450
Veluwezoom	1935	Woodland and heath	Bezoekerscentrum 'De Heurne' Heuvenseweg 5A 6991 JE Rheden	600
Kennemerduinen	1950	Coastal dune area	Militairenweg, 4 2051 Ev Overveen	1240
Schiermonnikoog	1984	Island coastal dunes	Gementehuis Schiermonnikoog Postbus 20, 9166 Schiermoonnikoog	5400
De Groote Peel	1985	Peat bog area	Lindanus Straat 2 6041 EC Roermond	1320
Dwingelderveld	1986	Heaths and woodland	Central State Office	3600
De Weerribben	1986	Water and peat swamp	Central State Office	3445
De Biesbosch	1987	Wooded marsh area	Central State Office	7100

National Landscapes and Landscape Zones

National Landscapes are intended to cover areas of 10 000 hectares and correspondingly contain not only land of conservation value, but also private land, agricultural land and settlement. Their objectives are similarly very broad, encompassing socio-cultural protection in some instances as well as natural history conservation. Recreation is also encouraged in appropriate areas, but only if it has an educational role to play.

Landscape Zones fulfil the same function as National Landscapes, but cover smaller areas. The maximum size of a Landscape Zone is set at 5000 hectares, with less emphasis being placed in outdoor recreation. In both areas, special financial encouragement is given to farmers to protect their traditional agricultural methods under the Environmentally Sensitive Areas (ESA) Directive. However, it has been noted (Central Council for Environmental Health, 1992) that the concept of both National

Landscapes and Landscape Zones have met some resistance from farmers, despite the ESA incentives. For this, and other reasons, a revised National Nature Policy Plan was published in 1989 (Department of Housing, Physical Planning and the Environment, 1989), which sought to resolve this apparent conflict between farmers and the land designation process. The plan concentrates upon interlinking small areas of high value within the larger areas, and of providing buffer zones to allow some flexibility to the tightness of the designation. In 1990, there were some 20 National Landscapes (covering 640 000 hectares) and 39 Landscape Zones (338 500 hectares).

Other designations

Large nature zones, nature reserves and natural monuments all cover slightly differing sizes, types and objectives for land designation. Many nature reserves, which are generally small, lie within the non-governmental or the private sector. Large nature zones, on the other hand, are broad designations of larger areas, up to 1000 hectares. In 1991, there were over 1500 Nature Reserves covering 314 000 hectares, of which around one-third were in non-governmental ownership.

It is also valuable to stress here that the Netherlands has begun to try to address the issue of the relationship between agriculture and nature conservation and how this can be improved to complement the land protected through designations. It is perceived that in a small and densely populated country such as the Netherlands this is a better long-term solution.

OTHER ISSUES

From much of the foregoing discussion is will be self-evident that the two overburdening issues in the conservation of the Natural environment within the Netherlands are the agriculture industry, and its relationship with conservation, and the management and control of water. Both of these have not only great impact on conservation, but also on the economy and life in the Netherlands.

Agriculture

The Dutch economy relies to a very great extent on the agricultural industry. While only 30% of the land area is arable agriculture, a further 35% is pasture, and all of it is very intensively farmed; there are few rough grazing areas that correspond to similar areas in more mountainous Member States. The number of land holdings is falling (184 000 to 132 000 from 1970 to 1987 respectively) but as elsewhere in Europe the land that remains in agriculture is being farmed more and more intensely so that overall output has not fallen despite land being taken out of agricultural production as part of set-aside and other programmes. For example, an interesting statistic is that between 1984 and 1988 the number of dairy farms was halved, while the number of cattle fell by 0.6 million, from 2.5 to 1.9 million (Ministry of Agriculture and Fisheries, various years).

This intensification, not only of the dairy industry, but also of other elements of the agricultural industry, is the single most concerning issue about the industry for environmentalists. The implications are felt in the quality of water courses (through fertilizer and herbicide creep for example) and in the very serious problem of disposing of animal waste and slurry; a big problem in a small country.

The two policies that are seeking to resolve the problems associated with the highly intensive agriculture in a small densely populated country are 'segregation' and 'integration'. Segregation of urban and rural land use, and integration of rural economic and land-use activity. Indeed, the Netherlands has been at the forefront of the process of integrated rural development; driven, it must be said, partly by the pressing need brought about by the factors discussed above. The Dutch approach of greater integration, has led to a unique management agreement for agricultural areas of high natural value (HNV) through the so-called 'Relation Papers' of 1993, and to further study of how the reform of the Common Agricultural Policy could be of benefit to nature conservation (Baldock and Beaufoy, 1993).

Water management

Around two-thirds of Dutch water is taken from groundwater sources, which is one of the highest in the European Community. The two problems, common to many Member States (but, ironically, predominantly those on the Mediterranean coasts) are water quality and quantity. The latter is an issue not because of low rainfall but because of the topography of the country. The regular supply of good quality water has only been maintained by boring deeper wells and by protecting the feeding grounds of these underwater sources from pollution. This has led to a large amount of expense being borne by the regional water companies. Indeed, the central government did try to push water prices up higher in an attempt to make consumers treat the resource more carefully. This was, at the most recent attempt, resisted by the water authorities.

The issue of water quality is divided between controlling the quality of ground water and the quality of surface water. The Protection of the Ground Act (1986) was designed to stop pollution of ground water sources, predominantly by restricting surface agricultural activity. The Surface Water Pollution Act predates the former Act. As early as 1870, the Dutch were concerned enough to enact strong regulation to protect the quality of surface drinking water.

The issue of quality of water is one of the driving forces behind the desire for greater integration of rural land uses mentioned above. There is no doubt that the issue will become increasingly important, not just in the Netherlands but across Europe.

Signing of conventions

The Netherlands has signed all of the significant nature conservation conventions mentioned in Chapter 6. Indeed, in most cases it was among the first Member States to do so.

Implementation of EC Directives

To a casual observer, the record of the Netherlands in implementing EC Directives presents a strange dichotomy. The foregoing analysis suggests that the Netherlands can be justifiably proud of its wide-ranging and indeed innovative environmental legislation. On the other hand, the Netherlands has, on four separate occasions, been condemned by the European Court of Justice for non-compliance.

The rationale for this apparent paradox is that, although the Netherlands has, in many cases, already had legislation in place which met the EC Directives, the formal process of compliance was held up by the length of the internal legislative process. In other words, the implementation of EC Directives was in almost all cases happening, but formal compliance was delayed in the parliamentary procedures.

Given this explanation of the paradox, it has been argued (Bennett, 1992) that the Dutch record of *implementation* of EC Directives is the best in Europe. Indeed, Bennett also argues that many in the Netherlands feel that EC policy is too conservative and it actually holds back the Dutch desire for better protection of the environment.

This fear is not only based upon the fact that many EC Directives are far less stringent than their Dutch counterparts but because 'it is not unusual in the Netherlands for compliance ... to require not only the formulation of new laws, but also the repeal of detailed existing legislation... and the re-organisation of long-established organisations and procedures' (Bennett,

1992). Against this background, it is possible that a growing body of opinion in the Netherlands may begin to question the benefit of EC Environmental Directives.

SUMMARY

The Dutch record of broadly based environmental protection is second to none in Europe. They have taken the lead in many areas of trying to integrate environmental considerations into mainstream economic activity. More specifically, the Dutch have also taken a leading role in integrating nature conservation into other activities, particularly agriculture (Baldock and Beaufoy, 1993). Indeed, in some European countries, the fact that responsibility for nature conservation lies within the Department or Ministry for Agriculture is a disadvantage and 'down values' nature conservation. In the Netherlands, this is not the case, because the environment is taken seriously, and has been for many years.

The basis for the Dutch concern for the environment (and this is also reflected in its land-use designations) is their relatively vulnerable position as a very low-lying country, with a high density of population. These characteristics mean that integration between agriculture and conservation is vital, and the potential for a serious land crisis resulting from pollution, mismanagement of natural resources or from activities beyond national boundaries is also made even more acute for the Netherlands where a large proportion of land is under sea-level, where the River Rhine enters the sea, carrying with it pollution from several countries, and where the dumping of waste into the North Sea affects a large part of the coastline.

Notwithstanding the pressures on land in the Netherlands, they have just above the European average amount of land designated for nature conservation.

REFERENCES

Aalders, M. (1992) *Organisational Structure*. DocTer, Milan.
Baldock, D. and Beaufoy, G. (1993) *Nature Conservation on the Common Agricultural Policy*. Report for the Ministry of Agriculture and Fisheries, Den Haag.
Bennett, G. (1992) *EC Policy and Implementation*. DocTer, Milan.
Brussaard, W. (1987) *The Rules of Physical Planning*. Ministry of Housing, Planning and the Environment, Den Haag.
Central Council for Environmental Health (1992) *The Environmental Year*. Government Publishing Office, Den Haag.

Department of Housing, Physical Planning and the Environment (1989) *National Nature Policy Plan* [Nationaal Natuurbeleidsplan]. Government Publishing Office, Den Haag.

Ministry of Agriculture and Fisheries (various years) *Agricultural Statistics*. Den Haag.

Portugal 19

Portugal has many social, political and geographical similarities with its Iberian neighbour, Spain. Portugal has a relatively recent history of democratic rule, which was formalized by the New Constitution of 1976. The biogeographical zones represented in Portugal are also similar to those of Spain, the most dominant being 'Mediterranean' with some 'Macronesian' influences in the extreme south-western corner. The proportion of the country covered by agriculture and forestry is slightly less than average, as too is the density of the population. Where Portugal does vary most significantly from the European average is in its Gross Domestic Product, which is 9.3 k per capita compared to a European average of 15.6 k. As a consequence, the emphasis for Portuguese activity since the new constitution was formed has been geared towards raising the economic standard of living, as well as introducing and facilitating the relatively new democratic processes. It is these issues that have dominated Portuguese socio-politics during its membership of the EC, and only recently has the environment become important.

POLITICAL STRUCTURE

The fact that the Portuguese constitution is only relatively young (from the new constitution of 1976) means that the process of legislating, and also the process of consolidating existing legislation, has been relatively short lived. Since 1974, when the revolution took place, the environment has taken a more important place in the legislative framework. This is explored more fully later in this chapter. However, at the same time that the political agenda was expanding, so too was the function and responsibility of government. Relatively small and bureaucratic State Cabinets were transformed into larger, policy-formulating Ministerial Departments. This reflects the new importance placed upon the democratic process as opposed to the administration of the State diktats.

National government

In keeping with many democracies in Europe, the Portuguese system is Presidential with the balance of power lying somewhere between the President and the Prime Minister and his/her government. The actual detail of specific areas of responsibility is contained within the 1976 constitution (Janvario, 1992). As well as a balance of responsibility between the President and the Prime Minister, there also exists a balance of responsibility and authority between the Government, the largest political grouping in the Parliament, headed by the Prime Minister and the Parliament as a whole (*Assemleia da Republica*, or AR). The Government has the power to draft 'decree laws' in matters which are not reserved for the full Parliament. The result of this balance of power is that, 'in truth the Government only functions as the supreme decision maker in carrying out general policy and in Public Administration' (Janvario, 1992). It is perhaps understandable that a country that came into the democratic process as recently as 1974 does not want to put too much power in any one group or individual.

The Prime Minister, who heads the government, is also supported by a cabinet of elected representatives, each one of which heads a ministerial department. These departments cover the areas of jurisdiction commonly found across Europe in one form or another. They include the Environment, Public Works and Planning and Territorial Administration for example.

Given the relatively recent creation of these large, well-resourced ministries, it is also not surprising that they have undergone a number of changes in areas of responsibility since 1974. The current structure for environmental administration, for example, dates back to 1986.

The inherited centralized system which predates the revolution of 1974 has led to a vacuum being present between National and local government. There is no equivalent, for example, to Spain's Regions, France's departments or Ireland's Counties. The next layer down is therefore the municipality or local level.

Local government

As there are no elected structures or organizations between the National government and the local, relatively small administrations of the municipalities, the gap has been partially filled by the National government's regionalization of some of its functions. The Regional departments, however, are not the start of a process of decentralization, but simply a delegation to regional departments of some of the administrative responsibilities of centrally devised policies. Furthermore, the various ministries (Education, Health, Industry and Agriculture in particular) have each devised their own geographical regions. Consequently, there is developing in Portugal a geographical and informational incompatibility and inconsistency of administration from National government (Garrett, 1992).

The municipal organizations themselves are democratically elected, but do not have any significant levels of power or responsibility. They are, therefore, responsible for local matters such as waste disposal, town planning and the administration of some National responsibilities at a local level.

ENVIRONMENTAL RESPONSIBILITIES

Since 1986, the Ministry that is responsible for environmental issues has been the Ministry of Planning and Territorial Administration. Indeed, it has been noted that, prior to 1974, the word 'environment' had not been mentioned *per se*, in any legislation or in any Ministerial or Cabinet responsibility (Garrett, 1992). The changes in emphasis only came with the new constitution and more recently, with Portugal's entry of the European Community. Prior to the formation of the new Ministry in 1986, environmental legislation was piecemeal and responsive, rather than proactive and policy led.

The Ministry of Planning and Territorial Administration (MPAT) has brought a new cohesion to environmental legislation and administration. Furthermore, given the foregoing analysis, it is really the only significant environmental agency that is managed by the government. For this reason the following discussion looks at the various components of the MPAT.

Ministry for Planning and Territorial Administration

The Ministry, or MPAT as it is commonly known, was formed in 1986 as both a reaction to increasing internal and external political pressures to put 'the environment' higher on the government's agenda, and also as a proactive measure to take the initiative in several emerging areas of importance. MPAT has a very broad remit, covering not only the environment and natural resources, but also physical planning; regional development and administration; and research and technology. Figure 19.1 shows the structural framework of the MPAT. From this it can be readily seen that the component of MPAT of most significance to us here is the State Secretariat for the Environment and Natural Resources (SEARN).

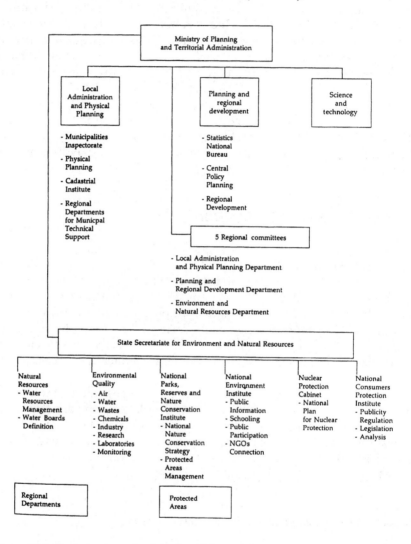

Figure 19.1 Organization of ministries with responsibility for the environment in Portugal

SEARN

The State Secretariat for the Environment and Natural Resources (SEARN) deals most directly with all environmental issues, from the quality of the environment, to protected areas and consumer protection and regulation. The single unifying law which draws together the functions of SEARN was passed in April 1987: The Environmental Framework Law (MPAT, 1987). Prior to this, legislation had dealt with individual components of the environmental patchwork. After 1987, the urgency was to consolidate existing legislation and meet the increasingly stringent standards of Europe.

It has been noted (Baldock *et al.*, 1988) that SEARN has flourished in relative terms compared to other components of the governmental structure and compared to other elements within MPAT. This has been due to the Secretariat's 'young, energetic and able first secretary' and due to the continued rise in importance of the environment within politics in general. The importance of SEARN within MPAT can be gauged from the fact that it is the Secretary of SEARN rather than the Minister for Planning and Territorial Administration who represents Portugal at the international level. Baldock *et al.* (1988) suggests that SEARN's first secretary 'is widely credited for the current level of attention accorded to environmental affairs'.

SNPRCN

Within the State Secretariat for the Environment, there is a specific service which deals with the administration and management of designated conservation areas. The National Service for Parks, Reserves and Nature Conservation (SNPRCN) has, within Europe, perhaps the most clearly defined remit of any government agency for the management and protection of nature and designated areas. While other countries struggle with multilayered levels of responsibility, Portugal's SNPRCN has few of these rivalries to contend with. While there is some overlap of responsibility with the Ministry of Agriculture (see below) the SNPRCN does have a clearly defined national role in both policy formulation and implementation. Its role is to plan for nature conservation at the national level, to propose the creation of protected areas and, subsequently, provide the structure and personnel for their management.

Other than the management and designating role of SNPRCN, the service is also responsible for the collection and collation of information and data upon species and habitat changes.

Other ministries

It would be naive and, indeed, incorrect to suggest that there is no duplication or overlap of responsibilities within Portuguese government. As has already been intimated, the Ministry of Agriculture has some areas of responsibility which overlap, if not directly compete with, those of

SNPRCN. The Ministry of Agriculture has control of hunting and, through its Forestry Service, controls and manages Parks and Hunting Reserves. Furthermore, as Table 19.1 shows, forestry is a very important and significant land use in Portugal, so the work of the Forestry Service clearly has a major impact upon nature conservation. There are also indications that the recent programme of afforestation has not only sought to increase the area of woodland, but also increase the recreational and hunting opportunities available. Forests, forest parks and hunting therefore appear to be increasingly complementary and/or antagonistic to the aims of SNPRCN.

Table 19.1 Land use in Portugal

Land area ('000 km²)	Arable/crop land ('000 km²)	% of land area	Wooded areas ('000 km²)	% of land area
92	36	39	31	34

LAND DESIGNATIONS

One of the more noticeable trends evident in Portugal is that, contrary to that found in most European countries, the rate of land designation at a National level has increased over recent years (Table 19.2). There are two main reasons for this. First, the recent democratic process is clearly still carrying with it the enthusiasm for the designation of conservation areas. Second, the National Government, as we have already seen, is far stronger vis-à-vis Regional government than in other countries. Hence, the surge of regionally based designations has not manifested itself in Portugal.

Table 19.2 Growth of designation in Portugal, 1974–88

Protected areas	1974		1980		1988	
	No.	Area (hectares)	No.	Area (hectares)	No.	Area (hectares)
National Parks	1	70 290	1	70 290	1	70 290
Natural Parks	0	–	4	210 082	5	218 082
Natural Reserves	0	–	6	57 469	8	70 384
Areas of Protected Landscape	0	–	0	–	5	85 766
Total	1	70 290	11	337 841	19	453 522

There is a wide range of designations which follows similar patterns to those found elsewhere: large parks that protect the overall integrity of areas, down to small sites that protect individual species or habitats.

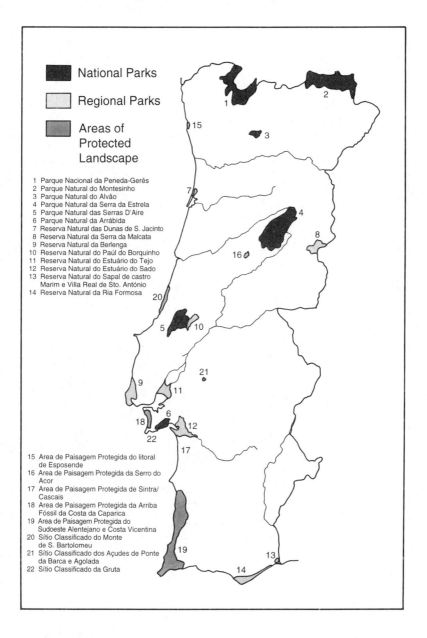

National Parks

Regional Parks

Areas of Protected Landscape

1 Parque Nacional da Peneda-Gerês
2 Parque Natural do Montesinho
3 Parque Natural do Alvâo
4 Parque Natural da Serra da Estrela
5 Parque Natural das Serras D'Aire
6 Parque Natural da Arrábida
7 Reserva Natural das Dunas de S. Jacinto
8 Reserva Natural da Serra da Malcata
9 Reserva Natural da Berlenga
10 Reserva Natural do Paúl do Borquinho
11 Reserva Natural do Estuário do Tejo
12 Reserva Natural do Estuário do Sado
13 Reserva Natural do Sapal de castro
   Marim e Villa Real de Sto. António
14 Reserva Natural da Ria Formosa

15 Area de Paisagem Protegida do litoral
   de Esposende
16 Area de Paisagem Protegida da Serro do
   Acor
17 Area de Paisagem Protegida de Sintra/
   Cascais
18 Area de Paisagem Protegida da Arriba
   Fóssil da Costa da Caparica
19 Area de Paisagem Protegida do
   Sudoeste Alentejano e Costa Vicentina
20 Sítio Classificado do Monte
   de S. Bartolomeu
21 Sítio Classificado dos Açudes de Ponte
   da Barca e Agolada
22 Sítio Classificado da Gruta

Figure 19.2 National and Regional Parks in Portugal.

Table 19.3 List of designated sites in Portugal (National Service of Parks, Reserves and Nature Conservation)

Type of area	Designation	Identification number	Legislation	Area (hectares)
National Park	Parque Nacional da Peneda-Gerês	1	Dec-Law 187/71 of 6 May	70 290
Natural Park	Parque Natural do Montesinho	2	Dec-Law 355/79 of 30 August	75 000
	Parque Natural do Alvão	3	Dec-Law 237/83 of 8 June	8 000
	Parque Natural da Serra da Estrela	4	Dec-Law 557/76 of 16 July and 167/79 of 4 June	100 000
	Parque Natural das Serras D'Aire	5	Dec-Law 188/79 of 4 May	34 000
	Parque Natural da Arrábida	6	Dec-Law 622/76 of 28 July	10 821
Natural Reserve	Reserva Natural das Dunas de S. Jacinto	7	Dec-Law 41/79 of 6 March and 55/80 of 26 March	666
	Reserva Natural da Serra da Malcata	8	Dec-Law 294/81 of 16 October	21 759
	Reserva Natural da Berlenga	9	Dec-Law 264/81 of 3 September	78
	Reserva Natural do Paúl do Borquinho	10	Dec-Law 198/80 of 24 June	529
	Reserva Natural do Estuário do Tejo	11	Dec-Law 565/75 of 19 July	14 563
	Reserva Natural do Estuário do Sado	12	Dec-Law 430/80 of 1 October	22 700
	Reserva Natural do Sapal de castro Marim e Villa Real de Sto. António	13	Dec-Law 162/75 of 27 March	2089
	Reserva Natural da Ria Formosa	14	Dec-Law 45/78 of 2 May	17 000
Area of protected landscape	Area de Paisagem Protegida do litoral de Esposende	15	Dec-Law 357/85 of 17 November	360
	Area de Paisagem Protegida da Serro do Acor	16	Dec-Law 67/82 of 3 March	388
	Area de Paisagem Protegida de Sintra/Cascais	17	Dec-Law 292/81 of 15 October	23 275
	Area de Paisagem Protegida da Arriba Fóssil da Costa da Caparica	18	Dec-Law 168/84 of 22 May	1 583
	Area de Paisagem Protegida do Sudoeste Alentejano e Costa Vicentina	19	Dec-Law 241/88 of 7 July	60 160
Classified spots and places	Sítio Classificado do Monte de S.Bartolomeu	20	Dec-Law 108/79 of 2 May	–
	Sítio Classificado dos Açudes de Ponte da Barca e Agolada	21	Dec-Law 197/80 of 24 June	–
	Sítio Classificado da Gruta	22	Dec-Law 140/79 of 21 May	–

National Parks and Nature Parks

There is just one National Park in Portugal which, perhaps ironically, was formed prior to the new constitution. The Park is in the north of the country (Figure 19.2) and adjoins a corresponding designation in Spain. The Park was founded in 1971 and covers over 70 000 hectares. Within the Park, the primary concerns are with nature and landscape conservation. Similarly, the Portuguese National Park designation also allows human settlements and some tourist developments.

Nature Parks are similar in size to the National Park, as Table 19.3 shows. The main difference between the two designations is in the objectives. The five Nature Parks not only seek to protect the natural environment, but they also allow for greater recreational, human and educational activity. Human settlements can be developed within Nature Parks, but only under tight regulations. Nature Parks, like National Parks, cover both publicly and privately owned land. Furthermore, the Parks also include several specific sites and Nature Reserves that add more precise protection to certain areas and habitats.

Nature Reserves

There are two types of Nature Reserve within Portugal: integral and partial. As the names imply, the former is more stringent in its protection than the latter. Both these designations, however, seek to protect as absolutely as possible components of the natural environment. Integral Nature Reserves exclude all human activity except for research and necessary management or administration and seek to protect the overall ecosystem or habitat. Partial Nature Reserves on the other hand are not so rigorous in their exclusion of human incursion because the designation seeks only to protect certain elements within the overall area, such as particular plant or animal species. Notwithstanding the precise and singular objectives of the Nature Reserves and the aim of total exclusion of human activity in some areas, some of the sites are surprisingly large compared to nature reserves or scientific sites in other countries. As Table 19.3 shows four out of the eight reserves are around or over 15 000 hectares in size. On average, though, the reserves are smaller than the National or Nature Parks.

Other designations

Three other designations concern us here: Recreation Reserves; Areas of Protected Landscape; Classified Sites and Places. All of these names and hence objectives behind the designations are relatively self-explanatory. Recreation Reserves allow higher levels of recreation and tourist activity than other designated areas, but they also seek to protect the natural environment and promote environmental education. (However, despite a relatively well-defined set of objectives, up until 1993 no Recreation Reserves had been designated.) The Areas of Protected Landscape cover five areas which are either urban or rural landscapes of cultural or traditional importance. Thus, almost by definition, the human element of these areas is critical to this traditional balance. Furthermore, for this same reason, these areas are attractive to tourists because of their natural beauty and their traditional lifestyles. The protected areas range in size from 360 hectares to over 60 000 hectares, reflecting the urban and rural range of their designations.

Finally, Classified Sites and Places are very small areas of great natural and cultural interest such as geological, archaeological or special species value. Only three such sites exist.

Overall, as Table 19.4 shows, some 4.9% of Portugal is protected in some way through land designations.

Table 19.4 Protected areas in Portugal

	'000 km²		
1980	1985	1990	1990 (% of total area)
2.5	3.8	4.5	4.9

Summary

It is worth summarizing the efforts made by Portugal since the revolution and subsequent new constitution in trying to bring some order to the collection of pieces of environmental legislation; more specifically the legislation dealing with land designations. The catalogue of types of designation is as comprehensive in Portugal as it is anywhere in Europe. The timescale over which it has been assembled and, more significantly, enacted is however much shorter than other countries. Notwithstanding this short timescale, the new constitution puts the designation of protected areas on the main political and environmental agenda. The progress that now needs to be made is in building up the actual designation – as we have seen, there is one designation that currently remains 'unused'. There does, none the less, appear to be the necessary political will in Portugal to make this happen.

OTHER ISSUES

As shown in Table 19.1, Portugal has one of the highest percentages of agricultural land in Europe. At 39%, it is on a par with Spain, and has less only than Italy and Denmark. Consequently, the impact of agricultural practices are very important to the overall balance of nature conservation. Of equal importance, but with different reasons, is the management of the water supply. The management of water is, currently, relatively disjointed in Portugal because no consolidating legislation has been passed. Therefore, the control and regulatory activities tend to be somewhat piecemeal.

The final area of importance is, in common with many if not all Mediterranean countries, tourism and recreation and the impact this has on the natural environment.

Agriculture

Agriculture in Portugal falls under the jurisdiction of the Ministry of Agriculture, Food and Fisheries (MAPA). Not only is this one of the largest Ministries, but it is also relatively old in that its importance predates the new constitution. The Ministry is responsible not only for agriculture, but also forestry and, importantly, hunting.

Pro rata, agriculture does not currently have a large impact on the environment compared to other European countries (Martins, 1992). However, in common with Portugal's Iberian neighbour Spain, this situation is changing as the pressure for agricultural intensification grows. Thus, the pressure is set to shift from one of the sheer size of the industry to one of size and those associated with high use of fertilizers, for example.

There is also likely to be an expansion in the overall area of land used for agriculture, because not only does the process of intensification bring new pressure on existing agricultural land, but it also tends to bring new land into use. This will be particularly noticeable in the interior of the country and some of the southern areas. This use of new land is becoming necessary because of the growth of Portugal's indigenous population and the growth in tourism.

Thus, the pressure from agriculture will move from one simply of the size of the industry to one of both size and intensity (Ministry of Planning and Territorial Administration).

Currently, the Portuguese agriculture industry is run by relatively old farmers (50% more than 55 years old) on small farms (average size 6.5 hectares) but still supporting some 23% of the population (Martins, 1992). The opportunity for intensification is therefore large. The current rural development plans of the National Government include: improvement of farm structure; modernization of methods; and capital intensification to support the incomes of the farmers (Organisation for Economic Co-operation and Development, 1988).

Forestry is managed by a specific Directorate within the Ministry of Agriculture, Food and Fisheries. Portugal has seen a rapid increase in the amount of forest cover in the country (Table 19.1). This has clearly led to some conflict between the forestry industry, the benefits to the national economy and nature conservation. Portugal, for example, has an important 'pool' of ancient Mediterranean forest species (just as most European countries have pockets of ancient and semi-natural woodlands). However, again in keeping with much of Europe, these local indigenous pools of species have been ignored and alien species have been used in the rapid afforestation pro-gramme (Martins, 1992). Also connected to this process of commercial afforestation is the risk of forest fires which increases as the density of the population increases. Large, monocultural blocks of, say, eucalyptus or alien pines are more susceptible to large forest fires than more open, natural forests.

The area at greatest risk from this problem is at the centre of Portugal, in the regions around Vila Real, Viseu and Castelo Branco. Recent legislation has sought to address these conflicts brought about by the forestry pro-gramme but, given the economic pressure to provide alternative or additional sources of income for Portugal's agricultural population, resolution to this problem remains difficult. This is made more difficult by the fact that over 75% of woodland in Portugal was privately owned and managed in 1989/90.

Water management

The management of water in Portugal is relatively disjointed, with no single agency responsible for either pollution control, regulation, collection or distri-bution. Even within the Secretariat for Environment and Natural Resources, there are two directorates which have powers over pollution control and water quality. This situation, and the overall situation surrounding the management of water, has carried over from the legislative position prior to the revolution and subsequent new constitution. This is self-evidently a serious problem in a country which, in common with many of its Mediterranean neighbours, has a very mixed pattern of availability and demand for water.

In some areas of Portugal, less than 40% of the overall population receives piped water. This situation predominates in the north of the coun-try. Around Lisbon, this figure rises to over 80%. The situation regarding the mains sewerage system is, however, less impressive with some areas, such as the rural north, only having 25% of discharges going into the sewerage network. Consequently, the water quality of some rivers and even ground-water is poor; a situation which becomes most critical in the estuaries of the main river systems where the administrative confusion and the problems of pollution combine to cause the greatest impact (MPAT, 1988).

Two other issues are of concern to conservationists in Portugal. First, the majority of surface water in Portugal is dependent upon Spanish manage-ment of the water resource. This is because the major Portuguese rivers (Duoro, Guadian, Minho and Tejo) all arise in the Spanish Sierras. Thus, the quality and quantity of Portuguese water is not entirely in its own hands. The second issue is that of salination of the groundwater supplies, particularly in aquifers that come under great seasonal pressure in tourist areas. Thus, the water quality of some underground supplies in the Algarve is poor, as it is in some of the Spanish Costas, and the Greek or Italian coastal aquifers. The knock-on effect of this on the natural environment is reflected in the impact that poor water quality has upon species diversity and habitats.

Tourism

The Portuguese tourist industry is regulated by the Ministry of Commerce and Tourism. The importance of the tourist industry for the national economy is shown by the emphasis placed upon it in the ministerial title. The industry has grown dramatically: from 1969 to 1989, the number of visitors rose from 1.2 million to 4.9 million, with over 85% of these being concentrated in the Algarve and Lisbon areas. The Ministry's role is therefore twofold. Not only must it promote and support the industry, but also regulate and approve the development of tourism infrastructure. The rural policy of Portugal is, in broad terms, attempting to level out the inequalities in the agricultural and rural economies. One of the main methods of doing this is through diversifying the rural economic base; a pattern found elsewhere in Europe. The search for rural economic activity other than agriculture has increased. 'Policies for roads, tourism, nature reserves and natural parks have particular significance' (Organisation for Economic Co-operation and Development, 1994). For this reason, capital grants are available, partly funded through the EC as elsewhere, to help the rural economy diversify into other areas. The potential conflict that this brings with nature conservation is discussed elsewhere in this book, but it is evident that the role of tourism needs to be clearly determined taking nature conservation into consideration. This problem is clear in the Algarve, where some 60% of incoming tourists stay where they are in Portugal, where 'local agriculture cannot supply the produce, there is an absence of infrastructure such as water supply or waste disposal and some habitats suffer from over-pressure' (Martins, 1992).

Signing of conventions

Given the late entry of Portugal into the European Community, it is a reflection of the country's commitment that it has signed all of the conventions mentioned in Chapter 6.

Implementation of EC Directives

The new constitution, as discussed above, contains the framework for tighter control of the environment and closer regulation. The large amount of work necessary since 1976 has, however meant that some slowing down of the implementation of the EC Directives has occurred. This is not necessarily a reflection on commitment, but on the time needed to cope with a new constitutional situation and a backlog of environmental legislation.

With Portugal's acceptance into the EC, there were time limits set for the implementation of some environmental Directives. However, no such 'derogations' existed for many nature conservation Directives. Whether or not it was because of this, is unclear, but by 1992 the Birds Directive had not been enacted. Notwithstanding this, the Portuguese government has made efforts to enact if not necessarily enforce most of the relevant EC Directives and Regulations.

SUMMARY

Portugal is, by any standard, a relatively young democracy, and as a result all issues that are influenced by politics (and as is made clear throughout this book, nature conservation is without doubt a political issue) have become involved in the process of democratization. As a result, in many instances, the priorities have been towards stabilizing the democracy, putting all legislation on a firm and new footing and only then moving forward with policies and plans. Given this late start, it is clear that Portugal has begun to understand many of the conservation issues that they are facing, and has very recently begun to put new legislation in place, particularly for some types of land designation.

The growth of the tourist industry must, however, be mentioned, not only because of the impact that it has had in Portugal, particularly in the Algarve, but also because of the broader principles involved. The concern of the Portuguese government to improve the economic conditions of the mainly rural workforce was, after 1976, understandable. This still remains a priority and consequently the push for the development of a tourist industry continues. The knock-on effects of this for nature conservation have been recognized, but not before some mistakes have been made.

This pattern is clearly not uncommon in many of the poorer Mediterranean countries and regions in Europe. What is perhaps equally important is that in Portugal these mistakes have been acknowledged and attempts are being made to resolve them.

REFERENCES

Baldock, D. *et al.* (1988) *The Organisation of Nature Conservation in Selected European Countries.* Institute of European Environmental Policy, London.

Garrett, C. (1992) *Organisational Structure.* DocTer, Milan.

Janvario, J. (1992) *Portuguese Environmental Legislation.* MPAT, Lisbon.

Martins, I.P. (1992) Agriculture and the Environment. DocTer, Milan.

Ministry of Planning and Territorial Administration (1987) *Lei no 11/87 de 7 de Abril – Bases do Ambiente.* MPAT, Lisbon.

Ministry of Planning and Territorial Administration (1988) *Ambiente 1988.* MPAT, Lisbon.

Ministry of Planning and Territorial Administration (1994) *Ambiente 1994.* MPAT, Lisbon.

Organisation for Economic Co-operation and Development (1988) *Recent Trends in Rural Development.* OECD, Paris.

Spain

Spain is one of Europe's largest countries; it covers 500 000 km² holding a population of 39 million. The north/south divide that is evident in other European (particularly Mediterranean) countries is also evident in Spain in that the northern part of the country, particularly around Madrid, Barcelona and the northern industrial towns, is relatively rich compared to the southern regions.

Like her westerly neighbour Portugal, Spain is a young democracy, with the new constitution having been formed in 1978, two years after that of Portugal, and three years after Greece.

The dominant biogeographical zone is 'Mediterranean', with areas of 'Alpine' being present in the north, and 'Macronesian' in the south-west. Furthermore, this general pattern is also given other characteristics by the fact that there is a large proportion of land in Spain over 1000 m, which brings with it some 'Alpine' features to many of these upland areas (Naylor, 1975).

A very large proportion of Spain is under forest or agriculture, and at 93% this is the highest in Europe. This somewhat surprising fact is explained by the Spanish definitions of these two land uses. Rough mountainous land and very poor quality scrubland is defined as having some agricultural value (which is perhaps an arguable point, given the extensive grazing of goats and other stock), and consequently similar dry or semi-arid land that would be excluded in, say, Greece is included in Spain's definition of 'agricultural'.

The proportion of land designated for nature conservation is 7.0% compared to an average of 8.4%, with both the Gross Domestic Product and the population density being similarly less than average.

The two politico-economic features of the Spanish period within the EC have been the moves towards Regional government on the one hand, and the perceived need to improve the economic condition of the rural population in the south, particularly through tourism, on the other. Both have had an impact upon nature conservation.

Plate 11 In southern Europe, the management of water is critical. Demands for pure water have increased, and its supply is difficult. This is not a road, but a dry riverbed, waiting for rain.

POLITICAL STRUCTURE

Spain's democracy is, in European terms, relatively modern. Partly as a consequence of this, and partly of a consequence of the regime which governed Spain prior to 1978, several major adjustments are still working their way through the Spanish political system. First, and perhaps most significantly, since 1980, the main responsibility for most aspects of government in Spain (and this necessarily includes nature conservation) has been devolved to the 17 autonomous Regions. The second effect is that Spain is one of the most recent members of the European Community, having signed the Treaty of Rome with effect from 1 January 1986. The politico-economic effect of this is still impacting upon the nation and its regions. Finally, with such an upheaval in the nature of government and its regionalization, there is inevitably a period of overlap with historic systems and mechanisms running alongside some more modern ones. For this reason, among others, the political structure in general, and the responsibilities of various agencies and levels of government, are often disjointed.

Regional and National government

Given the relatively recently formed democratic constitution of modern Spain (dating from 1978) and immediate (in political terms) acknowledgement of the recognition of the 17 autonomous Regions it is difficult if not impossible to separate out the issues of Regional and National government.

Figure 20.1 Regions in Spain.

The 1978 Constitution recognizes and guarantees the right to autonomy of the 17 Regions. The definition of a Region varies, but it covers islands, historical nationalities and other areas with identifiable cultural or economic characteristics or traditions. The regions are shown in Figure 20.1, and are: Andalusia; Aragon; Canary Islands; Cantabria; Castile-la-Mancha; Castile and Leon; Catalonia; Valencia; Estremadura; Galicia; Balearic Islands; La Rioja; Madrid; Navarre; the Basque country; Asturias and Murcia.

The role of central or national government is to provide national guidelines through basic laws or decrees. These do not remove the rights of the regions to introduce amending or supplementary regulations or laws. The importance of these basic laws varies according to the subject matter. Defence, for example, is still largely the responsibility of the national government, but others, including the environment, have been handed over almost exclusively to the Regions. As a consequence some areas of responsibility are apparently duplicated (to use a similar example, the responsibility for law and order lies with both national and regional law enforcement agencies). Conversely, in other areas agencies that were once exclusively responsible at national level are now only vestigial organizations with many of their legislative and executive responsibilities having been passed to the regions. One of these agencies related specifically to nature conservation, as discussed below.

The bulk of political power within Spain lies at the regional level. Each autonomous Region (*Communidades Autonomous*) has a Legislative Assembly (*Asamblea Legislaliva*) which is an elected body, elected by universal voting rights. The Legislative Assembly has a Governing Council (*Conserjo de Gobierno*) which is the executive and administrative agency of regional government. The Assembly elects a President from within its members.

The legislative framework by which each region governs its own affairs is, in part, built-up from internal 'organic' laws as much as from external decree and guidelines. It is around these areas that regional differences in interpretation of decrees occur. Indeed, it is also at this level, and partly as a result of these local historically important legislative and administrative frameworks that regional differences in executive responsibility occur. Thus, for example, responsibility for pollution control may lie with the Ministry of Public Works, Urbanism and Environment in one region, but may lie with a specially devised agency in another. This makes inter-regional co-ordination (for which state support is needed) difficult. Partly as a result of the need to co-ordinate responses to international initiatives despite regional variations, the national government still represents Spain at international conferences and conventions.

The final tier of government worthy of mention in this overview is the city council or *communidad*. Each urban area has its own locally elected council, which has a range of local and often very specific responsibilities. While most of these are 'administrative' (such as refuse collection, maintenance of open space or street lighting, for example) there are occasions that these responsibilities either overlap or are devolved from regional or, much less frequently, national government.

ENVIRONMENTAL RESPONSIBILITIES

Since 1980, the constitutional recognition of the autonomous regions has been translated into the transfer of authority for specific issues to the Regional Assemblies. This has inevitably included components of environmental responsibility in general, and responsibility for nature conservation in particular. Notwithstanding this transfer of power, the national government does retain several exclusive rights to initiate some environmental legislation, without prejudicing the Region's rights or competence to supplement the legislation. Furthermore, some agencies which before the process of regionalization had large organizations still remain in central government, but in a much changed and vestigial form. In order to fully understand the role of nature conservation agencies within central government, it is important to understand this shift in authority and responsibility.

National responsibilities

The main departmental responsibility within national government in Spain lies with the Ministry of Agriculture, within which there is a specialist institute for the conservation of nature (ICONA: *Instituto Nacional para la conservacion de la Natureza*). However, other ministries have some relevant areas of responsibility and, to act as a co-ordinating and discussion forum, an interdepartmental forum also exists.

Ministry of Agriculture

The Ministry of Agriculture is one of the largest within Spanish government, which reflects the fact that over 75% of the Spanish population derive their living from agriculture. One of the main organizations responsible for nature conservation (ICONA) has developed within the Ministry of Agriculture, and was itself a development of an older agency responsible for forestry within the Ministry.

ICONA

There are some grounds for suggesting that Spain led the way in the European Community with the creation of and legislation for National

Parks (see below). A law dealing specifically with National Parks in 1916 led to the first such parks being designated in Spain in 1918 in the north west and north east of the country. It is somewhat surprising, therefore, that ICONA (*Instituto Nacional para la Conservation de la Natureza*) was only constituted in 1971. Furthermore, ICONA is not exclusively concerned with nature conservation as the name suggests. Indeed, much of its main responsibility is with forestry and forestry management.

ICONA grew not only out of an increased awareness about the importance of nature conservation, but also the need to review hunting, game and fishing laws. Reorganization within the Ministry of Agriculture gave birth to ICONA. It has been argued, however (Baldock *et al.*, 1988), that ICONA never managed to lose its forestry background, and most of its energy and staff remain dedicated to forestry management.

CIMA

There are some five ministries directly involved in land-based conservation issues in Spain with many more agencies within these ministries. The Spanish government accepted in 1972 that this would almost inevitably lead to confusion and a lack of continuity. Thus, a Select Committee on the Environment (*Comision Delegada Del Gobierno para el Medio Ambiente*) and a corresponding working party (CIMA) were established.

CIMA (*Comision Interministerial del Medio Ambiente*) was set up to lead, promote and co-ordinate environmental policy in Spain. This naturally includes the land-based, nature conservation issues. Perhaps the most important function within this agenda is the co-ordination of ministerial activity. However, while the move was widely welcomed, the decisions and recommendations of the Commission are not legally binding, thus its ability is effectively restricted, despite the positive reasons for forming CIMA. Partly for this reason, and partly because the regionalization process exposed more fundamental problems with this means of co-ordination, CIMA in its original form was abolished in 1987. To date, no single substitute has been found or created to co-ordinate environmental or nature conservation issues. None the less, CIMA is worth mentioning here because it marked an attempt to draw together environmental policy at a National level.

Ministry of Public Works

The *Ministerio de Obras Publicas y Urbanismo* (MOPU) is the other ministry worth mentioning for its responsibility in nature conservation. Within MOPU, a new directorate was formed in 1980 which took on the responsibilities that ICONA did not absorb. Moreover, the directorate, DGMA (*Direccion General del Medio Ambiente*) now represents

Spain at international level on all environmental issues, and is responsible for implementing European legislation. Given the network of national agencies and levels of responsibility discussed here, this is inevitably a problem (Figure 20.2). A further role that DGMA has absorbed is that of widespread and continuous discussion with the non-governmental organizations.

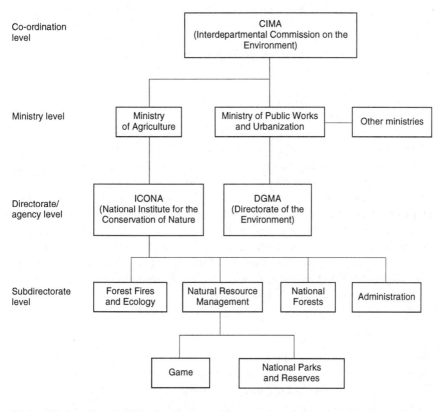

Co-ordination level — CIMA (Interdepartmental Commission on the Environment)

Ministry level — Ministry of Agriculture | Ministry of Public Works and Urbanization | Other ministries

Directorate/agency level — ICONA (National Institute for the Conservation of Nature | DGMA (Directorate of the Environment)

Subdirectorate level — Forest Fires and Ecology | Natural Resource Management | National Forests | Administration

Game | National Parks and Reserves

Regional level — Responsibilities for most forms of nature conservation have been transferred to the governments of the autonomous regions where a variety of arrangements are in place.

Figure 20.2 Organization of Nature Conservation in Spain.

Regional responsibilities

Most of the practical and implementary functions of nature conservation have been passed to the autonomous Regions. However, the Regions have local priorities, within which nature conservation takes a variety of levels of importance. Consequently, the organization and responsibility for nature conservation varies within each region. Some have simply moved the structures that were handed on from national government down to regional level. Thus, the structures of ICONA, for example, and its links with both forestry and agriculture remain. However, whereas prior to 1980, these agencies were regional offices of a national organization, no such direct link currently exists.

Some regions, such as Andalucia, Murcia and Asturias, have set up new agencies or cross-department agencies similar to CIMA (see above). These *Agencias de Medio Ambiente* have had varying degrees of success. By and large, however, the departmental fragmentation of nature conservation is repeated at regional level.

LAND DESIGNATIONS

There are four important categories of areas that are designated for nature conservation. The designatory system was established largely under the 1975 Act for the Protection of Natural Species, although as mentioned above, Spain was the first country within the European Community to have National Park legislation. Due to the timescale, some of the land designations are still managed by national government, while others have been passed to regional organizations, or indeed have only been designated after the regionalization process began. The four categories of land designations are: Integrated Reserves of Scientific Interest; National Parks; Nature Sites of National Interest; and Nature Parks.

National Parks

There are nine National Parks in Spain and, as has been identified elsewhere for countries within the EC, the process of designation of National Parks has slowed over recent years, although with the first National Park being designated in 1918, and the most recent in 1981, the pace of designation was never extremely quick!

Table 20.1 identifies the designation dates of the nine National Parks, while their locations are shown on Figure 20.3. The National Parks are the responsibility of National Government, with ICONA being the lead agency. The presence within the National Parks of ICONA staff varies in quantity, but it is clear from reports within ICONA that they feel that more field-based staff are needed (Ministerio de Obras Publicas y Urbanismo, 1982). To a certain extent, this is offset by joint working between the National Government and the autonomous Regions. The Regions do provide some management support, the quid pro quo for which is, however, an input into most important policy and management decisions. This can clearly cause some problems, because the objective of Spanish National Parks is to protect the natural environment, if necessary to the exclusion of human activity or access. If these objectives are administered inconsistently across the country, this leads to some confusion. A specific example would be the protection of endangered species, many of which are present exclusively in the National Park network. At a national level, these are some 300 species protected, theoretically with equal importance. Within regions, however, alternative lists have been prepared which tend to focus upon a fewer number of species often to permit hunting and which does not allow any level of consistency. Thus, the apparently clear line of responsibility for National Parks from ICONA is confused by the split of *de facto* responsibility with the regions.

Table 20.1 National Parks in Spain

Name	Year of foundation	Area (hectares)
Covadonga	1918	16 952
Ordesa y Monte Perdido	1918	34 463
Teide	1954	13 571
Caldera de Taburiente	1954	4 690
Aigües Tortes y Lago San Mauricio	1955	10 230
Doñana	1969	77 260
Tablas de Daimiel	1973	2 232
Timafaya	1974	5 107
Garajonay	1981	3 984

Nature Parks

Since 1978, most land designations in Spain have been Nature Parks. This is for a number of reasons. First, they tend to be smaller than National Parks (although one Nature Park – Sierra de Cazorla y Segura – is a massive 214 000 hectares). Second, the objectives of the Nature Parks are slightly less rigorous than those of the National Parks because public access and recreational activity is accepted to some extent although not always encouraged. However, undoubtedly the most important reason for the increase in pace of Nature Parks is that responsibility for designation lies solely with the Regions. Hence, with the increase in authority and power of the Regions comes the desire to designate their 'own' areas of conservation importance.

The pattern of designations is, however, similar to that of the National Parks. Figure 20.3 shows the distribution of both National Parks and Nature Parks. From this it is evident that the concentration in coastal and mountainous areas is common to both designations, with a strong concentration in the Canary Islands. Of the 58 Nature Parks designated by 1988, most fell into the category of mountain or coastline. To the list in Table 20.2, and almost forming a subcategory of its own, must be added some 29 new sites designated since 1988, all in the Canary Isles, with its 'Macronesian' biogeography.

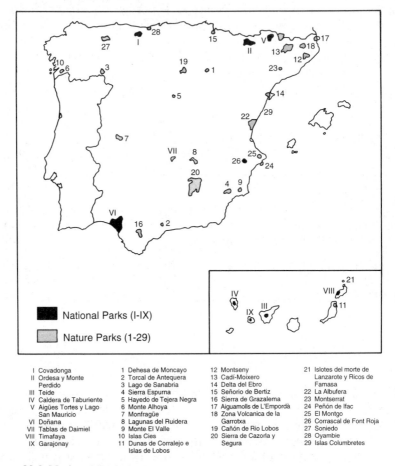

I	Covadonga	1	Dehesa de Moncayo	12	Montseny	21	Islotes del morte de
II	Ordesa y Monte	2	Torcal de Antequera	13	Cadí-Moixero		Lanzarote y Ricos de
	Perdido	3	Lago de Sanabria	14	Delta del Ebro		Famasa
III	Teide	4	Sierra Espurna	15	Señorio de Bertiz	22	La Albufera
IV	Caldera de Taburiente	5	Hayedo de Tejera Negra	16	Sierra de Grazalema	23	Montserrat
V	Aigües Tortes y Lago	6	Monte Alhoya	17	Aiguamolls de L'Empordà	24	Peñón de Ifac
	San Mauricio	7	Monfragüe	18	Zona Volcanica de la	25	El Montgo
VI	Doñana	8	Lagunas del Ruidera		Garrotxa	26	Corrascal de Font Roja
VII	Tablas de Daimiel	9	Monte El Valle	19	Cañón de Rio Lobos	27	Soniedo
VIII	Timafaya	10	Islas Cies	20	Sierra de Cazorla y	28	Oyambie
IX	Garajonay	11	Dunas de Corralejo e		Segura	29	Islas Columbretes
			Islas de Lobos				

Figure 20.3 National Parks in Spain.

In an effort to draw together the apparent competitiveness between National Parks and Nature Parks, ICONA has drawn up a list of some 700 sites, amounting to over three billion hectares, which are worthy of designated protection. The regional and national government are now embarking upon a long-term co-ordinated plan of designation which will clearly take many years to accomplish (Tario, 1992).

Table 20.2 Nature Parks in Spain

	Year of designation	Area (hectares)
Dehesa de Moncayo	1978	1 389
Torcal de Antequera	1978	1 200
Lago de Sanabria	1978	5 027
Sierra Espurna	1978	9 961
Hayedo de Tejera Negra	1978	1 641
Monte Alhoya	1978	745
Monfragüe	1979	17 852
Lagunas del Ruidera	1979	4 986
Monte El Valle	1979	1 900
Islas Cies	1980	483
Dunas de Corralejo e Islas de Lobos	1982	2 482
Montseny	1982	13 255
Cadí-Moixero	1983	41 342
Delta del Ebro	1983	5 900
Señorio de Bertiz	1984	2 040
Sierra de Grazalema	1984	47 120
Aiguamolls de L'Empordà	1985	4 624
Zona Volcanica de la Garrotxa	1985	12 228
Cañón de Rio Lobos	1986	9 580
Sierra de Cazorla y Segura	1986	214 336
Islotes del norte de Lanzarote y Riscos de Famasa	1986	1 722
La Albufera	1986	21 000
Montserrat	1987	3 440
Peñón de Ifac	1987	47
El Montgo	1987	2 800
Corrascal de Font Roja	1987	2 450
Soniedo	1988	30 000
Oyambie	1988	196
Islas Columbretes	1988	19

Other designations

The designations that seek to protect specific habitats are Integrated Reserves of Scientific Interest (22 sites) and Nature Sites of National Interest (74 sites). The former of these is by far the most highly protected, and concentrates upon very fragile ecosystems, often in unique locations. Consequently, most of the sites tend to be small, in the hundreds rather than the thousands of hectares in size. The Nature Sites of National Interest are equally small, but represent a second tier of habitats that require protection. However, it must be said that the total of 96 habitat protection sites is small relative to the size of Spain. Consequently, many of the overall 700 sites are habitat or species protection proposals.

Further, unique designations have been established for specific sites which merit particular protection. This is usually done through Royal Decree. Example of areas covered by special measures (control of hunting, or restricted development for example) include many forests, coastlines and specific areas such as the Murioellos or the Palmerla de Elche.

Table 20.3 Protected land in Spain

	'000 km²		
1980	1985	1990	1990 (% of total area)
16.8	17.0	35.1	7.0

OTHER ISSUES

Land use in Spain is dominated by agriculture and forestry, with around 72% of the land being covered by arable, crop and wooded land use (Table 20.4). In addition to this, there are large areas of rough grazing which account for an additional 10–12%; this is predominantly in the mountains of the south and north of the country. Furthermore, the country also has a thriving tourist industry, which makes great demands upon the natural resources of the country, particularly water and coastal environments. Consequently, there are many other factors which greatly influence nature conservation in Spain. These can clearly only be outlined here.

Table 20.4 Land use in Spain

Land area	Arable/crop land ('000 km²)	% of land area	Permanent grassland ('000 km²)	% of land area	Wooded areas ('000 km²)	% of land area
499	205	40	101	20	156	31

Agriculture

As is the case across Europe, Spanish agriculture is undergoing a prolonged period of dramatic reorganization. It has been estimated, for example, that around 500 000 workers will lose their jobs in agriculture between 1993 and 2003 (Quilez, 1993). The shift is from small family-run farms to larger corporately managed estates. This brings with it not only job losses but pressures for intensification, the scope of which in Spain is immense, with over 95% of the land being defined as agricultural in one form or another (Table 20.5). Since 1950, over 50% of workers have left the agricultural industry, and the process of intensification will mean that this trend continues, as outlined above. The need for additional water for irrigation will, in turn, cause environmental problems as large reservoirs are built in the relatively wet mountains, and many rivers consequently run dry.

Table 20.5 Distribution of agricultural area in Spain, 1986 (Anuario de Estadistica Agraria, 1986)

	Thousand hectares	% of total land
Agricultural areas	47 996	95.1
Cultivated terrain:		
non-irrigated	17 367	34.4
irrigated	3 053	6.1
Forested mountains	7 183	14.2
Non-forested mountains	3 601	7.1
Underwood	4 891	9.7
Meadows and pastures	6 652	13.2
Other agricultural areas	5 249	10.4
Non-agricultural areas	2 480	4.9
Total	50 476	100.0

Table 20.6 Area destined for various farm crops in Spain, 1986 (Anuario de Estadistica Agraria, 1986)

	Hectares	% of total land
Cereals	7 708 024	46.1
Legumes	417 839	2.5
Tubers	300 028	1.8
Industrial crops	1 296 129	7.7
Fodder	1 204 311	7.2
Vegetables and flowers	771 225	4.6
Fruit	1 136 716	6.8
Vineyards	1 572 723	9.4
Olive groves	2 205 917	13.2
Other	111 727	0.7
Total	16 724 639	100.0

Similarly, the environmental consequences of pollution from the process of intensification are increasing, and this is felt mostly in formerly valuable and remote areas of Spain such as the Sierra Nevada, Guadalquivir and the Jund Lagoon near Cadiz (Alvarez, 1992).

Water supply

The issues of importance in the supply of water are, in many instances, associated with the changes associated with agriculture. The increased demand for water from the dry areas of Spain has put a great strain not only on the infrastructure of water management, but also the natural environment.

The responsibility for managing water supply in Spain is held by 12 Regional Water Boards. Four of these are contiguous with and therefore administered by the autonomous Regions (Balearics, Canaries, Catalonia and Andalucia) but the others are separate entities and based upon natural watersheds rather than administrative boundaries. These organizations must work closely together to overcome the problems of geographic and monthly inequalities in supply. Furthermore, in order to raise the level of available water, the underground resources need to be exploited, and these again are geographically unevenly spread.

Given the scarcity of the resource, particularly in high tourist seasons, it is imperative that Spain's water is kept pure but, as is intimated above, chemical infiltration in intensive agricultural areas could pose a problem. Further problems are beginning to arise in coastal areas where over-exploitation of coastal aquifers has led to saline water seeping into the fresh supply, making them brackish (Ministerio de Obras Publicas y Urbanismo, 1988b).

Tourism

Other than agriculture, the industry that is having an increasingly signifi-cant impact on the environment is the tourist industry. The earliest legisla-tion specifically relating to tourism and tourism development dates back to 1963. This law was designed to stop the problems associated with large-scale and rapid urban development happening in tourist areas. While these are mainly concentrated on the coastal areas, they do, none the less, have an impact upon many designated areas (Ministerio de Obras Publicas y Urbanismo, 1982).

In recognition of this fact, the law on Protected Areas of 1975 specific-ally regulated tourist developments in National Parks, Nature Parks, Nature Areas of National Interest and Reserves of Scientific Interest. The impact of the tourist industry is therefore at a broader level than the specific designated sites.

The responsibility for tourism lies with the autonomous Regions and many have passed their own legislation to protect the natural environment and to curb some of the excesses of the tourist developments. The provision for tourism and recreation in natural environments is made both by the Regions and by the National government through ICONA. Similarly, both

Regional and National government give grants and subsidies to developers and individuals who wish to undertake tourist enterprises which add to the protection of the rural economy. As has been the case in Italy and Greece, however, the drive for economic regeneration has not always been sympathetic with the need for nature conservation.

Signing of conventions

Spain has signed all of the international conventions identified in Chapter 6.

Implementation of EC Directives

With the dramatic changes that were taking place internally at the time of Spain's accession to the European Community in 1986, the most important national priorities were the restructuring of the constitution and the devolution of authority and responsibility for a wide collection of issues to the autonomous Regions. Furthermore, the historic framework for formally adopting and implementing EC Directives was not in place. Consequently, there have been (and still are) many internal adjustments that have obstructed the adoption of EC Directives, and progress has been steady but slow. By 1992, 42 Directives has been adopted, with only one of these being directly relevant to wildlife and conservation. And, as we have seen elsewhere, adoption can be a long way from compliance or full integration.

Notwithstanding these shortcomings, Spain does appear committed to protecting the natural environment, particularly at the regional level. This concern and heightened awareness about the need for action have been partly brought about by the 'new found' political freedom of Spain, post-1986 and also by relatively recent problems arising out of the tourist industry and the pollution of the Mediterranean (Barrado, 1993).

SUMMARY

Spain's constitution is the most recent in the European Community. Furthermore, the creation of autonomous Regions has also been developing rapidly alongside and as part of the creation of this new constitution. This has not, it must be said, necessarily slowed the implementation of nature conservation legislation, but it has certainly added a clear regional and political dimension to the process. One obvious manifestation of this is the fact that no National Parks have been created since the creation of the new constitution, but many regional parks have. Indeed, one of the features of the moves towards autonomous Regions has been the transfer of power from the national government to these Regions. Included within this power is much of that associated with nature conservation. Consequently, much of the initiative now comes from the Regions.

This regional impetus not only appears in the designation of land, but also in the integration of nature conservation into wider development issues, particularly tourism and rural development. In the former case, it was the buildings associated with the tourist industry that in the 1970s and 1980s had such a dramatic effect on conservation, particularly along the coast. Some of these immediate conflicts have been resolved, but some of the longer-term problems associated with water supply, salination of aquifers and the disturbance of delicate habitats have yet to fully come to light. However, it is now evident that the Spanish government, at all levels, has a new commitment to address these difficult issues.

REFERENCES

Alvarez, A.G. (1992) *Agriculture and the Environment in Spain.* DocTer, Milan.

Baldock, D. *et al.* (1988) *The Organisation of Nature Conservation in Selected European Countries.* Institute of European Environmental Policy, London.

Barrado, A. (1993) Death throes of the Mediterranean. *Mediterranean Journal,* **37**.

Ministerio de Obras Publicas y Urbanismo (1982) *La proteccion juridica de los espacios natruales.* ICONA, Madrid.

Ministerio de Obras Publicas y Urbanismo (1988a) *Medio Ambiente en Espana.* DGMA, Madrid.

Ministerio de Obras Publicas y Urbanismo (1988b) *El agua en Espana.* DGMA, Madrid.

Naylor, J. (1975) *Andalucia.* Oxford University Press, Oxford.

Quilez, F.M. (1993) Union de Pequenos Agricultores: Annual review. *Mediterranean Journal,* **37**.

Tario, P.R. (1992) *Parks and Nature Reserves in Spain.* DocTer, Milan.

Sweden joined the European Community on 1 January 1995, along with its close neighbour Finland. (On that date the EC formally also became the EU). The Swedish economy, particularly the welfare economy, is very strong with an above-average GDP ($16.4 k compared to $15.6 k). This high national wealth is further compounded by the very low population density – second only to Finland and around only one-eighth of the EC average.

Sweden has a high proportion of forestry land, but a relatively low proportion of agricultural land; combined giving a slightly lower than average total value. The agricultural industry was seen as being one of the main benefactors on entry to the EC (*Sunday Times*, 1995).

The amount of formally protected land is relatively low (3.9% compared to 8.4% average) but this pattern is reflected in the other low population density countries.

In terms of the biogeography of Sweden, the country is split between 'Central European' and, in the north, 'Arctic', with a few pockets of 'Atlantic' on the exposed south-western coastline.

POLITICAL STRUCTURE

The management of government affairs in Sweden is somewhat different to that of the other countries of Europe in that much of the work of the government, at a national level, is carried out not only by a government-employed Civil Service, but by agencies and administrative boards. As a result, the actual ministries themselves are relatively small units that concentrate upon policy formulation and monitoring.

The sparsity of the population in Sweden dictates that most of the work on policy formulation is done at a National level, with little of the

National/Regional conflict seen elsewhere in Europe. This reflects the apparent trust in the National government felt at all levels (Orme, 1989), which is also reflected by the relative lack of non-governmental organizations (NGOs) within Sweden, particularly in the environmental sector.

National government

The ministries that manage the Swedish government are ultimately responsible to the monarchy, which, like most other monarchies in Europe, has a constitutional role to play rather than an active governmental role. The real administration, as elsewhere is undertaken by an elected parliament, the ruling party of which appoints the government, the day-to-day running of which is undertaken by ministers and Secretaries of State. The ministers reside over their respective departments which follow very similar 'patterns' to those found across Europe, e.g. Defence, Agriculture, Home Affairs and, most relevant for our purposes, a recently formed Ministry of Environment and Natural Resources.

The individual ministries promote and propose legislation that then goes before the Parliament for acceptance or rejection, and the ministries then become liable for its implementation.

The small size of the ministries, and their resultant ability to be very active in setting new standards and closely following international and national opinion means that many of the Swedish standards, in education, health care or environment, are exemplary for the rest of Europe. As shown below, this is particularly evident in some aspects of environmental legislation (European Community Committee of American Chamber of Commerce in Belgium, 1994).

Local government

Local government in Sweden mirrors the organizational arrangements at National level, with 24 countries and 286 municipalities having, in effect, local offices of both the ministry and the administrative boards. Local government is also managed by locally elected representatives who have certain local powers as of a right, but also certain statutory responsibilities handed to them by the National government.

ENVIRONMENTAL RESPONSIBILITIES

The main environmental concern of Sweden is the effect of air pollution on its forestry industry, although clearly there are many other issues that are relevant and important to the Swedish government. The importance of the issue of air pollution can, however, be judged from the fact that upon entry to the EC Sweden was able to negotiate a four-year lead-in period, after which other Member States needed to conform to current Swedish control standards. In short, all other countries must catch up with Swedish law. This is the reverse of the normal entry procedure. In other areas of environmental law, the two to three years building up to Sweden's entry into the EC was spent aligning EC law and Swedish law. During this period, it was also acknowledged by the European Environmental Agency that, in many cases, Swedish law was stricter than European law (European Environmental Agency, 1995).

Ministry of the Environment and Natural Resources

The Ministry of the Environment and Natural Resources was reorganized from the former Ministry of the Environment and Energy in 1991. Its role, as in common with all of the Swedish ministries, is to propose and monitor legislation. The key implementation agency in the Swedish environment is the Swedish Environmental Protection Agency. The Agency has a very broad remit, from nature conservation to air quality. This broad, single agency approach to environmental management is becoming common within Europe to reflect the increasing awareness that the term 'environment' is all encompassing. The management of nature conservation and flora and fauna protection sit alongside forestry and agriculture within the Department of Natural Resources in the Environment Protection Agency.

Without doubt, the main environmental concern of the Swedish government, and hence the most significant area of activity for the Environmental Protection Agency, is industrial and other emissions. Like many of its Scandinavian neighbours, Sweden has suffered particularly badly because of 'acid rain'. It has lost large areas of its indigenous forest stock as a result of air- and water-borne pollution. Within this broad objective, there are clearly some implications for flora and fauna. The Climate Change Act of 1993, for example, has as part of its overall aim the protection of the country's natural history resource as well as the economic timber resource.

The Ministry of the Environment and Natural Resources was instrumental not only in negotiating on Sweden's behalf to keep its own internal stringent environmental measures, but was responsible for helping to raise European levels of control. After four years of EC Membership, European standards should have risen to the Swedish standards on many issues, but particularly those on emissions and pollution control (Swedish Environmental Protection Agency, 1995b).

A further concern of the Environmental Protection Agency is that of 'integrating environmental thinking into every sector of society and helping each sector assume responsibility for identifying its environmental problems' (Annerberg, 1992). Again, this policy is shown particularly in the forestry industry, where over 80 000 employees of the industry have attended biodiversity courses (Annerberg, 1992).

Environmental Advisory Council

In common with many European countries, Sweden has begun to broaden the amount of discussion that formally takes place about the environment. One such vehicle for achieving this debate is the Environment Advisory Council. This group is attached to the Ministry of the Environment and Natural Resources (it is chaired by them and the Ministry provides the Secretariat) and it brings together ministers from other departments along with non-governmental organizations, the research and university sector, some of the government's own agencies and other environmental control organizations. The main objective of the agency is to provide a forum for discussion about the whole spectrum of environmental issues. This includes forthcoming environmental legislation as well as wider issues. The Advisory Council is not an executive group, and it does not have the power or the resources to enact any of its proposals. It does, however, provide a very useful function in allowing free debate about items that are of wide interest to many organizations and people in Sweden.

Local government

The main policy and organizational responsibility for nature conservation falls at a National level. The role of the local government authorities is to pursue these policies, predominantly through the local land-use plans and the implementation of the recommendations, reports and advice of the Environmental Protection Agency.

The physical planning process at local government level in Sweden has two distinct characteristics which simplifies into Stockholm and the rest of Sweden. Given the sparse population in most of Sweden, the issue of integrated rural planning is the most important outside of the capital city. The role of local government is to ensure that all relevant issues are included in the rural plans.

At a more specific level, each county also has a conservation unit, which is responsible to the county administration but also in direct contact with the Environmental Protection Agency. The role of the conservation unit is to advise the county authorities on conservation issues, and also to initiate, designate and manage Nature Reserves in the country. In some instances, this responsibility has been further delegated to community or neighbourhood levels, although this is the exception rather than the rule.

Other agencies, such as the Swedish Forest Service and the Environmental Advisory Council, have county offices for their operations, and have some direct responsibility. For example, the Forest Service manages nature reserves that are on public land.

LAND DESIGNATIONS

Much of Sweden is sparsely populated wilderness, and the country contains some of the few areas of 'Arctic' biotope in the European Union. Furthermore, a large part of the country is also very mountainous. Both of these facts are reflected in the designations of protected areas within Sweden. The third critical factor is the amount of forestry (both coniferous and deciduous) in Sweden. It is from this background that land-based environmental protection started and for this reason the Swedish Forest Service, mentioned above, manages all National Parks on behalf of the State.

There are two significant forms of land designations within Sweden: National Parks and Nature Reserves.

National Parks

There are 23 National Parks in Sweden, nine established as early as 1909, with the most recent wave of designation occurring in 1988/89 (Table 21.1).

Table 21.1 National Parks in Sweden

Name	Main habitat	Founded	Area (hectares)
Vadvetjakka	Arctic delta	1920	2 630
Abisko	Arctic tundra	1909	7 700
Stora Sjofallet	High mountain range	1909	127 800
Padjelanta	High mountain moorland	1962	198 400
Sarek	High mountain range	1909	197 000
Muddus	Arctic lake and bog	1942	49 340
Reljekaise	Mountain birch forests	1909	15 340
Bjornlandet	Virgin forest	1991	1 100
Skuleskogen	Coastal mountains	1984	2 360
Sanfjallet	Coniferous forests	1990	10 300
Hamra	Coniferous forests	1909	28
Tofsingdalen	Boulder fields	1930	1 615
Angso	Island/coastal	1909	168
Tyresta	Lowland pine forests	1993	2 000
Garphyttan	Medieval cultivated landscape	1909	111
Djuro	Lake/lake islands	1991	4 480
Tiveden	Coniferous forest/boulder field	1983	1 350
Gotska Sandon	Island/coastal	1909	4 490
Norra Kvill	Virgin coniferous forest	1927	114
Bla Jungfrun	Granite/glacial boulder field	1926	198
Store Mosse	Lowland bog	1982	7 850
Dalby Soderskog	Deciduous forest	1918	36
Stenshuvud	Rocky outcrops	1986	390

This is in contrast with many other European countries which have slowed down their designation rate for National Parks and increased rates for Local or Regional Parks.

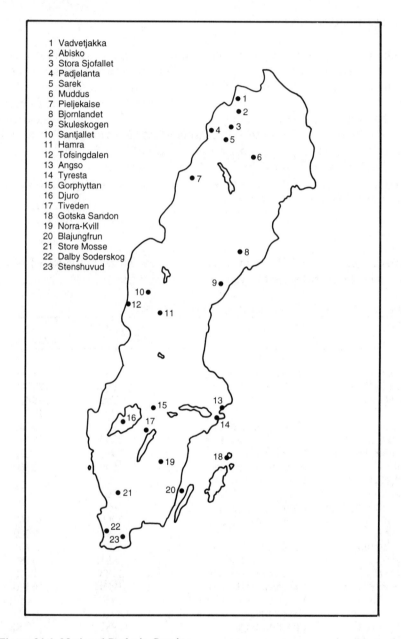

1 Vadvetjakka
2 Abisko
3 Stora Sjofallet
4 Padjelanta
5 Sarek
6 Muddus
7 Pieljekaise
8 Bjornlandet
9 Skuleskogen
10 Santjallet
11 Hamra
12 Tofsingdalen
13 Angso
14 Tyresta
15 Gorphyttan
16 Djuro
17 Tiveden
18 Gotska Sandon
19 Norra-Kvill
20 Blajungfrun
21 Store Mosse
22 Dalby Soderskog
23 Stenshuvud

Figure 21.1 National Parks in Sweden.

The National Parks of Sweden (Figure 21.1) include six inside the Arctic Circle, and a seventh just south of this line. These northern-most Parks are some of the only true 'Arctic' habitats within the European Community, and reflect three of the significant landscapes of northern Europe: mountains, fjord coastline and flat bogs.

The total area covered by the National Parks is around 6300 km^2 and individually they range in size from just 28 hectares to 198 000 hectares. Other than the mountain, coastline and bogs mentioned above, the fourth habitat type that is extensively covered by Swedish National Parks is forest and woodland. Indeed, in simple terms, the Parks South of the Arctic Circle tend to correspond to the relatively lower-lying country and are predominantly woodland or forest. However, even within the overall context of 'woodland' there are several distinct variations: deciduous/coniferous; coastal pine forests; scrub birch woodland and so on.

The underlying principles of designations for National Park status are that the land must be owned by the State, large (average size is around 10 000 hectares) and be relatively untouched by human land management activity. Designation allows for landscape and habitat protection, and also some level of informal recreation. This latter point is relatively unusual, with the UK being the only other country in the EC to legislate for recreational provision rather than simply allow it on an *ad hoc* basis.

Management of the National Parks is through the Environmental Protection Agency, which then delegates responsibility to the Forestry Board, usually at county level. In only one case, that of Gotska Sandon on the islands of south-eastern Sweden, does the Agency manage the sites directly (Swedish Environmental Protection Agency, 1993).

All National Parks are managed through an integrated management plan which is drawn up by the managing authority but which has to be agreed by the Environmental Protection Agency.

Nature Reserves

Nature reserves cover around 5.5% of Sweden, despite being much smaller than the National Parks. In all there are around 1400 Nature Reserves, which seek to protect small sites of biological, botanical or geological interest. However, unlike many countries, the Swedish Nature Reserves also allow for designation on educational and recreational grounds. It has been estimated, for example, that as few as 15% of the country's nature reserves have been designated for purely scientific conservation reasons (Orme, 1989). Thus, the use of the Nature Reserve designation is much more flexible in Sweden than elsewhere, and is often used to protect the areas of natural land around centres of population.

Nature Reserves are designated on both state/county-owned land and on private land. In the former instances, management is usually through the same mechanisms as those used in National Parks. In cases where Nature Reserves are on private land, the management is through an agreement with the landowner, who will be offered incentives and recompense for any financial loss caused by designation.

Other designations

It was partly as a result of the fact that the designation of Nature Reserves was being compromised that two new designations have been introduced over recent years. These are conservation areas and landscape management areas.

Conservation Areas are similar to nature reserves but are less restrictive. They are relatively small areas which have some wildlife or natural merit, but where human activity has compromised the natural integrity. The designation seeks to protect the remaining value of the site while allowing some level of human activity, particularly recreation.

Landscape Management areas are larger areas where existing land use continues, but where voluntary agreements are made between government and landowners to either continue with existing traditional methods of land management or where appropriate (and possible) adopt new methods of land management. Although there are no financial incentives for landowners who enter into these agreements, there is support in the form of advice and information.

Two other, very specific designations are worthy of note: Wildlife Sanctuaries are designated to protect threatened species and are set at the county level, with guidance from the national Environmental Protection Agency. Natural Monuments relate to single objects (glaciers, or trees for example) that are outstanding examples of the natural world. Again, these are designated at the county level, with guidance from the national Agency.

OTHER ISSUES

There are several land-based issues which are important in Sweden, but perhaps one particular concern is more relevant in Sweden than any other European Community country, other than Finland: so-called acid rain. Given the dependence of the Swedish economy on forestry and the large number of National Parks that are centred upon deciduous or coniferous woodland (Table 21.1) the Swedish environment is susceptible to any influence which is damaging to the woodland stock. For this reason, the Swedish government has been insistent both prior to and after its entry to the EC that air-quality standards are maintained and improved across Europe.

Agriculture

There are two main trends within Swedish agriculture which impact upon the Swedish natural environment. Whilst these trends are not unique to Sweden they do have characteristics which are significant. First, given the importance of fresh water habitats in Sweden, any impact on the chemical balance of the lakes will be very damaging. The numerous, often large bodies of inland water in southern Sweden are historically very poor in nutrients, and their ecosystems have developed accordingly. Any increase in eutrophication, therefore, however small, will be quickly felt. The drive for more intensive agriculture has begun to be felt in these lakes, and consequently in the rivers. Given the delicate, semi-Arctic nature of many Swedish habitats, such changes will be difficult to reverse.

The second issue arising out of recent agricultural practice is common across Europe. Agricultural intensification has begun to cause land-use problems in some valuable wildlife areas, particularly in the south of the country. While it must be accepted that this process has not been as dramatic as elsewhere in Europe, it has reached a stage where public concern is being expressed (Orme, 1989).

Economic development

The intensification of agriculture can in some ways be seen as an element of the wider economic development in Sweden. However, there are many other elements to the debate which in Sweden are caused by the sparse and often harsh condition in which many rural communities live, particularly in the north of the country. The importance of these rural areas in cultural, political and economic terms is large and for this reason the population in these sparsely populated areas has considerable political influence. One consequence of this is that there is an increasing potential for conflict between the economic requirements of the rural areas and the natural history interests. Two cases in point are hunting and large capital developments (such as hydro-electric plants or timber processing factories) inside National Parks.

Hunting is part of the traditional culture of many northern European communities, but the species hunted often include valuable wildlife such as the brown bear. Swedish legislation has attempted to minimize this conflict, and such legislation dates back as far as 1938. Furthermore, the Swedish Hunters Association (*Svenska Jajoreforbundet*) liaises with the Environmental Protection Agency. None the less, at a community level, hunting is still perceived as an integral part of the way of life of many Swedish people.

The capital projects are in many instances supported by government and trades unions because they bring much valued jobs to the rural areas. These capital projects include not only clearly defined economic developments but also tourism, and road and infrastructure schemes. This has led some organizations to call for zoning of National Parks to curb and if possible stop development of any kind in the true wilderness areas. This would not only include larger-scale development but relatively minor intrusions such as recreation and off-road vehicular access.

Non-governmental agencies

While Sweden does not have the tradition of voluntary sector activity of, say the United Kingdom or Italy, there are a few relatively large national agencies which have not only begun to become more influential but have also begun to broaden their areas of activity. The Swedish Society for the Conservation of Nature (SSCN, *Svenska Naturrardsforeningen*) does own and manage a few nature reserves, but its main function is as a commentator on proposed legislation and a means of generating public awareness, interest and involvement in nature conservation.

The Swedish Ornithological Society (*Sveriges Ornitologiska Forening*) is the second largest non-governmental organization concerned with nature conservation. Recently the Society has broadened its concern from species to habitats. As a result, the Society, along with SSCN, has been able to draw upon the deepening public interests and concern for the environment which has grown as a result of the acid-rain problem. By building upon this, the two societies hope to develop a greater level of understanding about some of the more detailed elements of nature conservation such as species and habitats protection (Swedish Society for the Conservation of Nature, 1995).

Signing of conventions

Sweden had signed all the international conventions mentioned in Chapter 6 prior to it joining the European Community in 1995.

Implementation of EC policy

The legal process of aligning Swedish law with European law has clearly not had chance to be fully implemented. None the less, prior to Sweden joining the European Community and as part of the precondition of membership, the Swedish government had to identify areas of legislation that complied with or exceeded European requirements. As a general rule, it was evident in this process that Swedish law was in many cases more rigorous than European law. Indeed, it was a cause of concern in Sweden that their own constraints on air and water pollution would be compromised by membership of the European Community. As a consequence, the formal process of matching Swedish and European legislation is not perceived as presenting serious problems (Swedish Environmental Protection Agency, 1995a).

SUMMARY

Swedish environmental standards have been at the forefront of European standards for many years. Even prior to the date of joining the European Community, legislation in Sweden was rigorous. This has continued to be the case since, with the European Community legally bound in some areas to tighten European legislation.

The most important concern of Sweden is the problem of acid rain, which has economic as well as ecological repercussions. The environmental movement in Sweden has expanded general concern about acid rain into a wider public awareness of broader ecological issues. This is reflected in official as well as informal debate and integration between ecological and other agencies.

REFERENCES

Annerberg, R. (1992) *The Protection of Nature*. Enviro, Swedish Environmental Protection Agency, Stockholm.
European Environmental Agency (1995) *Annual Report*. Copenhagen.
Hanneberg, P. (1995) *Editorial Comment*. Enviro Swedish Environmental Protection Agency, Stockholm.
Sunday Times (1995) *Expanded EC poses problems for Europe*, 10 March, 18.
Swedish Environmental Protection Agency (1993) *National Parks in Sweden*. Enviro, Swedish Environmental Protection Agency, Stockholm.
Swedish Environmental Protection Agency (1995a) *EU Policy and the Swedish Experience*. Enviro, Swedish Environmental Protection Agency, Stockholm.

Swedish Environmental Protection Agency (1995b) *Country Study*. Enviro, Swedish Environmental Protection Agency, Stockholm.

Swedish Society for the Conservation of Nature (1995) *Annual Report*. SSCN, Stockholm.

The United Kingdom | 22

Situated at the North Western edge of the European Community, the United Kingdom is made up of four separate constituent parts: England, Scotland, Wales and Northern Ireland. As a result, it is politically and ecologically relatively complex. Different legislative procedures are used in Scotland and Northern Ireland from England and Wales. Consequently, the enactment of legislation often needs three separate Acts of Parliament; a situation similar to other European Countries.

Ecologically, the United Kingdom has two main biogeographical zones: 'Atlantic' and 'Continental'.

The United Kingdom is a relatively densely populated country, which puts pressure on the available land. Furthermore, the process of agricultural intensification started earlier here than elsewhere in Europe. Consequently, the interests of nature conservation have long been an important political issue in the United Kingdom. This concern has also had its roots in the long history of industrialization and urbanization, which again started earlier in Britain than in most European countries.

The amount of land protected for nature conservation is around the European average, as too is the Gross Domestic Product per capita.

POLITICAL STRUCTURE

The political structure of Britain has, during the course of its membership of the European Community, had several adjustments made to it at the local level but has remained consistent at the national level. This is true not only for the actual political process and parliamentary procedures, but also by and large the departmental and administrative processes that underpin the political systems. This does not mean to say, however, that tension and overlap do not exist or that this consistency has managed to eradicate over-lap of responsibility. There still exists in the United Kingdom a variety of political relationships which remain the focus of considerable attention. Not least among these is the pressure for a greater degree of independence and autonomy in Wales and Scotland and the unresolved issues surround-ing Northern Ireland and its relationships with the UK and Eire.

Plate 12 Like most of Europe, the United Kingdom has many National Parks in remote, upland areas.

National government

National Government in the United Kingdom is based upon two 'Houses'. One, the House of Commons, consists of elected representatives from all over the United Kingdom. The other, the House of Lords, is a non-elected House with both hereditary and nominated peers, acting as a balance to the work of the House of Commons. The political party with the largest repre-sentation in the House of Commons form the government which, constitu-tionally, acts on behalf of the monarch. Needless to say, there is much debate about the role of the non-elected House in defining public policy and law.

National government is supported in its policy implementation by a professional Civil Service which is divided into departments or ministries, each one of which is headed by a member of the government as a Secretary of State. The ministries are similar to those found across Europe and include the Environment; Agriculture Food and Fisheries; Education; Health and Trade and Industry.

In Scotland, Wales and Northern Ireland, a Secretary of State represents the government and administers all the government's affairs through departmentalized offices, such as the Welsh Office or the Scottish Office.

This situation is further complicated by the fact that Scotland and Northern Ireland have different legal systems to England and Wales and, consequently, in some cases individual pieces of legislation have to be enacted for these areas which mirror the legislation in England and Wales, but which take account of the local legal circumstances.

Local government

There has long been heated discussion about the shape of local government in the United Kingdom. In 1969, a Royal Commission suggested that regionally elected local councils were the best option, but these never materialized. The system that is currently in place is therefore one of County Councils managing strategic issues in England, Wales and Northern Ireland, but Regions taking on this role in Scotland. These bodies are locally elected, and supported by their own locally funded professional administration. (There are exceptions to this general rule, particularly in urban areas of England where Metropolitan Districts take on the strategic role.) In the Counties and Regions there exists a second tier of District and Borough Councils. These are again locally elected, and supported by a professional administration.

This combination of two-tier systems in most of the United Kingdom, and single-tier system in the major conurbations in England is currently under review again, with the preference for single-tier or unitary authorities becoming increasingly popular. Ironically, this is a reflection of some of the recommendations of the 1969 Royal Commission (Richards, 1973). As a result of the 1994 review, many regions and counties have been abolished to leave a 'patchwork' of coverage.

Needless to say, there exist areas of confusion and potential conflict between the various levels of National and local government, particularly if they are run by different political parties.

A further significant factor at local level is the organization of National government offices in the Regions. Other than the situation on Scotland, Wales and Northern Ireland, England is divided into eight Regions for the administration of central government policy. The County and District Authorities deal with the government office in their particular region, staffed by Civil Servants. The regional government office can comment on and if necessary overrule strategic and other plans of the local authorities. Again, this is an area for questions to be raised. As Robson (1994) asks 'Are the Regional Offices advocates of the regions or dispensers of Central government policy, and what is their relationship with local authorities and other relevant organisations?'

Other levels of government

There is a further level of government in most parts of the United Kingdom, namely the Town or Parish Council. Unlike other areas of Europe, however, this very local, often municipal layer of authority does not have any significant powers and responsibilities, nor does it have any full-time administrative support, except at a very low level.

ENVIRONMENTAL RESPONSIBILITIES

The above system of national and local government is reflected in the wide variety of agencies within the United Kingdom with responsibility for various aspects of the environment. The picture is further complicated by central government trends to let agencies deal with policy advice and grant administrations rather than dealing directly with these issues from within the Civil Service. Consequently, there is a large number of government agencies working with environmental issues.

National government

Since 1970, the Department of Environment has been the governmental department dealing with environmental issues. Prior to this, a variety of departments and ministries dealt with various issues such as housing, public works and environmental pollution. Figure 22.1 shows the departmental breakdown of responsibilities, from which it can be seen that most of the agencies and responsibilities refer back to the Department of Environment.

The Department of Environment has a wide range of executive, advisory and policy-making powers. These are implemented through various channels. The Department, for example, has the power to call in strategic and other planning documents and ask for them to be revised if they do not reflect central government policy. These documents are, by and large, prepared by local government bodies. At a different level, the Department directly controls the agencies that are responsible for regulating the environmental performance of industry and service providers. Thus, the Inspectorate of Pollution and the National Rivers Authority regulate, among other things, industry. Finally, the Department also runs a number of advisory bodies, such as English Nature which advises both Central Government and other agencies on nature conservation issues.

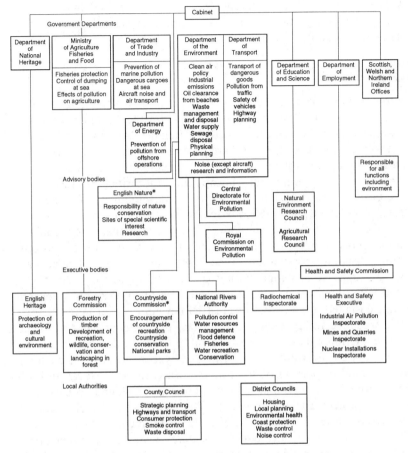

Figure 22.1 Governmental structure for environmental protection.

This relatively simple model is confused by the fact that some of the advisory agencies do have other powers (such as the Countryside Commission, which advises and offers grant support for landscape conservation and countryside recreation) and some of the regulatory agencies also have executive powers. Furthermore, different arrangements exist in Scotland, Wales and Northern Ireland.

Other departments do have a variety of environmental responsibilities. Most relevant here is the role of the Ministry of Agriculture, Food and Fisheries, and their work through the Forestry Commission and Forestry Enterprise (the advisory and executive section of the National Forestry Industry respectively).

In short, therefore, the National government is served by a variety of advisory, regulatory and/or executive agencies, each dealing with specific parts of the overall environmental agenda.

Local government

The role of local government in environmental management varies according to the level of the organization and whether or nor it is within England/Wales or Scotland or Northern Ireland. Broadly speaking, however, there are two functions that are performed by the local authorities: a strategic or planning role; and an executive and regulatory role.

The County, Regional and Metropolitan authorities produce strategic plans, based on land use and infrastructure developments, for their areas. These are reviewed and often revised by central government. The plans also go out to public consultation. The eventual plan then guides the planning process for a prescribed period of time. Consequent decisions on planning or land-use issues must then fit into this plan or risk refusal at the approval stage. It has long been argued (Cullingworth, 1990) that the United Kingdom has the most advanced form of local planning system in Europe, designed to guide but not restrict development of land.

The executive and regulatory role of local government is not restricted to land-use planning issues. Some central policies and legislation on the environment are, for example, implemented by local government such as the environmental inspection of food or factories. Similarly, local authorities take positive steps to manage their affairs and influence others around them, to protect the environment. The delivery of local Agenda 21 initiatives is, for example, the role of local government.

At the lower end of the hierarchy local authorities at the district or borough level are responsible for environmental issues such as street cleaning, refuse collection and the maintenance of open space and parks.

Other agencies

Non-governmental and charitable organizations are very active within the environment in the United Kingdom, and some of these organizations are very large both in terms of their financial resources and the land that they control. For example, the National Trust for England and Wales is the third largest landowner in the country, after the State and the monarchy. The Trust's sister organization, the National Trust for Scotland, is similarly active. The Royal Society for the Protection of Birds is one of the world's largest environmental charities, as too is the World Wide Fund for Nature. Both are based in the United Kingdom. Between them, these three NGOs raised some £96 million in 1991/92 (Charities Aid Foundation, 1993).

At the lower end of the scale, local charities operate in each county or district. County Conservation Trusts, for example, manage local reserves and conserve wildlife interests in other ways (Bromley, 1990). Furthermore, international charities such as Friends of the Earth and Greenpeace also operate United Kingdom branches.

The other agencies worthy of mention have already been touched upon. Central government is increasingly implementing its environmental functions through agencies that lie outside but still controlled by the Department of Environment. The main ones that concern us here are English Nature and the Countryside Commission (or the joint bodies that operate within Wales, Scotland and Northern Ireland). These agencies are funded entirely by central government and therefore seek to implement government policy, but also act as independent advisers to the government on nature conservation and landscape conservation respectively. Both agencies also offer grants to other groups (most usually, local authorities and NGOs) to undertake work which meets the broad objectives of nature or landscape conservation.

LAND DESIGNATIONS

The United Kingdom has a variety of land designations which reflect not only the variety of agencies involved in the process of conservation designation but also the various systems that operate in the various constituent parts of the country. In broad terms there are the larger national designations which are similar to those that are found in other countries in the European Community; at a local level, a number of agencies also help to designate and manage sites that represent a second tier of regionally important sites.

National Parks

The National Parks of England and Wales (there is no such designation in Scotland and Northern Ireland) are designated as a consequence of the 1949 National Parks and Access to the Countryside Act (Department of the Environment, 1949). There are 10 such Parks, with two other areas having similar functions but not being fully designated at National Parks. Figure 22.2 and Table 22.1 give relevant details.

The designation of National Park status is to protect and enhance the natural landscape, provide for informal recreation and to safeguard traditional land uses such as agriculture and forestry. In their aims, therefore, the National Parks of England and Wales have more in common with, say, French Regional Parks than other countries' National Parks. The National Parks vary in size, from 580 km² to 2240 km² and most of the land is in

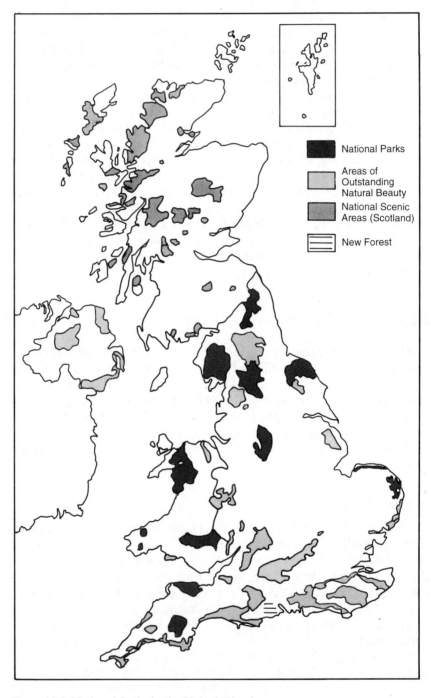

Figure 22.2 National Parks in the United Kingdom.

Table 22.1 National Parks in England and Wales

Name	Year of institution	Area (hectares)	Resident population (1981)
Brecon Beacons	1957	134 400	37 000
Dartmoor	1951	94 500	30 000
Exmoor	1954	68 632	10 000
Lake District	1951	224 300	40 000
Northumberland	1956	103 100	2 000
North York Moors	1951	143 221	22 000
Peak District	1952	143 000	37 000
Pembrokeshire Coast	1952	58 350	21 000
Snowdonia	1951	217 100	24 000
Yorkshire Dales	1954	176 113	17 000
Broads Authority	1989	28 880	5 000
New Forest	N/A	37 500	13 000

some form of private ownership, with agriculture, forestry or rough grazing being the dominant land uses. In common with many European countries, the UK's National Parks are largely to be found in mountainous and upland areas and, again in common with many countries, the move to designate areas of land has slowed considerably, with no National Parks having been designated since 1957.

Since that date, however, the Norfolk Broads has been established as a designated area with comparable powers to a National Park (so is unofficially acknowledged as the 11th National Park) and the New Forest (an area of Crown Land, managed by the Forestry Commission, among others) is often acknowledged as the 12th National Park.

The ten National Parks and the Broads are administered by local boards that represent a balance of local and national interests, and are funded at around 50–60% by central government through the Countryside Commission (Countryside Commission, 1991).

Areas of Outstanding Natural Beauty

Areas of Outstanding Natural Beauty (AONBs) were also devised under the 1949 Act. They are found only in England, Wales and Northern Ireland, with some 39 areas covering from 16 km² to 2000 km². AONBs are very similar to National Parks in that they seek to protect valuable landscapes and traditional land uses, and in the fact that most land is in private ownership. There is, however, no remit to provide for recreational access in AONBs, nor is there a specific board established to oversee the management of the areas and develop management and conservation plans.

National Scenic Areas

National Scenic Areas (NSAs) are found only in Scotland and fall some way between the National Parks and AONBs of England and Wales. Designated in 1972, the 40 NSAs vary in size from 9 km² to over 1000 km². The range of sites is wide, with coastal and lowland areas being represented alongside the mountainous areas and Europe's most westerly designated site, St Kilda, which is over 200 km to the west of the Scottish mainland (also a World Heritage Site). The weakness of the NSAs is that, unlike English or Welsh National Parks, no statutory powers exist for landscape protection for the local authorities.

National Nature Reserves and Sites of Special Scientific Interest

The final national land designation worthy of individual note are National Nature Reserves (NNRs) and Sites of Special Scientific Interest (SSSIs). The UK agencies draw a clear distinction between landscape conservation and habitat or wildlife conservation. The previous land designations are concerned predominantly with landscapes; NNRs and SSSIs are concerned with wildlife conservation. There are around 200 National Nature Reserves, of an average 700 hectares in size, and some 4000 Sites of Special Scientific Interest, of around 300 hectares on average. Designation is to protect a habitat or species, with the ownership often left in private hands and a series of management measures enforced by the central government agencies.

Other designations

The United Kingdom has a very wide variety of land designations, which is a result of the various different systems and organizations involved. Others worthy of note include the following.

1. Environmentally Sensitive Areas which, alongside other similar designations in Europe resulting from Regulation 797/85 of the European Commission, seek to protect environmentally important land from the pressure of agricultural intensification. In so doing, monies from the Common Agricultural Policy are directed into conservation.
2. Heritage Coastlines, designated in England and Wales since 1972, now cover some 1493 km of coast particularly in Wales and South Western England. Most Heritage Coasts coincide with coastal areas of National Parks and AONBs and much is owned by the National Trust (see above).
3. Local Nature Reserves fall into several types; they are often owned and managed by NGOs; designated by local authorities; or dedicated voluntarily by private landowners.

This list is not exhaustive, but does reflect the wide variety of designations used in the United Kingdom, and which accounts for it having one of the highest levels of designated land in Europe. (Table 22.2)

Table 22.2 Land designations in the United Kingdom

	'000 km²			
1970	1980	1985	1989	1989 % of total area
13	13.2	15.5	25.7	10.6

OTHER ISSUES

Parts of the United Kingdom are very densely populated, and overall it is one of the most densely populated within the European Community. Consequently, the issues surrounding resource management (such as water) are important. Conversely, despite the high population density some 80% of the country is still defined as agricultural, so the farming industry and its associated changes also have an important bearing on nature conservation.

Agriculture

The agricultural surpluses of the 1970s and 1980s resulted in a number of measures being introduced as we have seen earlier. In the United Kingdom this manifested itself in several ways that are common to those found in other areas of the Community. 'Set-aside', for example, was designated simply to take land out of production but was not linked to any proposals to use the set-aside land for any ecological or natural history purpose (Bower, 1987). A further experiment was through the designation of Environmentally Sensitive Areas which were identified in agricultural areas of the country where 'traditional' farming methods were seen as being the means of protecting the natural history and landscape integrity of an area.

Notwithstanding these localized or other initiatives, farming patterns are following those witnessed elsewhere in Europe with more intensive agricultural methods being used on large farms, with fewer opportunities for nature conservation interest to be enmeshed within overall agricultural methods. At a wider level, agriculture and support through capital or other grants is now seen as part of a broader socio-economic environment within rural areas. As elsewhere, agriculture is no longer the mainstay of many rural economies, although in some areas this is still the case. Farm diversification into tourist or recreational ventures is encouraged in capital grants for example, which could have a detrimental impact on the natural environment. However, within the United Kingdom there is an official view at least that 'By working together, government departments have developed complementary policies designed to encourage growth and diversification of the rural economy' (Organisation for Economic Co-operation and Development, 1988).

Water management

Water 'collection' and supply is managed by a series of regionally organized private companies, based upon the former publicly owned Regional Water Authorities. The quality of water and associated environments is monitored by one agency (the Environment Agency) and prices and commercial standards by another. Over 99% of households in the United Kingdom receive direct supplies and the main issue is not usually the level of supply and demand (as it is in, say drier or more seasonally variable areas such as countries with large tourist industries) but in the quality of the water supply. This is an important issue for nature conservation for a number of reasons. First, control of the upland catchment areas, usually in the wetter west of the country, means that public access and control of wildlife can be affected in a desire to control possible sources of pollution. Treatment of large bodies of water to improve drinking quality also results in changes to the ecosystem within the water system. In areas where water is taken from underground aquifers the hydrology of associated wetlands is seriously affected, especially during the drier summer months. This is particularly acute on the four remaining areas of lowland bog, where active pump drainage of the bogs is destroying these ancient habitats, for example the Somerset levels and the Humber levels (Baldock, 1984).

Tourism and recreation

The conflict between recreation and nature conservation in the United Kingdom is in some ways greater than elsewhere in Europe because of the objectives behind the designation of National Parks and National Scenic Areas in Scotland. These areas are designated to promote the recreational enjoyment of them as well as protect the landscape. Thus, some of the National Parks in Britain are the busiest in Europe if not the world with two (the Lake District in northern England and the Peak District in central England) receiving over 20 million visitors a year. Similarly, much of Britain's coastline is important for nature conservation and as a tourist/recreational destination. As a consequence of this, many local authorities have taken on a management responsibility to try to resolve these conflicts as have the authorities responsible for managing the National Parks or National Scenic Areas and, to a lesser extent, the other areas of land designation identified above.

Signing of conventions

The United Kingdom has signed all of the major international conventions discussed in Chapter 6.

Implementation of EC Directives

It has been argued (Haigh, 1992) that the British government's privatization of many functions associated with the environment, particularly the water industry, has focused a lot of attention on the environmental performance of the United Kingdom government and its agencies.

This implementation is either directly through Acts of Parliament (such as the Wildlife and Countryside Act) or, more usually, through purely administrative procedures. These have been queried because the process simply involves the relevant central government department (usually the Department of Environment) informing local authorities of the relevant Directive and nominating them as the competent authority. The obvious flaws in this are now leading to pressure to implement more by direct Acts or issue of Regulations rather than rely upon administrative methods which could be seen as simply passing responsibility onto local government, often without extra resources.

A required outcome of this shift is that the controversy over the non-compliance by the United Kingdom of EC Directives will be overcome by much clearer and more specific implementation. For example, compliance with the Habitats Directive will be through amending relevant planning and wildlife legislation, not by issuing an advisory note through the Department of Environment to local authorities.

SUMMARY

The United Kingdom has long had an ambiguous relationship with Europe and one of the subsequent points of conflict for this ambiguity has been the environment. While this has not specifically focused upon nature conservation *per se*, it clearly has been an issue. The quality of water, pollution on bathing beaches and the levels of permissible dumping of waste in the North Sea have all been issues of conflict between the European Commission and the United Kingdom government.

Notwithstanding this potential discord, the United Kingdom has also got a long history of nature conservation, within which, perhaps more so than elsewhere in Europe, the voluntary or non-governmental sector has been particularly influential. Several of the largest non-governmental agencies in Europe either started in the United Kingdom or are based solely there. These include the Royal Society for the Protection of Birds, the World Wide Fund for Nature and the National Trust. Equally strong have been the non-governmental pressures for access to and an understanding of the environment. As a consequence, National Parks in the United Kingdom, more so than anywhere else in Europe, have been established with not only conservation but also public enjoyment in their remit.

Another characteristic of the United Kingdom system of nature conservation is that there are clear distinctions drawn between the various strands of conservation: landscape, wildlife and heritage/culture. Again, as a consequence, National Parks and Country Parks do not have the protection of flora and fauna as a sole objective.

Finally, while the relationship between local/regional government and national government is not as complex as in, say, Belgium, France or Spain, there are none the less frictions which have often resulted in responsibilities being passed to local government without resources being available to meet these new responsibilities. As elsewhere, this relationship has not been resolved and, as a consequence, in some instances the environment will suffer.

REFERENCES

Baldock, D. (1984) *Wetland Drainage in Europe*. International Institute for Environment and Development, London.

Bower, J. (1987) *Removing Land from Agriculture*. CPRE, London.

Bromley, P. (1990) *Countryside Management*. E. & F.N. Spon, London.

Charities Aid Foundation (1993) *Charity Trends*. CAF, London.

Countryside Commission (1991) *Fit for the Future*. Cheltenham.

Cullingworth, J.B. (1990) *Town and Country Planning in England and Wales*. Allen & Unwin, London.

Department of the Environment (1949) *National Parks and Access to the Countryside Act*. DoE, London.

Haigh, N. (1992) EC policy and implementation, in *European Environmental Yearbook*, DocTer, Milan.

Organisation for Economic Co-operation and Development (1988) *Trends in Rural Policy Making*. OECD, Paris.

Richards, P.G. (1973) *The Reformed Local Government System*. Allen & Unwin, London.

Robson, B. (1994) Missed chance to make a regional statement. *Planning*, **1079**, 9.

PART THREE

Conclusions

Developments | 23

This part of the book can only map out some of the trends that will carry us forward into the next decade, and consequently put forward some broad conclusions about the development of nature conservation in Europe, both at the macro, community level and at the micro, individual Member State level. It is only possible to present the wider picture, of necessity. The conclusions, presented in this chapter, are therefore those that are clearly distinguishable from the vantage point of distance in both time and geographic spread. It is often difficult to attain that perspective when dealing day by day with the problems associated with National Park or Nature Reserve management. Similarly, it is also difficult to predict how policy introduced at an international level will impact upon national methods of working, or what problems such a policy will meet in its implementation; problems that may arise not just because of a lack of willingness to make change, but also simply because the systems used to manage nature conservation within Member States may not be able to accommodate the new legislation.

In these two chapters, the opportunity is taken to explore where the European Community is going. More specifically, it is perhaps only possible to examine some of the issues that will influence the development of nature conservation policy and practice within Europe. These influences come from a variety of sources, including moves within the Community and some global influences. Similarly, these issues will not all be led by environmental concerns; the expansion of the European Community, for example, is not driven by environmental concerns, but by socio-economic considerations as well as defence and security concerns. The following discussion is therefore wide ranging but, of necessity, brief.

Plate 13 The Unesco definition of a World Heritage site combines natural heritage with artificial and cultural heritage as here at Hadrian's Wall in northern England.

Plate 14 Coniferous woodland is one of the commonest habitats in much of northern Europe.

EXPANSION OF THE COMMUNITY

With the entry into the Community on 1 January 1995 of Finland, Sweden and Austria, the first steps were made along the often promoted route of broadening the European Community. The other part of this debate is, however, not just about broadening the Community, but deepening it as well. With the decline and ultimate demise of the Communist bloc, led by the Soviet Union, at the end of the 1980s it was thought that, even within the European Community, the emerging states and countries would join the EC sooner rather than later (European Commission, 1991). In this way the 'broadening' process would be speeded up. However, with the resultant conflicts arising in some of the emergent nations, particularly Russia, the economic and social upheaval attendant in the reunification of Germany, and the pressure to 'deepen' the Community through the Maastricht Treaty, this move to include the Eastern European countries in the Community has slowed down considerably.

Within western Europe, also, the three most recent entrants mark the end of the foreseeable expansion. Consequently the growth of the European Community in geographic terms looks set to be relatively slow in the early part of the 21st century. This, therefore, suggests that the attention will shift to the speed and mechanisms through which deeper Community interaction can take place. Moves towards full economic and social integration are foremost in Member States. Consequently, the initiative set up through the Habitats Directives and Econet will eventually be deepened, and, in the longer term, expanded geographically, first to the three new Member States and subsequently to any further Member States.

SUBSIDIARITY

Consequential to the broader/deeper debate is the notion of subsidiarity; a much quoted and variously interpreted Euro-concept if ever there was one! Talk of a 'multispeed', 'twin-track' or 'opt-out' Europe is driven by the varying concerns of the Member States that European legislation and government will take away from the 'individual States' their local national sovereignty and power. The principle of subsidiarity is that any decision that can be made at a national level will be made at a national level, or at an even smaller geographic basis such as the Region or County level. However, even this principle has not clarified the argument (*The European*, 1994) and countries are seeking clarification on the right *not* to follow certain types of legislation (such as the United Kingdom's opt-out of social legislation arising from the Maastricht Treaty). Indeed, it has been argued that the Norwegian rejection of membership of the European Community in late 1994 in the national referendum was caused by the Norwegian population's fear that European legislation would undermine the Norwegian way of life (*The Times*, 1994). This is a reflection of the issue that lies at the heart of the subsidiarity debate.

The implications for this for environmental legislation, and particularly for nature conservation, is that there will inevitably be more debate between Member States and the European Commission about the legal competence of the Commission to make legislation and subsequently how this is to be interpreted at the local level. It is possible that the principle of subsidiarity could be tested legally on environmental issues: a Member State could well question whether some environmental legislation should best be made at a National level rather than at a European level. If such a challenge were to take place on nature conservation and habitat designation, an integrated and co-ordinated Econet would falter. While no such challenge is currently being discussed publicly, it may well arise, whether or not it focuses on the environment, as the issue in question.

There is no doubt that the issues surrounding the concept of subsidiarity (only the European Community could have created a world like that!) will lie at the centre of much debate within Europe. At its most obvious extreme, the discussions about a 'seamless state' with a single currency is either the vision or the nightmare of individuals and countries within Europe. At another extreme, it is giving renewed hope to separatist democratic politicians in many countries, who see the concept of a federal network of regions as being a different result of the subsidiarity debate. Thus areas such as Scotland in the United Kingdom, Brittany in France and the Basque region in Spain are seeing renewed calls for independence within Europe.

INTEGRATED RURAL DEVELOPMENT

A different trend that is not, perhaps, new but is witnessing renewed emphasis is that of integrated rural policy making. Many countries across the world, and not just in Europe, have rediscovered the need to plan for a multi-use, multifunctional countryside which does not seek just to zone different economic, cultural and ecological land uses, but seeks to integrate these into a land-use policy.

This broad movement can be summarized from a report by OECD (Organisation for Economic Co-operation and Development, 1993):

Rural areas have increasingly faced economic adjustments and migration pressures, while many metropolitan centres have grown to dis-economic and socially unhealthy levels. The environmental effects have been significant. The challenge for rural development policy is to improve the balance of economic opportunities and social conditions between rural and urban areas – whilst not destroying the rural heritage and environment.

The success or otherwise of these plans depends largely upon the actual or perceived economic viability of an area. In other words, if an area sees itself as being an economically underdeveloped region, then economic regeneration is often the most important consideration in any land-use plan. Consequently, it is justified to suggest that such a plan is not, strictly speaking, integrated. It is for this reason that, while the 'greening' of many economic policies is to be welcomed, the safeguard of ecologically based land designation is also necessary. As has often been discovered in the recent past, the process of including environmental considerations in economic decision making is very difficult (Pearce and Turner, 1992).

There are several manifestations of this greater concern for the broader natural environment, rather than just with pockets of it. The revisions being made to the Common Agriculture Policy for example (Baldock *et al.*, 1993), the theme of the fifth European Community Environmental Action Programme (Towards Sustainability), and the growth of 'green tourism' as a means of directly linking environmental protection and economic growth (World Tourism Organisation, 1992) are all examples of policy integration.

REGIONALIZATION

The final trend that is worthy of short review here is, in many ways, linked to the three preceding trends. The European Commission is keen to promote the subnational level of government and non-governmental activity. Consequently, the Single European Act established a new Committee within the Commission structure: the Committee of the Regions (COR). The guiding framework within which Regional working will operate is 'Europe 2000 plus', a policy guideline produced by the European Commission. Within this document, there is a long-term commitment to regional planning. In turn, this has socio-political and environmental implications for the whole of Europe. Rivalries between National and (where they exist) Regional governments will continue, and some areas (such as Scotland and Brittany) could well see 'independence' within a regionalized Europe. Conversely, the move could well promote closer and more tightly focused planning and co-operation between public, private and voluntary organizations. If this were to happen, the vision of integrated rural planning across Europe may become a reality. As if to emphasize the environmental significance of the process of regionalization, the environment was chosen as one of the first themes to be addressed by COR (Morphet, 1995). The debate that surrounds the relationship between COR and the formal systems and structures within the EC will continue and it is likely they will continue for a long period of time. It is also likely that the pressure for more power to be allocated to regional bodies will increase. We only have to remember the competition that exists between regions and central governments within individual member states to realize that the 'regional voice' within Europe is becoming increasingly loud.

FIFTH ENVIRONMENTAL ACTION PROGRAMME

The importance of the fifth Environmental Action Programme is stressed in Chapter 5. It is worth emphasizing here just how significant this programme actually is and how it puts down important way-markers for future policy development.

The fifth Environmental Action Programme marked a departure from the former areas of concern for the EC policy makers. Gone were the constraints imposed by the need to have an environmental policy on the grounds that it contributed to an equalization of economic performance across Europe. Gone too was the focus on species-based protection of the natural environment. In its place came a desire to see environmental protection as an underpinning base for all activity. The concept of sustainability became paramount, and so too did the needs of the environment in agricultural legislation, economic legislation and social legislation. In some ways, this deflected the previously central focus of the EC, namely protecting species and sites, into a wider agenda. It would be easy to think that this meant a reduction in the importance of site-based and species-based protection. However, the development of Natura 2000 (Chapter 6) and Econet (Chapter 6) indicates that this is not the case. Notwithstanding this, the fifth Environmental Action Programme does indicate a broadening of the environmental agenda, and a willingness on the part of the EC to begin to place the environment at the centre of all its legislation. Against this background, the fifth Action Programme marks a new direction for the EC.

EUROPEAN ENVIRONMENTAL AGENCY

A further marker for future developments within the EC is the establishment of the European Environmental Agency (EEA) which was formed in 1990 but only became operational in 1993, and only found its permanent location in Copenhagen in 1995. The need to create a comprehensive data base on the environment and to compare best practice across Europe lies at the heart of the Agency's work. Several priority areas have been identified for the Agency, including land use and natural resources. The full agenda does, however, reflect the broadly based concerns of the EC outlined above. The implications of the work of the Agency will be that there will be greater co-operation across Europe and this will increasingly be mandatory in the awarding of environmental grants from Europe. Recipients of grants will be expected to establish joint working arrangements with agencies in other EC Member States. The LIFE Programme, for example, was an environmental funding programme running from 1992 to 1995 with budgets of around 70 million ECU per annum. An integral requirement of all projects (45% of which were for 'the protection of habitats and nature') was that they linked with partners in at least two other EC countries. Pan-European links will become the norm in future, rather than the exception.

NATURE CONSERVATION

It may seem somewhat strange to have a section in this chapter dedicated to nature conservation, when the whole book is concerned with nature conservation; however, it is clearly worth noting some of the significant European and international trends in nature conservation. Furthermore, it is also worth identifying some of the more important points within individual Member States.

The first point worthy of note is that over the years since the EC was first formed, very significant strides have been made. Information flows relatively freely, and consistency has become more important in the way that information is collected and presented. The development of Econet and Natura 2000 as defined in Chapter 6, clearly shows how this increased consistency can be brought to good effect to create a cohesive, pan-European strategy (IBM, 1992). This cohesion will undoubtedly increase both in its extent (i.e. by covering a wider geographical area as other countries seek to join the EC) and in depth (i.e. by ensuring that the cohesion covers more issues). In this context, the environment is part of the debate about the future of Europe: does it go deeper or wider? However, in the case of the environment, it looks set to do both (European Commission, 1994).

A further similar point to this is that not only has the EC at an overall level made significant advances, but individual Member States have also made significant strides. In only the mid-1980s many European countries were being openly criticized for clearly ignoring environmental considerations when pursuing economic development. Most now build in environmental assessments at a very early stage of proposals. Whether or not these assessments and other controls would have been created without the 'push' from the EC may never be known, but the fact of the matter is that they do now exist. It is also the case that all countries acknowledge that more could and should be done to protect the environment. If Part Two seems a little harsh in places about the performance of individual countries, it is in part because these countries themselves are also indicating that more could be done. Even the countries which embrace environmental protection most enthusiastically, such as Denmark, the Netherlands and Sweden, acknowledge that they could perform better. By so doing, the best performers will continue to lead the way for other countries.

In southern Europe too, where some of the strongest criticism has been levelled at conservation suffering because of the drive for economic development, there have been significant improvements in nature conservation. Organizational structures have been put into place, the regions particularly have been very active in land-use designations, and, while the number of National Parks being designated has declined, there has been an increase in the number of Regional Parks or their equivalent being created. The Regional Planning process in Portugal, for example, is set to increase the amount of protected land from 5% to 8% between 1995 and 1999 (Enderby, 1995).

All of this does not mean, however, that problems do not continue to exist. The very issue of regionalization which has forced the pace in some conservation issues also serves to confuse the issue at other levels. The continued debate around the role of the regions will also have affects upon the ability of some countries to address conservation issues. Furthermore, the other conflicts which surround nature conservation continue, with agriculture, economic development and, at a more specific level, hunting and transport policies having a severely damaging effect upon the natural, cultural and heritage environments. The headline 'Species at risk as Minister backs hunters' (*Sunday Times*, 1994) is hardly designed to make conservationists feel optimistic.

The pressure for improvements in nature conservation and the organizations established to manage the process will continue to bring about positive change.

SUSTAINABILITY

The concepts of sustainability and Agenda 21 are relatively recent additions to the lexicon of conservationists. They became commonplace with the Rio Summit of 1992, and by the late 1990s were beginning to embrace many aspects of environmentalism including nature conservation. In Europe, this drive for sustainability covers many issues, and forms the basis of the fifth Environmental Action Programme. The main concerns cover the sustainability of our urban areas (Ave, Monet and Klein, 1994), agriculture (Knapman, 1994) and other issues. It will increasingly become the underpinning criterion for any decision and development proposal that comes forward in Europe and, as we have already seen, lies at the heart of the fifth Environmental Action Programme. As a theoretical subject, there is no doubt that sustainability is gaining ground. What is unclear, however, is what this means in practice, particularly at the local or subregional level.

How is sustainability to manifest itself? For this reason, it is increasingly likely that land managers, along with all other environmental disciplines, will be expected to view their own work against the backdrop of sustainability, and also to show in detail how it contributes towards sustainability.

AGRICULTURE

The bulk of the EC budget is still spent upon the Common Agricultural Policy (CAP), particularly for intervention prices paid for produce. Despite the best intentions of the McSharry proposals (Chapter 5) and the Programmes and Directives for Environmentally Sensitive Farming and Countryside Protection in Less Favoured Areas, the CAP still, on the whole, supports intensive agricultural production. Even the concept of set-aside was not, it is now commonly accepted, a success in meeting broader environmental objectives, although it did reduce agricultural production which was its primary objective (Baldock *et al.*, 1993).

For these reasons, the CAP will be under continued pressure to revise its workings so as to deliver environmental objectives as well as agricultural- or production-based ones. The debate, in the last decade of the 20th century, is still stuck in the analysis of what effects changes to CAP will actually have upon the agriculture industry in various countries. And, as is evident from the analysis of the individual Member States, the political and economic power of the agriculture industry is strong in most EC countries.

TAXATION AND FINANCES

There were a number of initiatives in the 1990s that started to introduce the concept of environmental taxation and the 'sustainable' resourcing of environmental management. Some countries have special taxes upon the use of non-renewable resources, and many are introducing specific taxes aimed at reducing waste; one example is 'land-fill' tax, which is aimed at discouraging simply dumping waste into costly and environmentally damaging land-fill sites.

At a European level, the Delors White Paper of December 1993 was entitled 'Growth, Competitiveness and Employment'. Within this paper the broad issue of shifting taxation from people to natural resources is given thorough coverage. The issue is most definitely back on the European agenda (Morphet, 1994).

Where this debate will leave nature conservation and land management in general is, as yet, unclear. However, it will increasingly become a role of conservationists not only to know the intricacies of their own discipline, but

to have opinions and views as to how their work can be environmentally
and financially sustained into the future.

REFERENCES

Ave, G., Monet, R. and Klein, V. (1994) *The Cultural and Economic Conditions of Decision Making for the Sustainable City*. European Commission DGXII, Brussels.

Baldock, D., Beaufoy, G., Bennett, G. and Clark, J. (1993) *Nature Conservation and New Directions in the EC Common Agricultural Policy*. IEEP, London.

Enderby, C. (1995) Portuguese reforms to speed schemes approval. *Planning*, September, 113–37.

European Commission (1991) *The Community and its Eastern neighbours*. European Commission, Brussels.

European Commission (1994) *Promoting Biodiversity in the European Community*. European Commission, DGXI, Brussels.

IBM (1992) *Parcs nationaux; l'Europe dono toute sa nature*. IBM, Paris.

Knapman, D. (1994) Towards a more sustainable style of rural development. *Planning*, January, 1034–35.

Morphet, J. (1995) *European regions shape view on spatial planning. Planning*, January, 10–11.

Organisation for Economic Co-operation and Development (1993) *What Future Our Countryside?* OECD, Paris.

Pearce, D. and Turner, K. (1992) *Benefits, Estimates and Environmental Decision Making*. OECD, Paris.

Sunday Times (1994) Species at risk as Minister backs hunters. August.

The European (1994) Subsidiarity it rises again. May.

The Times (1994) Norway says no. August.

World Tourism Organisation (1992) *The Development of National Parks and Protected Areas for Tourism*. WTO, Madrid.

As the French author, Alexander Dumas, once said, 'All generalisations are dangerous ... including this one.' None the less, an overview of some of the strands of the foregoing chapter, and indeed the whole book, is necessary. These conclusions cover a variety of broad subject areas, within which there are clearly many individual elements and examples.

There are many common threads that can be identified within all the European Member States, and indeed at the Community level. The first and most important thread is the real and identifiable progress that has been made on many fronts and issues. All Member States now have a framework of nature conservation legislation, and a hierarchy of land designations through which landscapes, habitats and species are protected as well as, in some countries, historically and culturally important landscapes and sites. This general observation is perhaps also worth noting as a common thread. All the Member States have, to a greater or lesser extent, based their nature conservation policies upon the designation of sites and areas where conservation is of primary importance. Some Member States, such as Denmark and Holland, hold less importance to this site-based work than, say the United Kingdom or Germany and attach equal importance to wider environmental legislation. However, all Member States do have a site-based system of management which will remain a cornerstone of conservation into the next century.

At a more negative level, it is also evident that the European Community has struggled to find a coherent organizational framework within which nature conservation can find a secure and efficient place. This has been greatly improved with the Single European Act and the subsequent changes in 'competence' brought about at Maastricht. However, the general conclusion must be that the environment (in common with all issues it must be said) does get severely compromised in the wider political and organizational wrangles within Europe. Consequently, the environment is not best served.

This pattern is mirrored at individual Member State level, where a variety of constraints conspire to restrict the effectiveness and efficiency of the agencies trying to conserve the environment. It would be unfair to suggest for one instant that these constraints were there solely to thwart the work of conservationists. However, it is evident that this is one of the repercussions. A common thread is that in many instances the role of nature conservation is split between several agencies, and in many instances, between several government departments. Furthermore, because of historical or other reasons, some nature conservation departments are situated within ministries or departments that could be seen as having conflicting interests to those of nature conservation: Agriculture and Forestry are two such examples.

Wider political issues also compromise nature conservation, and the best and commonest example of this is the conflict which occurs between regions and central government, particularly where the process of regionalization has not yet settled down. In these circumstances, general uncertainty and conflict prevail, which quite obviously manifests itself in complexity at the level of implementation. It is very easy in the circumstances for conservationists to believe that they are unique in suffering because of political uncertainty. Clearly they are not, but it is also true that nature conservation is not 'top of the agenda' when regional and central governments debate their levels of responsibility.

A physical manifestation of this shift from central to regional power structures in many European countries has been the relative reduction in the rate of designations of National Parks and their equivalent and the corresponding increase in some countries of Regional Parks (France, Spain and Italy, for example). A further point arising out of the organizational arrangements for conservation in individual countries is that parks and areas are designated for a wide variety of reasons. In some instances, the concepts of wildlife and landscape are separated (as in the UK for example) whereas in others, no such distinction is drawn (the Netherlands for instance). In the case of Greece, the concepts of cultural and natural heritage are mixed (e.g. Mount Olympus National Park) and are organizationally linked.

Through this labyrinth of designations, the EC and Member States have attempted to bring about some element of consistency through their various strategies and network proposals. Environmentalists would stress the importance of variety; managers require some degree of order. Slowly the two are coming together!

Outside the role of government, the work of the non-governmental organizations (NGOs) has always been important in the world of environmentalism. Throughout Europe, this is the case to a lesser or greater extent.

What is also clear is that increasingly the NGOs will play a greater role in not only the development of policy, but also the implementation of these policies. The EC itself is keen to involve what are termed 'social partners' in many of its initiatives. This generic term includes trade unions, NGOs, charities, community groups and so on. Furthermore, the ways in which these social partners will be involved will in itself increase. For example, the NGOs are being encouraged to network across Europe to share experience and to increase their own levels of expertise.

Finally, the sustainability debate will seriously influence the work of nature conservationists. Not only is their work already being seen against this background, but also their own views may, in future, be subsumed into a wider agenda. For this reason, the process of land designations *may* now be seen as less important as wider environmental policies gain in importance. However, the two will always be complementary and in many instances, parks and other similarly designated areas can show how localized models of sustainability can work. National Parks which, in some of their peripheral areas, support suitable economic activity as well as protect the landscape and the natural and cultural environment, surely show examples of best practice which the rest of Europe and the world can draw upon.

REFERENCES

Morphet, J. (1994) Green dialogue on the agenda. *Planning*, December, 1097–98.

References

There are several texts which provide background and additional information for individual Member States. The following list gives some of those which have been referred to most often in the preceding chapters. Further specialist references are also given for each Member State.

GENERAL

Baldock, D. *et al.*, (1988) *The Organisation of Nature Conservation in Selected European Countries.* Institute of European Environmental Policy, London.

DocTer International (1992) *European Environmental Yearbook.* DocTer, Milan.

European Committee of the American Chambers of Commerce. *European Union Environment Guide.* ECACC, Brussels.

Falk, N. (1992) *Voluntary Work and the Environment.* European Foundation for the Improvement of Working and Living Conditions. Shankhill, Dublin.

O.E.C.D. (1994) *Environmental Indicators*, OECD, Paris.

Orme, E. (1989) *Nature Conservation and the role of the Land Manager.* College of Estate Management, Reading.

APPENDICES

Appendix A
Rio Declaration on Environment and Development (Agenda 21)

Principle 1: Human beings are at the centre of concerns for sustainable development. They are entitled to a healthy and productive life in harmony with nature.

Principle 2: States have, in accordance with the Charter of the United Nations and the principles of international law, the sovereign right to exploit their own environmental and developmental policies, and the responsibility to ensure that activities within their jurisdiction or control do not cause damage to the environment or other States or of areas beyond the limits of national jurisdiction.

Principle 3: The right to development must be fulfilled so as to equitably meet developmental and environmental needs of present and future generations.

Principle 4: In order to achieve sustainable development, environmental protection shall constitute an integral part of the development process and cannot be considered in isolation from it.

Principle 5: All States and all people shall co-operate in the essential task of eradicating poverty as an indispensable requirement of sustainable development in order to decrease the disparities in standards of living and better meet the needs of the majority of the people of the world.

Principle 6: The special situation and needs of developing countries, particularly the least developed and those most environmentally vulnerable, shall be given special priority. International actions in the field of environment and development should also address the interests and needs of all countries.

Principle 7: States shall co-operate in spirit of global partnership to conserve, protect and restore the health and integrity of the earth's eco-system. In view of the different contributions to global environmental degradation, States have common but differentiated responsibilities. The developed countries acknowledge the responsibility that they bear in the international pursuit of sustainable development in view of the pressures their societies place on the global environment and of the technologies and financial resources they command.

Principle 8: To achieve sustainable development and a higher quality of life for all people, States should reduce and eliminate unsustainable patterns of production and consumption and promote appropriate demographic policies.

Principle 9: States should co-operate to strengthen endogenous capacity, building for sustainable development by improving scientific understanding through exchanges and scientific and technological knowledge, and by enhancing the development, adaptation, diffusion and transfer of technologies, including new and innovative technologies.

Principle 10: **Environmental issues are best handled with the participation of all concerned citizens, at the relevant level.** At the national level, each individual shall have appropriate access to information concerning the environment that is held by public authorities, including information on hazardous materials and activities in their communities, and the opportunity to participate in decision-making processes. **States shall facilitate and encourage public awareness and participation by making information widely available.** Effective access to judicial and administrative proceeding, including redress and remedy, shall be provided.

Principle 11: States shall enact effective environmental legislation. Environmental standards, management objectives and priorities should reflect the environmental and developmental context to which they apply. Standards applied by some countries may be inappropriate and of unwarranted economic and social cost of other countries, in particular developing countries.

Principle 12: States should co-operate to promote a supportive and open international economic system that would lead to economic growth and sustainable development in all countries, to better address the problems of environmental degradation. Trade policy measures for environmental purposes should not constitute a means of arbitrary or unjustifiable discrimination or a disguised restriction on international trade. Unilateral actions to deal with environmental challenges outside the jurisdiction of the importing country should be avoided. Environmental measures addressing transboundary or global environmental problems should, as far as possible, be based on an international consensus.

Principle 13: States shall develop national law regarding liability and compensation for the victims of pollution and other environmental damage. States shall also co-operate in an expeditious and more determined manner to develop further international law regarding liability and compensation for adverse effects of environmental damage caused by activities within their jurisdiction or control to areas beyond their jurisdiction.

Principle 14: States should effectively co-operate to discourage or prevent the relocation and transfer to other States of any activities and substances that cause severe environmental degradation or are found to be harmful to human health.

Principle 15: In order to protect the environment, the precautionary approach shall be widely applied by States according to their capabilities. Where there are threats of serious or irreversible damage, lack of full scientific certainty shall not be used as a reason for postponing cost-effective measures to prevent environmental degradation.

Principle 16: National authorities should endeavour to promote the internationalization of environmental costs and the use of economic instruments, taking into account the approach that the polluter should, in principle, bear the cost of pollution, with due regard to the public interest and without distorting international trade and investment.

Principle 17: Environmental impact assessment, as a national instrument, shall be undertaken for proposed activities that are likely to have a significant adverse impact on the environment and are subject to a decision of a competent national authority.

Principle 18: States shall immediately notify other states of any natural disasters or other emergencies that are likely to produce sudden harmful effects on the environment of those States. Every effort shall be made by the international community to help States so afflicted.

Principle 19: States shall provide prior and timely notification and relevant information to potentially affected States on activities that may have a significant adverse transboundary environmental effect and shall consult with those States at an early stage and in good faith.

Principle 20: Women have a vital role in environmental management and development. Their full participation is therefore essential to achieve sustainable development.

Principle 21: The creativity, ideals and courage of the youth of the world should be mobilized to forge a global partnership in order to achieve sustainable development and ensure a better future for all.

Principle 22: Indigenous people and their communities, and other local communities, have a vital role in environmental management and development because of their knowledge and traditional practices. States should recognize and duly support their identity, culture and interests and enable their effective participation in the achievement of sustainable development.

Principle 23: The environment and natural resources of people under oppression, domination and occupation shall be protected.

Principle 24: Warfare is inherently destructive of sustainable development. States shall therefore respect international law, providing protection for the environment in times of armed conflict and co-operate in its further development as necessary.

Principle 25: Peace, development and environment protection are inter-dependent and indivisible.

Principle 26: States shall resolve all their environmental disputes peacefully and by appropriate means in accordance with the Charter of the United Nations.

Principle 27: States and people shall co-operate in good faith and in a spirit of partnership in the fulfilment of the principles embodied in the Declaration and the further development of international law in the field of sustainable development.

Appendix B
Glossary of abbreviations

ACE	Action by the Community Regulation, 1984.
ACP	African and Caribbean States.
CAF	Charities Aid Foundation.
CAP	Common Agricultural Policy.
CBI	Confederation of British Industry.
CEPS	Centre for European Policy Studies.
CITES	(Washington) Convention on International Trade in Endangered Species.
COR	Committee of the Regions.
COREPER	Committee of Permanent Representation.
CORINE	Decision on Information on the State of the Environment, 1985.
CPRE	Council for the Protection of Rural England.
DG	Directorate-General.
EAGGF	European Agricultural Guidance and Guarantee Fund.
EAP	Environmental Action Programme.
ECBH	Euro group for the Conservation of Birds and Habitats.
ECU	European Currency Unit.
EEA	European Environmental Agency.
EEB	European Environmental Bureau.
EFTA	European Free Trade Association.
EIONET	European Environmental Information and Observation Network.
ERDF	Economic Regional Development Fund.
ESA	Environmentally Sensitive Area.
ESF	European Social Fund.
FAO	Food and Agriculture Organisation of the United Nations.
FEA	Federal Environmental Agency.

FEOFA	Collective term for EC agricultural funds.
GATT	General Agreement on Trade and Tariffs.
GDP	Gross Domestic Product.
HMSO	Her Majesty's Stationery Office.
ICAN	International Conservation Network.
IDP	Integrated Development Programme.
IEEP	Institute of European Environmental Policy.
IFAW	International Fund for Animal Welfare.
IUCN	International Union for the Conservation of Nature and Natural Resources.
MAB	Man and the Biosphere Programme.
MEP	Member of European Parliament.
NCC	Nature Conservancy Council.
NGO	Non-governmental organization.
OECD	Organisation for Economic Co-operation and Development.
OJ	*Official Journal* of the European Community.
RSPB	Royal Society for the Protection of Birds.
SAC	Special Area of Conservation.
SEA	Single European Act.
SPA	Special Protection Area.
UN	United Nations.
UNCED	United Nations Conference on Environment and Development.
UNEP	United Nations Environment Programme.
UNESCO	United Nations Education, Science and Cultural Organisation.
WCS	World Conservation Strategy.
WTO	World Tourism Organisation.
WWF	World Wide Fund for Nature.

Index

Agenda 21, 100, 106, 341
Agriculture
   Austria 128
   communities 14
   Denmark 152–3
   France 179–81
   Germany 195
   Greece 210
   Irish Republic 224–5
   Italy 240–1
   Luxembourg 251
   Netherlands 262–3
   policy 13–16, 24, 62–3, 333, 336
   Portugal 277–8
   Spain 292–3
   Sweden 305
   United Kingdom 319–20

Berne Convention 66, 98–9
Birds Directive 64–5
Bonn Convention 66, 98

Canberra Convention 66, 99
CITES *see* Washington Convention
Collective procedures 42–3
Common Agricultural Policy 14, 29, 57,
   74–8
Conventions 94–7
CORINE 69–70
Council of Europe 19, 69, 85–8, 96
Council of Ministers 37–8
Court of Justice 40–1
Cultural heritage 211–12

DDT 20
Directorates General 30–1, 39, 48–50

Eastern Europe 327–8
Environmental Action Programming
   55–9, 330–1
Environmental Impact Assessment 21,
   68–9
Environmental Information Agreement
   61–2, 63
Environmentalism 17–19
Environmental responsibility
   Austria 122–4
   Belgium 135–6
   Denmark 146–8
   Finland 157–9
   France 169–74
   Germany 188–90
   Greece 203–6
   Irish Republic 217–20
   Italy 232–6
   Luxembourg 247–9
   Netherlands 256–60
   Portugal 269–72
   Spain 285–8
   Sweden 298–301
   United Kingdom 312–15
European Coal and Steel Community
   29
European Commission 39–40
European Community
   budgets 45–6
   external relationships 7, 10, 23
   formation 7–9, 11–26

programmes 46–7
types of legislation 43–4
European Environmental Agency 78–9, 330–1
European Environmental Bureau 91
European Parliament 36–7
European Year of the Environment 8

Forestry 138, 174, 208, 251
Formal compliance 44–5
Friends of the Earth 22

GATT 77, 91
Government structure
  Austria 120–2
  Belgium 131–5
  Denmark 144–6
  Finland 156–7
  France 166–9
  Germany 186–8
  Greece 200–3
  Irish Republic 215-17
  Italy 229–32
  Luxembourg 245–7
  Netherlands 254–6
  Portugal 267–9
  Spain 282–5
  Sweden 297–8
  United Kingdom 309–12
Greenpeace 22

Habitats directive 71–3
Hunting 180, 241

Industrialization 13
International Union for Conservation (IUCN) 87–9, 95, 102

Land designations
  Austria 124–7
  Belgium 136–40
  Denmark 150–2
  Finland 159–63
  France 174–9
  Germany 190–4
  Greece 206–9
  Irish Republic 220–4
  Italy 236–40
  Luxembourg 249–50
  Netherlands 260–2
  Portugal 272–6
  Spain 288–92

Sweden 301–4
United Kingdom 315–19
Landscape protection 127, 194, 261, 318
L.I.F.E. 50–1

Maastricht Treaty 32, 34–6
Man and biosphere 102–4
Manshott Plan 14, 75
McSharry reform 78

National Parks 125–6, 137, 160–1, 175–6, 191–2, 206–7, 221–2, 236, 249, 260–1, 272–4, 288, 301–13, 316–18, 336
Natura 2000 70, 73, 106–7, 331
Nature Reserves 126–7, 137, 162, 176–7, 192, 223, 239, 275, 289–90, 304, 318, 331
Non-governmental Organization 58–9, 90–2, 124, 206–7, 220, 306–7

Organization for Economic Co-operation and Development (OECD) 58–9, 108, 116

Paris Convention 96–7
Polluter pays 52, 62

Qualified majority 38–9, 42

Ramsar Convention 63–4, 79, 95
Regional parks 178, 238, 274–5
Regionalization 329–30
Rio summit 58, 99–101
Royal Society for the Protection of Birds 92
Rural communities 14
Rural development 163, 305, 328–30, 341

Set-aside 76–7, 333
Single European Act 8, 12, 17, 31–4
Social cohesion 32–3
Subsidiarity 327–8
Sustainability 332–3

Taxation 333–4
Tourism 23, 25, 181, 196, 279, 294–5, 320
Treaty of Paris 29
Treaty of Rome 8, 10, 12, 17, 28, 29–31

UNESCO 100, 104

United Nations 89–91
United States of America 17, 29
Urban planning 15–17
Urbanization 15, 23, 25

Washington Convention 67, 97–8

Water management 140–1, 153, 163,
    180, 195–6, 210–11, 225, 241–2,
    250, 263–4, 278–9, 294, 320
World conservation strategy 104
World heritage conservation 95–6
World Wide Fund for Nature 22